Ultimate Salesforce Data Cloud for Customer Experience

Explore, Implement, and Elevate B2C Experiences Through Customer Data Innovations Using Salesforce Data Cloud

Gourab Mukherjee

www.orangeava.com

First published: January 2024

Published by: Orange Education Pvt Ltd, AVA™

Address: 9, Daryaganj, Delhi, 110002

ISBN: 978-93-88590-99-0

www.orangeava.com

Dedicated To

My beloved Parents:

Hemanta Kumar Mukherjee
Barna Mukherjee

and

My wife Biyanka Bhattacharya

About the Author

Gourab Mukherjee is a certified Salesforce Consultant with more than 5 years of experience in helping Fortune 500 clients leverage the Salesforce Platform to its potential. He has worked on various Salesforce implementation projects, including Salesforce Data Cloud. He has an MBA degree from K J Somaiya Institute of Management, Mumbai, and a B.Tech in Electrical Engineering from Heritage Institute of Technology, Kolkata.

As a certified Salesforce professional, he holds a range of Salesforce certifications. He is passionate about creating great customer experiences and Salesforce is his weapon of choice.

He is a prolific writer, contributing to major websites, including Salesforceben.com - one of the most popular websites for Salesforce professionals. The writing bug bit him early in his life, and although he dreams of writing a novel someday, for now, he is focused on writing business and technology articles. He is a thought leader in creating stellar customer experiences and data-driven decision-making for organizations.

He is an avid reader who enjoys reading books from various genres such as mystery, thriller, and non-fiction, including biographies and autobiographies, as well as books on businesses and start-ups. Additionally, he closely follows the start-up industry and is interested in reading and exploring new technologies. As a car and bike enthusiast, he keeps himself regularly updated on the latest launches. He is particularly passionate about the EV sector and has high hopes that India will one day become an EV hub for the world. He loves watching movies and TV shows for passive entertainment, preferring character-driven stories. Also, he loves playing cricket and football, and during the winter season, badminton.

He is multilingual and speaks English, Hindi, Bengali, German, and Spanish. Although his German and Spanish are a little rusty, he is fluent in the other three languages. He was a top performer in the TCS training program as well as a silver medalist in the MBA program at K J Somaiya Institute of Management. He has also won many accolades for his work in Brillio.

In his leisure time, he enjoys catching up with his family and close friends, reading books, watching binge-worthy TV shows or good movies, or going for long drives. He currently lives in Kolkata with his family.

About the Technical Reviewer

Kunal Parikh is a seasoned tech professional with a strong background in systems management and a passion for all things Salesforce. With a knack for transforming ideas into actionable strategies, Kunal has earned the title of "Salesforce Champion" through his dedication to mastering the Salesforce ecosystem.

Having honed his skills in the world of technology, Kunal's journey has been marked by a commitment to continuous learning and innovation. His proficiency in Salesforce Marketing Cloud, in particular, is a testament to his expertise in crafting targeted marketing solutions that drive results.

Beyond the digital realm, Kunal is known for his friendly and social personality. He thrives on connecting with others and building meaningful relationships, both personally and professionally. When he's not immersed in the world of tech, you can often find him socializing with friends and colleagues or cheering on his favorite cricket team with unwavering enthusiasm.

Kunal Parikh is a true enthusiast, bringing his technical acumen, management skills, and passion for Salesforce to every endeavor. Whether in the realm of systems management, Salesforce Marketing Cloud, or the world of sports, he's a dedicated professional who continues to make a significant impact in his field.

Acknowledgements

There are a few people I want to thank for the continued and ongoing support they have given me during the writing of this book. First and foremost, I would like to thank my parents and my wife for continuously encouraging me for writing the book – I could have never completed this book without their support.

I am grateful to the Salesforce partner learning course and the resources provided by them which helped me understand the concepts in Salesforce Data Cloud. Along with that, I am grateful to the Brillio Pvt. Limited where I started my Salesforce journey and where I was part of different Salesforce projects, including ones on Data Cloud.

I gratefully acknowledge Mrs. Sonali Biswas who worked with me throughout the journey of writing this book, chapter by chapter and guiding me throughout the process. Without her feedback, it would have been difficult to move ahead. I also thank Mr. Kunal Parikh for his technical scrutiny for this book.

My gratitude also goes to the publishing team for being supportive throughout the writing process and providing me with ample time for me to work on the book. They provided me with the freedom to be creative with the content of the book. Without that, this book would not have seen the light of day.

Preface

During my first interaction with an ecommerce platform, I added a few products to the shopping cart but didn't check them out as I was apprehensive about whether the product would be delivered. Minutes later I got an e-mail from the same ecommerce company asking me what went wrong as I had not bought the product. They had even provided a customer care number that I could call to clarify any issues. I was surprised.

How did they know we had abandoned the cart and did not check out? How did they link that behavior to my email id? How did they send the reminder mail so quickly within a few minutes? This was back when I was a college student. E-commerce and digital marketing were in their nascent stage in India and it was natural for me to get intrigued.

I am sure that many already have experience with this. You explore a product but do not buy it and then you receive an email reminder, you like an Instagram reel about cars and now you see more reels about cars when you swipe down on Instagram reels. You browse some shoes on a website and the next time you open Facebook, you see the same shoe being promoted in your feed. You view a category of videos on YouTube and now you are recommended more videos from that creator or that genre. Some companies like Netflix take it to the next level where they show you a video clip from a movie or a series that will most likely result in you watching the content.

How do companies do this? How do they personalize the experience for millions of customers at scale and within minutes of action being taken? How do they make us spend more time on their apps rather than doing something else with that time?

Customer Data Platform (CDP) answers all of the above-mentioned questions. The Customer Data Platform is a tool that helps you capture user behavior data at scale. With further analysis and modeling of that data using algorithms, companies build highly personalized experiences for users.

A personalized experience is the key to increasing user retention, daily active users, and user engagement rates, and as a result of, increasing monetization per user. If you are in the business of creating experiences for users, you need to take

Customer Data Platforms very seriously. With a CDP, you will be able to create highly personalized experiences and as a result, user engagement will improve.

So who should read this book? Why should you care about reading it? Did you make a mistake in choosing it? Let me answer that first before you put it down.

This book is meant for anyone who wants to get started on understanding customer data platforms and how they work. It is intended for anyone who aspires to become a technical and functional consultant or a solution architect helping companies understand and implement a CDP. It is meant for anyone interested in the latest Salesforce offering: Salesforce Data Cloud which is going to revolutionize the CDP industry.

Last but not least, this book is for anyone who wants to revise the concepts in the Data Cloud certification exam and earn the certification.

Here is a sneak peek of the book:

Chapter 1: Introducing Salesforce Platform

The first chapter introduces the Salesforce platform to the reader, explains its benefits and clarifies some basic concepts around the platform which will set the context for what comes in the successive chapters. We will also discuss the Salesforce architecture and data model.

Chapter 2: Introduction to Customer Data Platform

This chapter will introduce the reader to the concept of CDP and why it is so important today. The chapter will help readers understand the challenges faced by companies in delivering a great customer experience.

Chapter 3: Salesforce Data Cloud for Customer Experience

This chapter will introduce the reader to the Salesforce Genie and why it is a revolution in the CDP world.

Chapter 4: Salesforce Data Cloud Architecture

This chapter introduces the reader to the Salesforce Genie architecture. We will delve into a detailed examination of the key building blocks of Salesforce Genie and understand how they interact with each other.

Chapter 5: Implementing a Customer Data Platform

This chapter discusses the steps involved in implementing a Customer Data Platform (CDP) solution. We will understand the step-by-step approach for implementing a CDP solution, covering topics such as choosing a CDP vendor, creating business use cases to get traction from business leaders for your CDP project, creating a steering team, tracking plan, and implementing the tracking plan among other steps.

Chapter 6: Implementing Salesforce Data Cloud

This chapter will walk you through the implementation steps for Salesforce Data Cloud. We will introduce the Salesforce recommended way of implementing Data Cloud.

Chapter 7: Data Security and Privacy

This chapter explores the multifaceted world of data security and privacy, shedding light on the fundamental concepts, challenges, and solutions for protecting data in an increasingly interconnected and data-driven world. We delve into the principles, best practices, and technologies employed to ensure the confidentiality, integrity, and availability of data, as well as the legal and ethical considerations surrounding data privacy.

Chapter 8: Success Stories with Salesforce Data Cloud

In this chapter, we will study a few organizations that have successfully implemented a CDP solution or a Salesforce Data Cloud solution. We will understand their motivations for implementing Data Cloud, how they went about implementing it, and understand the outcome it had on their business.

Chapter 9: The Way Forward for Creating Great Customer Experiences

In this chapter, we will discuss the emerging trends in the world of customer experience management.

Chapter 10: Preparation for the Salesforce Data Cloud Consultant Exam

In this chapter, we will explain how to begin your preparation for the exam, go through the exam guide, and discuss in brief how to prepare for each section, tips, and finally some mock questions with their solutions and explanations.

Get a Free eBook

We hope you are enjoying your recently purchased book! Your feedback is incredibly valuable to us, and to all other readers looking for great books.

If you found this book helpful or enjoyable, we would truly appreciate it, if you could take a moment to leave a short review with a 5 star rating on Amazon. It helps us grow, and lets other readers discover our books.

As a thank you, we would love to send you a free digital copy of this book, and a **30%** discount code on your next cart value on our official websites:

www.orangeava.com

www.orangeava.in (For Indian Subcontinent)

Here's how:

Leave a review for the book on Amazon.

Take a screenshot of your review, and send an email to **info@orangeava.com** (it can be just the confirmation screen).

Once, we receive your screenshot, we will send you the digital file, within 24 hours.

Thank you so much for your support – it means a lot to us!

Downloading the code bundles and colored images

Please follow the links or scan the QR codes to download the
Code Bundles and Images of the book:

https://github.com/ava-orange-education/Ultimate-Salesforce-Data-Cloud-for-Customer-Experience

The code bundles and images of the book are also hosted on
https://rebrand.ly/d2795e7

In case there's an update to the code, it will be updated on the existing GitHub repository.

Errata

We take immense pride in our work at **Orange Education Pvt Ltd,** and follow best practices to ensure the accuracy of our content to provide an indulging reading experience to our subscribers. Our readers are our mirrors, and we use their inputs to reflect and improve upon human errors, if any, that may have occurred during the publishing processes involved. To let us maintain the quality and help us reach out to any readers who might be having difficulties due to any unforeseen errors, please write to us at :

errata@orangeava.com

Your support, suggestions, and feedback are highly appreciated.

DID YOU KNOW

Did you know that Orange Education Pvt Ltd offers eBook versions of every book published, with PDF and ePub files available? You can upgrade to the eBook version at **www.orangeava.com** and as a print book customer, you are entitled to a discount on the eBook copy. Get in touch with us at: **info@orangeava.com** for more details.

At **www.orangeava.com**, you can also read a collection of free technical articles, sign up for a range of free newsletters, and receive exclusive discounts and offers on AVA™ Books and eBooks.

PIRACY

If you come across any illegal copies of our works in any form on the internet, we would be grateful if you would provide us with the location address or website name. Please contact us at **info@orangeava.com** with a link to the material.

ARE YOU INTERESTED IN AUTHORING WITH US?

If there is a topic that you have expertise in, and you are interested in either writing or contributing to a book, please write to us at **business@orangeava.com**. We are on a journey to help developers and tech professionals to gain insights on the present technological advancements and innovations happening across the globe and build a community that believes Knowledge is best acquired by sharing and learning with others. Please reach out to us to learn what our audience demands and how you can be part of this educational reform. We also welcome ideas from tech experts and help them build learning and development content for their domains.

REVIEWS

Please leave a review. Once you have read and used this book, why not leave a review on the site that you purchased it from? Potential readers can then see and use your unbiased opinion to make purchase decisions. We at Orange Education would love to know what you think about our products, and our authors can learn from your feedback. Thank you!

For more information about Orange Education, please visit **www.orangeava.com**.

Table of Contents

CHAPTER 1
Introducing Salesforce Platform

Introduction

This chapter talks about the Salesforce platform. Before we can start discussing Salesforce Data Cloud, which is a real-time customer data platform from Salesforce, we need to understand the Salesforce core platform. We will discuss in depth the key Salesforce concepts, its architecture, data model, security model, and so on. This will help you understand how Salesforce works and how Salesforce Data Cloud leverages the platform's capabilities to unlock customer value.

In this chapter, we will understand what customer relationship management (CRM) software is and why Salesforce is rated as the top CRM software. We will touch on the topic of the Salesforce ecosystem of applications. We will discuss the basic concepts to help you understand the Salesforce platform and proceed to understand the technical architecture. We will delve into the data model and the security model and finally understand the Customer 360 vision of Salesforce.

This chapter will prepare you for what comes in later chapters. It is recommended reading this chapter carefully if you are new to the Salesforce platform. Understanding the key concept is very important; otherwise you might feel lost in the later chapters. Those who are already familiar with the Salesforce platform and have worked previously in different Salesforce applications like the Sales Cloud, Service Cloud, and so on can either give this chapter a quick read or glance to revise the key concepts or skip it. You can revisit this if you are stuck somewhere.

Note: Salesforce Genie is now known as Salesforce Customer Data Cloud or Data Cloud.

Structure

In this chapter, the following topics will be covered:

- Introducing CRM Platform
- Salesforce: One of the top CRM Applications
- Salesforce Ecosystem of Applications
- Basic concepts to understand the Salesforce Platform
- Salesforce Technical Architecture
- Salesforce Data Model
- Salesforce Security Model
- Salesforce Customer 360

Introducing CRM Platform

If you are new to the concept of a Customer Relationship Management Platform, you have every right to be confused. Let's clear up that confusion now.

According to Salesforce, a CRM is "*a technology for managing all your company's relationships and interactions with customers and potential customers*".

Let us clarify. When a business deals with its potential customers or clients, the interaction follows a journey known as the customer journey. For example, one such customer journey can be like this: A sales representative will reach out to potential customers. In the first meeting, the client may have shown some interest in the product or service sold by the representative, but they are not yet sure whether they will buy it. Then the sales representative may contact the client again for a product demo. Then, in the third meeting, the client may agree to buy and therefore wants to get a quote from the representative. After some negotiations, they will agree to a price and then sign the contract. Once the contract is signed, the product is delivered or the service rendered. After delivery, a bill is generated and sent to the client. The client pays the bill, and revenue is recognized by the company.

Figure 1.1: *Salesforce Sales Cloud home page*

It is possible to manage this workflow on spreadsheets and documents if the company is just starting with a few clients in the range of 10–50. But once the number of client interactions becomes larger than that, running into hundreds, it gets difficult to manage. Transparency is lost, communication is broken, and the process fails. Today, a lot of enterprise sales happen online and across geographies. In an era of online selling, selling without a CRM tool becomes very challenging. Managing your sales process using ad hoc tools becomes difficult. So, a CRM tool is a one-stop solution for managing the relationship with your potential customers.

Selling your product or service is just one part of the business. Next comes the more important part, that is, the delivery of the sold product or service. You need to manage order fulfillment, service delivery, invoicing, payment recognition, and so on. Depending on the experience your customer has after buying from you, they would either buy again or leave you for a competitor. A CRM also helps in managing the after-sales relationship with customers. This relationship management is very important for organizations to win renewal deals. So a CRM tool is a one-stop solution for managing the relationship with your customers as well.

Now go ahead and read the definition of CRM again. It will start to make more sense.

So, if a company is growing and has a lot of customers to cater to, it cannot manage with spreadsheets. That is the time when they invest in good CRM software that will not only help them manage the sales process but also the after-sales process.

Here are the top five benefits of using a CRM tool:

- Improved productivity of employees
- Increased collaboration
- Accurate reporting on business metrics
- Single source of information
- Improved buying experience for customers

Almost all companies have a CRM tool in place for managing customer relationships. Without that, it is difficult to function.

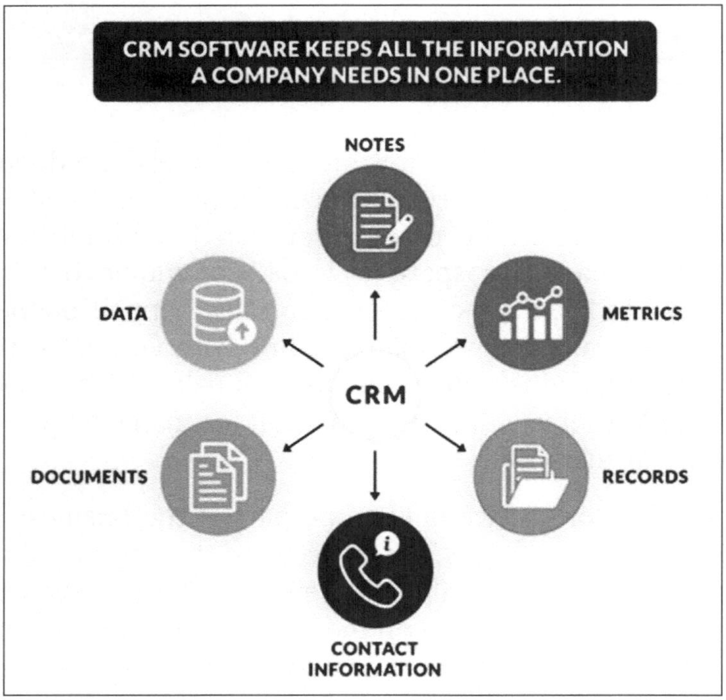

Figure 1.2: *CRM helps to provide a single source for your customer-related information*

What we have described is a basic requirement of a CRM tool. The CRM tools we have today do much more for example, they help sales agent understand the probability of winning a deal using artificial intelligence, give prompt reminders to follow up with a client, and enhance collaboration in an era of virtual selling among others. Life is much easier selling using a CRM tool.

There are many CRM software available in the market, each catering to different audiences. Some are suitable for small companies with 100-500 employees; some are more suited for big enterprises. CRM tools are available based on the revenue or the complexity involved in the selling process. There are on-premise CRM tools, which means your company has to provide the servers and other infrastructure to install and run the CRM tools. On-premise tools are used by companies that are in highly regulated industries or by government institutions. There are also many Software as a Service (SaaS)-based CRM tools. These do not require you to provide infrastructure. You just need to buy the user licenses, and then you can log in to their portals and start using them. These SaaS CRM tools are more popular today. Salesforce was the first company to provide SaaS-based CRM software and has not looked back since then.

For the scope of this book, we will focus only on SaaS CRM tools, as they are more popular today. We will not discuss on-premise CRM solutions.

Among many SaaS CRMs, here are the top SaaS CRM tools available today:

- Salesforce
- Microsoft Dynamics 365
- SAP C/4 HANA
- Oracle CX Cloud
- Zoho (for smaller companies)

In terms of market share, Salesforce has the largest share. It is one of the most popular CRM tools in the market today.

Salesforce: One of the top CRM Applications

As mentioned earlier, Salesforce is the pioneer in providing SaaS CRM software. It was the first to provide cloud-based CRM software. There was no need to maintain the infrastructure for running the software. All you needed was an internet connection. You could log in to Salesforce using the internet and use the tool. This gave it a head start when the world of technology was shifting from on-premise to cloud technology. Back then, Siebel was the number one CRM, but it was costly to build and maintain. Salesforce provided a cloud-based and relatively affordable version of a CRM.

In 1999, Marc Benioff started Salesforce with the idea that CRM software should be affordable, available to the masses 24/7, and based on the global cloud platform. With its affordable cost compared with other options available at that time, and its easy-to-use and user-friendly features, it soon started becoming popular. Its growth was phenomenal. The company extended its offering from Sales Cloud (for managing sales process) to Service Cloud (for managing customer care representatives) to Marketing Cloud and Pardot (for B2C and B2B marketing, respectively). As it saw opportunities in the market, it kept on improving its product lines, either by building the product in-house or through acquisitions.

Back then, creating a quote for a sales representative was a difficult and time-consuming task especially if the products were complicated in nature. SteelBricks CPQ (configure, price, and quote) software helped sales users create quotes seamlessly and send them to their customers. Salesforce acquired SteelBricks CPQ and later renamed it Salesforce CPQ. Similarly, it kept acquiring companies to expand its product lines, acquiring Demandware to create Commerce cloud, and acquiring Tableau to create Tableau CRM and Slack for communication, among others.

Salesforce also provides easy-to-integrate features with other leading applications like ERP solutions, billing solutions, marketing platforms, and so on.

One of Salesforce's design policies is to use less code and more point-and-click-based development. This is the reason why Salesforce is very easy to use and customize, even for those who don't know how to code. It is very user-friendly for business users and non-technical users. Business users can do a lot of the work themselves without using any technical help. This helped Salesforce become very popular among business users.

In the year 2022, Salesforce had a revenue of $26.5 billion. It has the highest market share among CRM players. (Source: **https://www.statista.com/statistics/972598/crm-applications-vendors-market-share-worldwide/#:~:text=Salesforce%20is%20the%20leading%20vendor,percent%20shares%20of%20the%20market**.)

Here are the top five reasons why Salesforce is one of the top CRM tools:

- It is scalable and fits the requirements of small companies as well as large global enterprises
- Its user interface is user-friendly and easy to customize without the need for extensive coding
- It provides powerful process automation tools which even business users can use to create process automation

- Salesforce has a lot of applications for managing different business processes like sales, service, marketing, commerce, order management, and so on. So you don't need to have separate software vendors for different business processes.
- It has a well-developed partner ecosystem called the Salesforce AppExchange where one can find applications for various business needs which are not present in the core Salesforce platform, as well as consultants who can help you implement and get the most out of your Salesforce application. Salesforce AppExchange is like a Google Play Store or an Apple store from where you can install applications. We will have a detailed discussion about Salesforce AppExchange later.

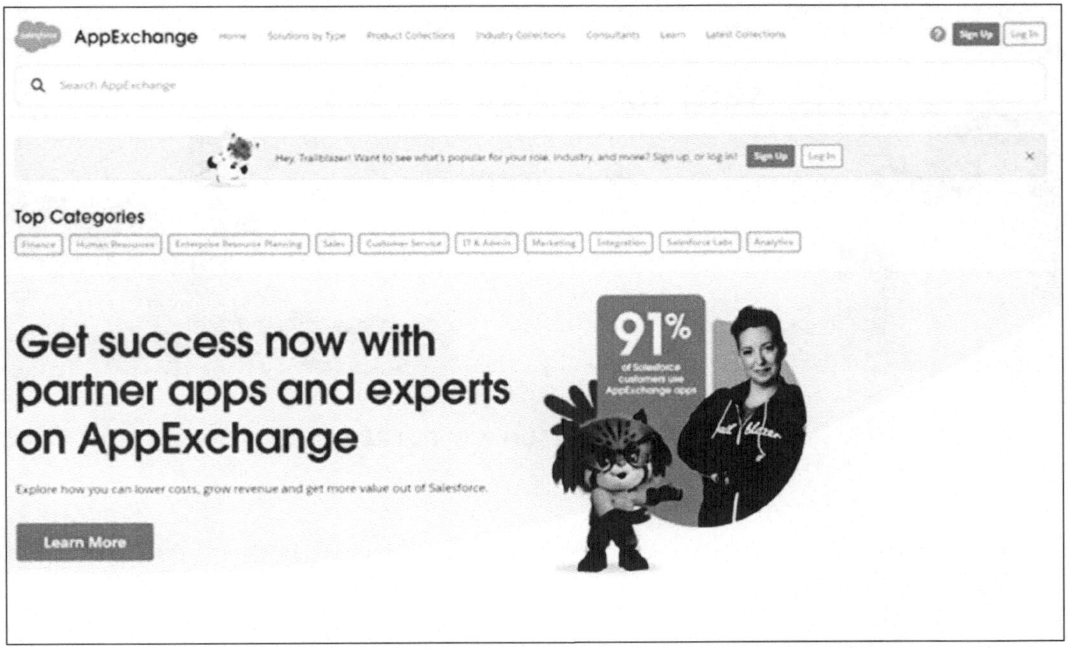

***Figure 1.3**: Salesforce AppExchange Website* (**https://appexchange.salesforce.com/**)

Salesforce has a few core philosophies to which it adheres. First, it wants to make its platforms very easy to use and customize. It has many out-of-the-box solutions as well as provides many tools using which you can customize the CRM applications by using clicks and no code. Salesforce's *Click and no Code* philosophy helps it become popular among business users as well as those who are not very hands-on with coding. Salesforce is easy to learn and easy to get started with. It has a dedicated website for gamified learning called Salesforce Trailhead(**https://trailhead.salesforce.com/**). Using trailhead, anyone can learn Salesforce very easily.

Along with learning Salesforce from Trailhead, it is a good idea to create your own free developer org to practice what we teach in this book as well as what you will learn in trailhead. Creating a Salesforce developer account is completely free, and you don't need to share any card details.

You can sign up for a free developer account by providing the relevant information on this page: **https://developer.salesforce.com/signup.**

Our suggestion will be to create the account and keep it handy. You can check out the concepts on the org as we discuss them in this book.

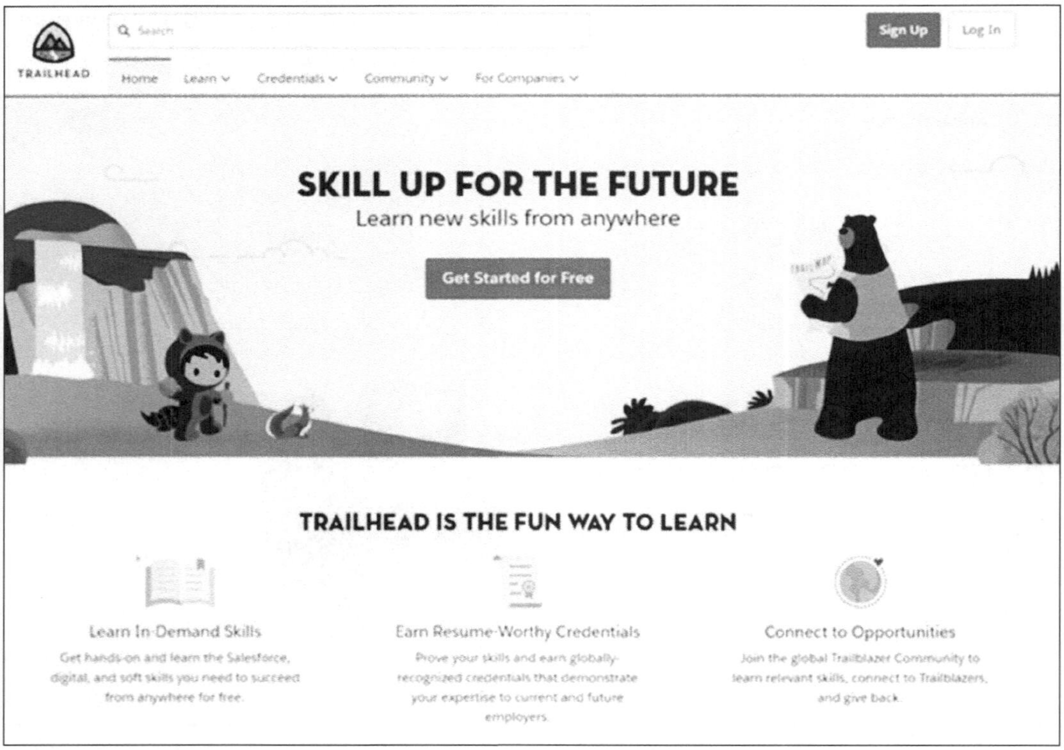

Figure 1.4: *Salesforce Trailhead Website*-**https://trailhead.salesforce.com/**

The second important philosophy it has is to provide companies with a 360-degree view of their customers. Salesforce has applications that help you holistically understand your customers. From marketing to sales to order management to customer service to analytics, it helps you track what is going on with your customers all within the same platform. This unlocks immense value for companies that use Salesforce.

Salesforce Ecosystem of Applications

Now that you have understood the CRM applications and also why Salesforce is very popular among CRM applications, it is time to dig deeper into the Salesforce ecosystem. As we have pointed out earlier, Salesforce is not just one application but an ecosystem of applications, either built by Salesforce themselves or by Salesforce partners. Together, they make the Salesforce platform very powerful and capable of handling unique business processes.

Let's take a look at the following diagram:

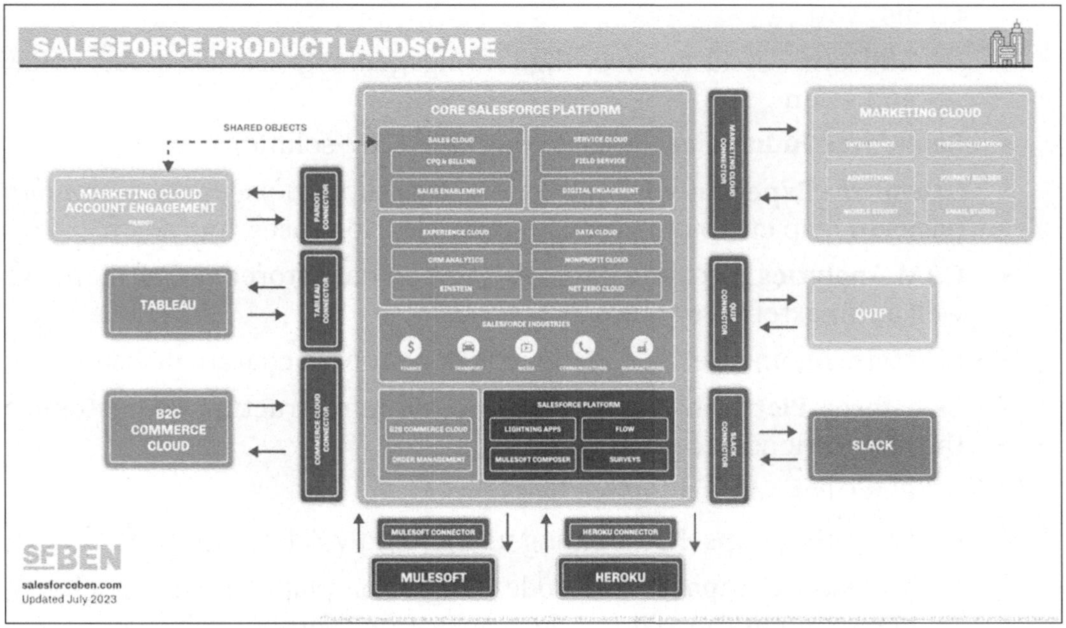

***Figure 1.5**: Salesforce ecosystem of applications.*
Source: **https://www.salesforceben.com/salesforce-products/**

Even for those who have experience working on the Salesforce platform, it is difficult to wrap their heads around all the different Salesforce products. One of the reasons for the confusion is due to the ever-changing names of the products. By the time you get habituated to the name of a product, Salesforce will decide to change the name or package the same product differently. The name changes because of changing industry needs. So, it just might be the case that when you are reading the book, the names are already changed. In any case, whatever the future name, the functionalities of the core product remain the same sans some upgrades.

Core Salesforce Platform

Back to the Salesforce products. In the middle, there is the core Salesforce platform. This forms the base of the Salesforce products. It has the following applications:

- **Sales Cloud**: For managing Sales processes
  - Add-ons- CPQ and Billing, High-velocity sales, Lightning Dialer, and so on
- **Service Cloud**: For managing service processes and customer support teams
  - Add-ons- Field service, digital engagement, service cloud voice, and so on
- **Salesforce Industries**: Industry-specific CRM solutions
- **Salesforce Experience Cloud**: For creating support pages or community pages to help customers read help articles, log cases, and so on
- **CRM Analytics**: For providing analytics on data stored in Salesforce as well as on external systems
- **Einstein**: Augmented AI to help in making more accurate decisions
- **Salesforce Platform**: Providing the basic infrastructure to customize the applications. It consists of:
  - **Flow**: For automating business processes
  - **Lightning Apps**: For creating user-friendly Salesforce apps
  - **Mulesoft Composer**: No-code integration platform which helps to create integration with other applications without using code
  - **Heroku**: Cloud platform as a service

Marketing Cloud

On the right-hand side of the diagram, we can see the Marketing Cloud products. Marketing cloud products are connected with the core Salesforce platform using the Marketing Cloud connector.

- **Marketing Cloud Intelligence (formerly known as Datorama):** For holistic reporting from all the marketing channels
- **Marketing Cloud Personalization (formerly Interaction studio):** helps to create personalized experiences for customers

- **Marketing Cloud Advertising (formerly Advertising studio):** provides access to different advertising platforms like Instagram, Facebook, Twitter Google, and so on, from the Salesforce platform.
- **Journey Builder:** helps to build powerful marketing journeys
- **Email Studio:** For email marketing
- **Mobile Studio:** For mobile marketing
- **Marketing Cloud Customer Data Platform (formerly Salesforce CDP):** for unifying customer data

Marketing Cloud Account Engagement (formerly known as Pardot)

It is used for B2B email marketing, landing page generation, lead generation, and so on, available through Pardot connector.

Tableau

It is used for analytics using the data stored in the Salesforce database as well as in the external database.

Commerce Cloud

It is used for creating B2C and B2B digital storefronts for e-commerce. It provides all the functionalities that are required to build an e-commerce store. It is available through the Commerce Cloud connector.

Salesforce Data Cloud Customer Data Cloud

So where does Salesforce Data Cloud customer data cloud fit in? For the purpose of this book, we will call Salesforce Data Cloud Customer Data Cloud as Salesforce Data Cloud. Salesforce Data Cloud is a relatively new addition to the Salesforce product portfolio. Salesforce Data Cloud is an active common layer across the core applications as well as other Salesforce products, which will help to bring in data from different Salesforce products as well as from external systems into a single repository. This helps to create a 360-degree view of the customer. Salesforce CDP did the same thing earlier. But Salesforce Data Cloud can do it at scale and on a real-time basis. Customer data is continuously updated with new data from any of the Salesforce products and then fed into the repository. Your data remains fresh all the time. This helps make Salesforce an integrated CRM platform.

To visualize Salesforce Data Cloud as part of the Salesforce product portfolio, we need to look at the following diagram:

***Figure 1.6**: Salesforce Data Cloud connects all Salesforce and other third-party applications together through a common data repository*
(source- **https://www.v2sa.com/salesforce-Data Cloud-and-marketing-clouds-customer-data-platform/#:~:text=Where%20does%20Data Cloud%20fit%20in,can%20differentiate%20within%20an%20organization.**)

Salesforce Data Cloud takes a central position among the Salesforce products wherein it connects all the different Salesforce applications and other third-party applications together. It brings the data from different applications, whether they are from Salesforce or from other third-party applications, and provides common storage for this data. The data then can be unified and sent to different applications for solving business use cases.

We will discuss more on Salesforce Data Cloud in the later chapters. For now, it is enough to understand that Salesforce Data Cloud helps to bring real-time data from different systems and enables Salesforce to provide a 360-degree view of the customer.

Basic concepts to understand the Salesforce Platform

In the course of the book, we will be using terms to refer to different things in the Salesforce platform. It is important to familiarize yourself with these terms to improve comprehension and avoid confusion. Revisit this part of the book if there is any confusion with any of the basic concepts.

We will start with some basic definitions of terms used in the Salesforce ecosystem and then move on to more complicated concepts.

- **App**: Short for application. This causes some confusion among those new to the platform. Salesforce is a CRM application. But when we use the term apps, it refers not to the core Salesforce application but to the internal applications available inside the Salesforce platform. An app is a collection of tabs, reports, dashboards, and pages specific to a business process. So inside Salesforce, you will find a Sales app for Sales users, a Service app for service people, marketing apps for marketing people, and so on. It helps to distinguish between different business processes.
- **Object**: Salesforce uses relational databases to store information in the form of tables. A table in Salesforce is called an object. An object stores data about one aspect of the business. For example, an account object stores data about the client account, like the name, address, type of client, and so on. Case object stores data about a service request like case type, name, and so on. An object is made up of fields that are similar to columns on a table. Each row of data in that table is called a record. So an object is made up of fields and records. Objects are of two types: Standard objects are those that come pre-populated in a Salesforce org and custom objects are those that are created by companies for specific use cases.
- **Organization**: Organization (the short version is org) is a deployment of Salesforce specific to a company (hence called an organization). It contains all the licenses your company has purchased, any purchased apps, data, and so on.
- **Salesforce Lightning Platform**: Refers to the platform as a service (PaaS) offering from Salesforce. But when the term Salesforce lightning is used, it usually refers to the latest version of Salesforce with the updated UI. The previous version of Salesforce was Salesforce Classic. It is recommended to use Salesforce Lightning for using Salesforce going forward.
- **Tab**: A tab provides easy access to an object inside a Salesforce app in *Figure 1.7:*

Figure 1.7: *Sales App home page: Home, Opportunities, and Account are all tabs*

- **Salesforce Admin**: Refers to the Salesforce administrator user who is in charge of maintaining the Salesforce org for a company. This is a super user who can do any changes in the org. Therefore, only a few users are kept as Salesforce admins, as they have the greatest privilege in the org. They help with new user creation, changing permissions, and giving access to users, among other tasks.
- **Page Layout**: Refers to the design of the Salesforce page that you see on the screen. Using the page layout tool, you can design the look of the page and change the sections on the page, the different fields, buttons, and links that will be visible on the page. You can also set up different page layouts for different groups of users so that the users see only those buttons, fields, and so on that are relevant to them. For each object, you have at least one or more page layouts that are customizable according to business needs.
- **Salesforce Native Apps**: Refers to those Salesforce apps that are developed on the Salesforce platform and hence available directly in Salesforce without the need for integration. Both Salesforce as well as Salesforce partners develop Salesforce native apps.

Salesforce Technical Architecture

Now we will talk about the Salesforce technical architecture.

Salesforce is a multi-tenant cloud platform. Heroku is the cloud platform as a service that is powering Salesforce.

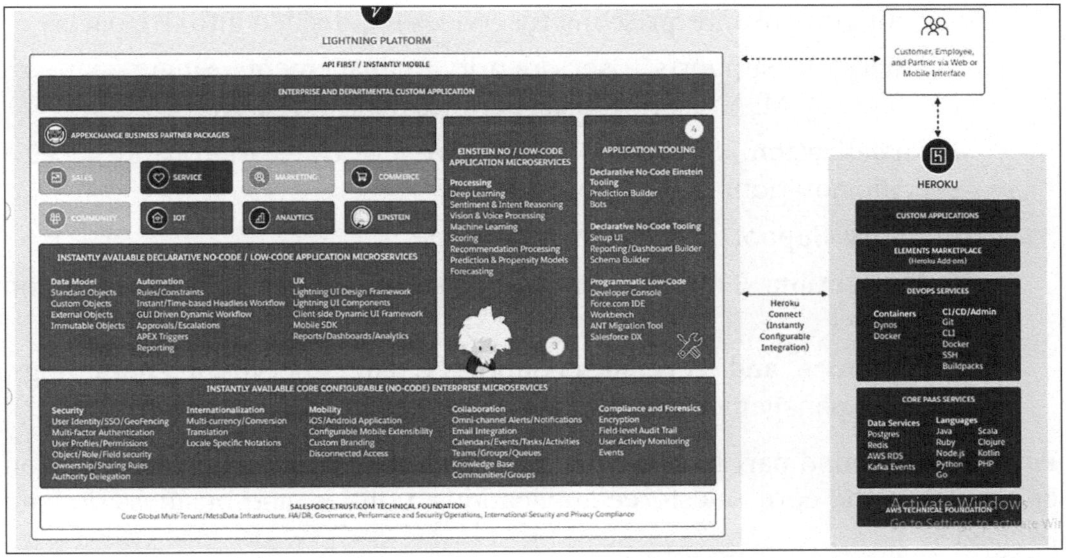

Figure 1.8: *Salesforce architecture diagram-source* (**https://www.salesforce.com/eu/products/platform/architecture/**)

As you can see in the diagram, there are two main blocks. One is the Salesforce lightning platform, which we will refer to as the core Salesforce platform and the second block is the Heroku platform which is a PaaS (Platform as a Service) offering from Salesforce. The two integrate seamlessly with Heroku Connect. The lightning platform is an API and mobile-first platform. It is where the bulk of the Salesforce features are available.

Let us break up the Salesforce architecture into six parts:

Part 1: The first part is the instantly available core configurable (No-Code) Enterprise microservices. You start building with a fully secure platform filled with microservices and mobility.

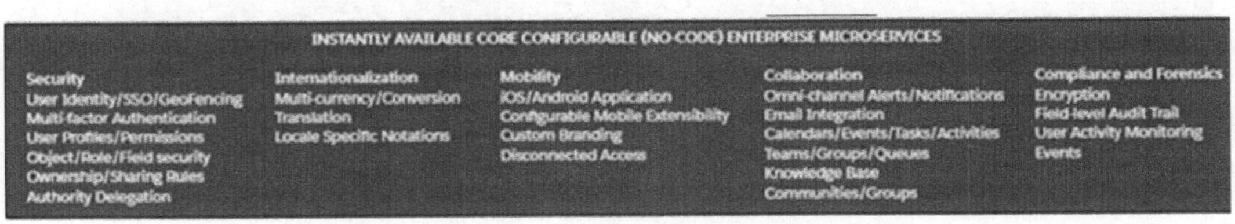

Figure 1.9: *Enterprise Microservices*

The Salesforce platform is highly configurable with no-code tools as well as with custom code. Let's talk more about the no-code tools. Later, we will discuss how we can customize Salesforce using code.

The core configurable enterprise microservices are divided into five parts:

- **Security**: It supports User Identity management, Single sign-on, Geofencing, MFA, User profiles, permissions, and so on
- **Internalization**: Supports multi-currency, translation, and locale-specific notations
- **Mobility**: Supports mobile-first apps
- **Collaboration**: Supports various tools to help teams collaborate on Salesforce
- **Compliance and Forensics**: Supports data encryption, audit logs, change management, user activity monitoring, and so on

Part 2: The second part is Salesforce Clouds and AppExchange partners. You can build on the core Salesforce applications, utilities, and business domain packages.

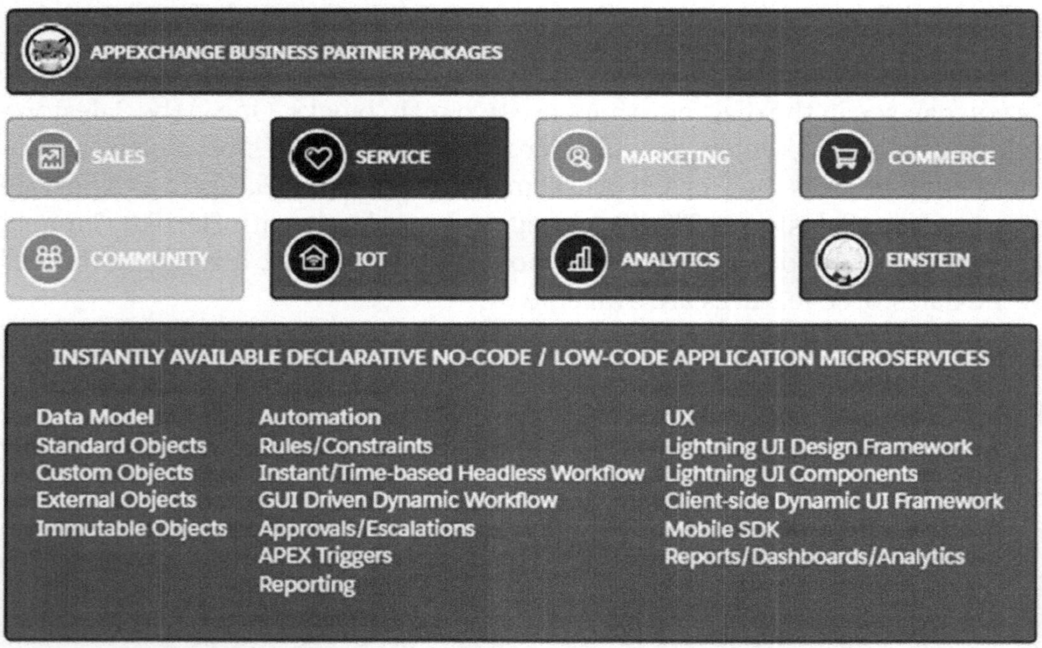

***Figure 1.10**: Salesforce Clouds and AppExchange packages*

On the top of the preceding diagram, you can see the different cloud solutions provided by Salesforce, namely Sales, Service, Marketing, Commerce, Community (now called Experience), IOT, Analytics, and Einstein cloud. These offerings provide out of the box solutions for companies using the plug-and-play model. Several business use cases are solved by out-of-the-box solutions.

Salesforce AppExchange is a platform where one can find applications for various business needs which are not present in the core Salesforce platform, as well as consultants who can help you to implement and get the most out of your Salesforce application. You can install any of the Salesforce AppExchange packages to solve specific business needs.

These core offerings are supported by the declarative No-code/ Low-code application microservices.

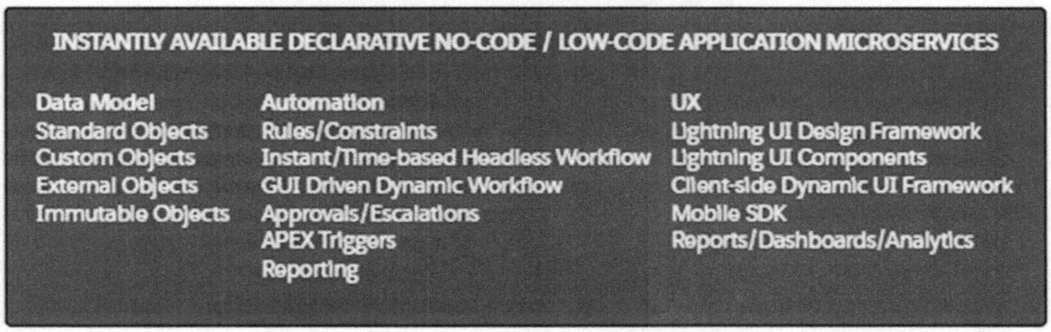

Figure 1.11: *No-code/Low-code application microservices*

To customize Salesforce to solve specific business use cases, Salesforce provides low-code/no-code solutions. There are three parts:

- **Data Model**: We will discuss the data model later. For now, it is important to note that you can create custom objects, external objects, and immutable objects, apart from the existing standard objects, to meet your business use cases.
- **Automation**: Salesforce provides many automation tools to improve the productivity of users. Process automation can be built without the need for extensive coding.
- **UX**: Salesforce provides tools to make changes to the UI using No-code/Low-code. It provides Lightning UI framework, UI components, and mobile SDK, among others to improve the UX.

Part 3: Use AI to build intelligent automation powered by Salesforce Einstein

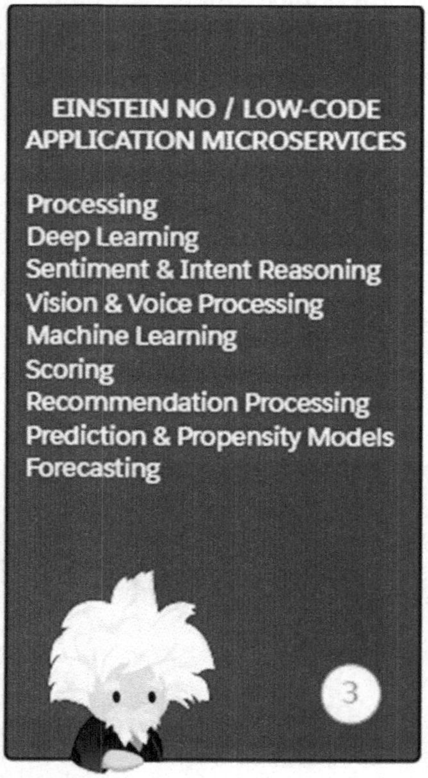

Figure 1.12: *Einstein No/low-code services*

Salesforce provides machine learning and citizen data science tools to help make intelligent decisions based on Salesforce data through Salesforce Einstein. Einstein tools make it easy for business users to perform machine learning and data science using only clicks and no code. This reduces the dependency a business user will have on a machine learning engineer or a data engineer or a data analyst. Einstein provides:

- Processing
- Deep Learning
- Sentiment and Intent Reasoning
- Vision and voice processing
- Machine Learning
- Lead Scoring
- Forecasting
- Recommendation processing

Part 4: Application Tooling- Utilize a full suite of development tools for both declarative no-code as well as low-code development.

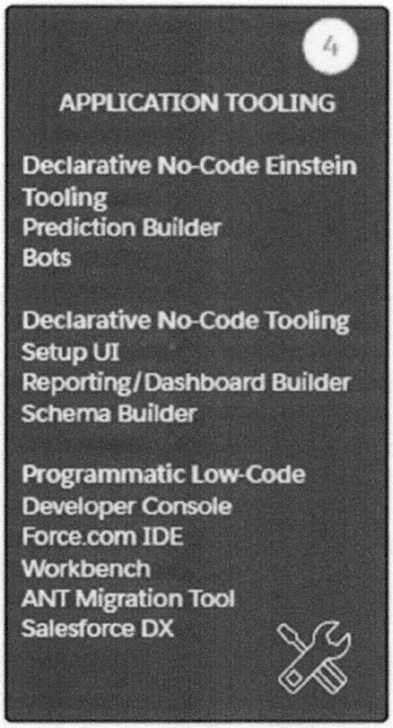

***Figure 1.13**: Application Tooling*

Salesforce provides the following to build on the Salesforce platform:

- No code Data science tools
- Prediction builder
- No code Einstein bots
- Setup UI
- Reporting/Dashboard Builder
- Schema Builder
- Developer Console
- Force.com IDE
- Workbench
- ANT migration tool
- Salesforce DX

Part 5: PaaS-based Applications- Salesforce provides users with Heroku which is a platform as a Service application.

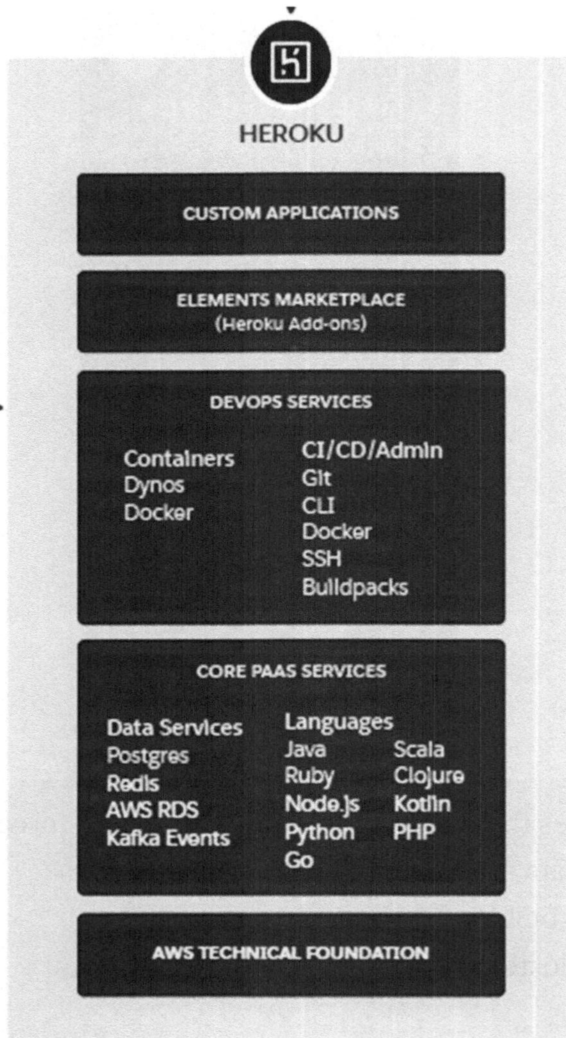

***Figure 1.14**: PaaS-based Applications*

You can design your own application and even sell your applications by becoming an AppExchange partner. Build enterprise-grade secure applications with Salesforce which provide:

- Custom Applications
- Elements marketplace
- DevOps services

- Core PaaS Services
- AWS technical foundation

Part 6: Connection between Heroku and Core Salesforce platform

Salesforce provides instantly configurable integration between the lightning platform and the Heroku platform so that you can leverage the data irrespective of its location. You can maximize programming models for maximum efficiency and agility without integration.

Salesforce Data Model

Now we will talk about the Salesforce data model. Understanding the Salesforce data model is very crucial in order to appreciate the synergies Salesforce gets when it shares the same data model among its products. This makes the Salesforce platform very powerful across different business use cases.

The data model refers to the way Salesforce stores and retrieves data. It also refers to the type of relationships you can create in the data. As already mentioned earlier, Salesforce stores data in the form of objects. Objects are like tables, where fields refer to the columns in a table and a record refers to a row of data. Let us discuss them in more detail.

All the business data is stored as objects. There are five types of objects in Salesforce namely standard objects, custom objects, external objects, platform events, and big objects. The three important ones to know are the first three in that list.

- **Standard Objects:** Objects that are part of the default Salesforce package are called standard objects. They come preinstalled when you subscribe to a Salesforce product. For example, Accounts, Contact, Opportunities, Cases, Products, and so on are all standard objects. Standard objects are created based on the research Salesforce has done in understanding and standardizing business processes. Almost all Salesforce customers use standard objects like Accounts to hold customer information, Opportunities to hold potential deals information, Contact to hold customer contacts information, and so on.

- **Custom Objects**: Custom objects, as the name suggests, are created by businesses to store information specific to their own business use case. Every business is different, and no two businesses, even in the same industry, will have the same objects. Therefore, in Salesforce, you can create your own custom objects. For example, you can create a custom object named property to store information about properties.
- **External Objects:** External objects are similar to custom objects except they are used to store data that is outside Salesforce. You can have data outside Salesforce but you can refer to that data inside Salesforce via external objects.

You can create relationships between objects in order to relate one object to another. The following types of relationships are available in Salesforce:

- **Master-Detail Relationships:** This is the type of relationship where one object acts as the parent (Master) of another object. We create a master-detail relationship between two or more objects when one object depends on another and cannot exist without the master. The detail object gets its properties, including security settings from the master object. For example, for every contact record, you need an account record. A contact cannot exist with an account. So Account is the master and Contact is the detail object. There are many details about master-detail relationships, but we won't be covering that in this book. To know more about this type of relationship between objects, you can refer to the Salesforce documentation.
- **Look-up Relationship**: If there cannot be a master-detail relationship, that is, one can exist independently without the other, then you can create a look-up relationship if you want to access one object's data on another object. Through a lookup relationship, you create a lookup field using which you can access any field on the other object. Lookup relationships can be one-to-one or one-to-many.

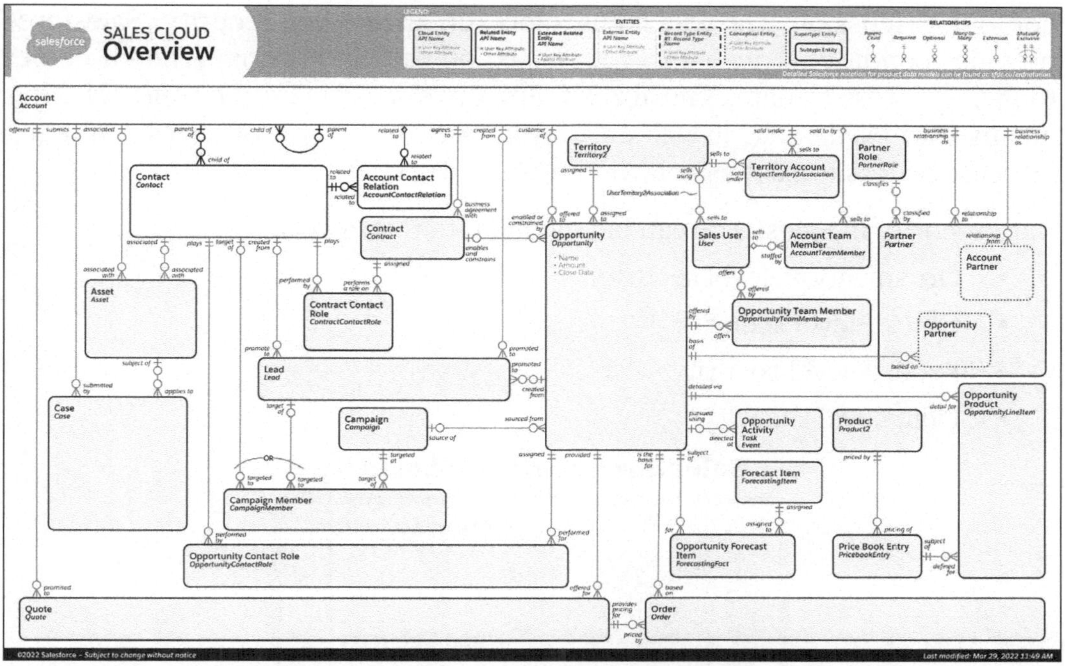

Figure 1.15: *Salesforce Data model example*
(*Source*: **https://architect.salesforce.com/diagrams/template-gallery/sales-cloud-overview-data-model**)

An example of a typical Sales cloud data model can be seen in *Figure 1.15*. Using the legend, you can infer that several different types of relationships are created. This is how a Salesforce architect will design the data model before they start creating objects and fields in Salesforce.

Salesforce Security Model

Now that we understand how Salesforce stores data, it is essential to discuss how Salesforce provides data security. Since Salesforce is a multi-tenant cloud platform, Salesforce takes the security of its customer data very seriously.

Salesforce has the industry's best security for its platform. The infrastructure layer comes with data duplication, disaster recovery planning, and backup facilities. Network services are equipped with encryption in transit and advanced threat detection features. Salesforce shield provides Platform Encryption, Event Monitoring, and Field Audit Trail. Salesforce in its security documentation states the following, "*Salesforce offers customers a robust data processing addendum containing strong privacy commitments*".

For our discussion, we will focus more on data-level security. Salesforce provides conditional access to data based on certain criteria. When it comes to giving access to data, Salesforce follows a less is the better approach. This means that by default, it will start with the lowest level of access. You can increase access to data as and when required.

Data security in Salesforce can be divided into four levels:

- Organization-level security
- Object-level security
- Record-level security
- Field-level security

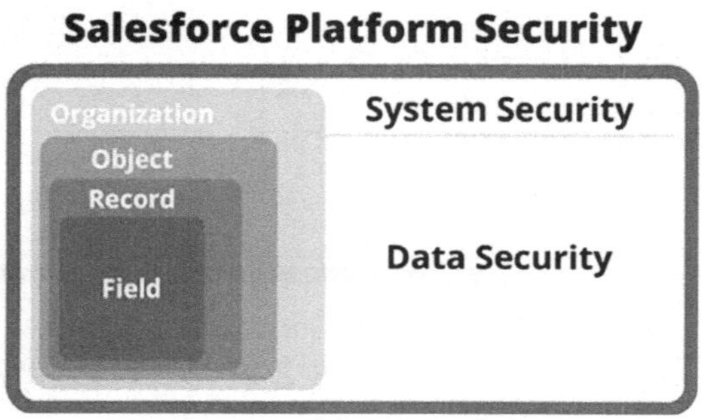

Figure 1.16: *Salesforce Security Model*

Let's talk about each of these four levels in detail.

Organization-level security

The top level of security is organization-level security. Organization-level security controls who has access to Salesforce and from where they can connect to Salesforce. Security in this layer is in the form of user credentials like user id and password, along with multi-factor authentication using a mobile phone application called Authenticator, through which a user has to enter a code along with the user id and password to log in. IP ranges are another layer of security using which Salesforce restricts the IP from which users can log in as well as the time during which users can log in. For example, you can restrict customer service reps from logging in after their shifts are over.

Object-level Security

The next level of security is object-level security. You can control who can view what objects in Salesforce. This is done through profiles and permission sets explained as follows:

Profiles: Profiles control what a user can or cannot do with objects and data, what they can do in the application, and whether they have access to certain page layouts, fields, and so on. Every user is given a profile. You can either choose from the standard profiles available in Salesforce or create a custom profile.

To see the profiles available in your org, click the gear icon on your Salesforce org home page and then search for `Profiles` in the quick find box.

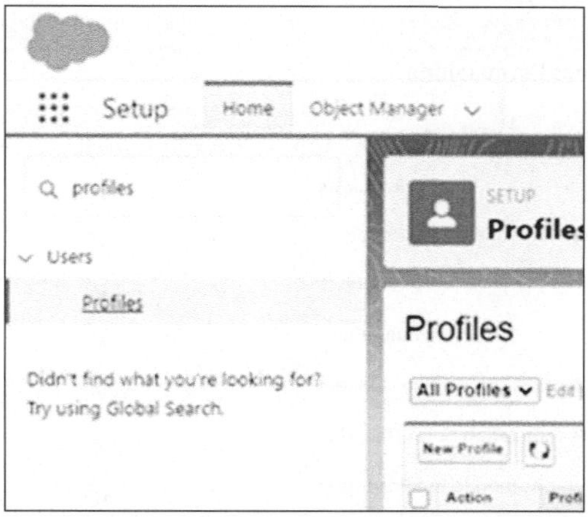

Figure 1.17: *Salesforce quick find box*

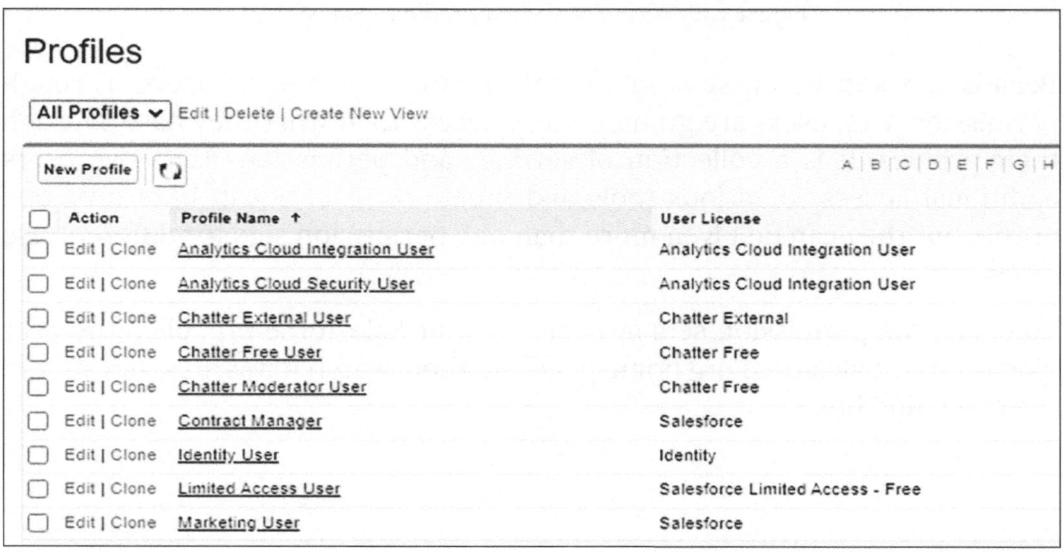

Profiles

All Profiles | Edit | Delete | Create New View

New Profile

Action	Profile Name ↑	User License
Edit | Clone	Analytics Cloud Integration User	Analytics Cloud Integration User
Edit | Clone	Analytics Cloud Security User	Analytics Cloud Integration User
Edit | Clone	Chatter External User	Chatter External
Edit | Clone	Chatter Free User	Chatter Free
Edit | Clone	Chatter Moderator User	Chatter Free
Edit | Clone	Contract Manager	Salesforce
Edit | Clone	Identity User	Identity
Edit | Clone	Limited Access User	Salesforce Limited Access - Free
Edit | Clone	Marketing User	Salesforce

Figure 1.18: *Profiles in Salesforce*

As you can see in the preceding image, there are a number of profiles available out of the box from Salesforce. You can also create custom profiles according to business needs. On the column named custom, those that have a checkmark on the custom column are custom profiles.

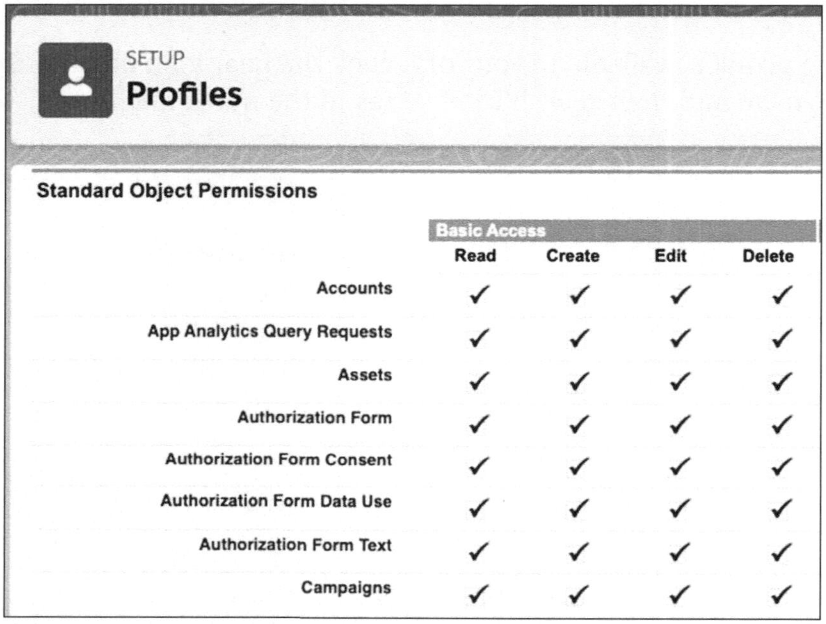

***Figure 1.19**: Permissions in a profile in Salesforce*

Permission set: Permission sets grant additional access to users. Through permission sets, users are granted more access than what they have through their profiles. It is a collection of settings and permissions that give users additional access to various tools and functions. A user can have only one profile but they can be given more than one permission sets for different use cases.

To check the permission sets available in your Salesforce org, click the gear icon on your Salesforce org home page and then search for `permission sets` in the quick find box.

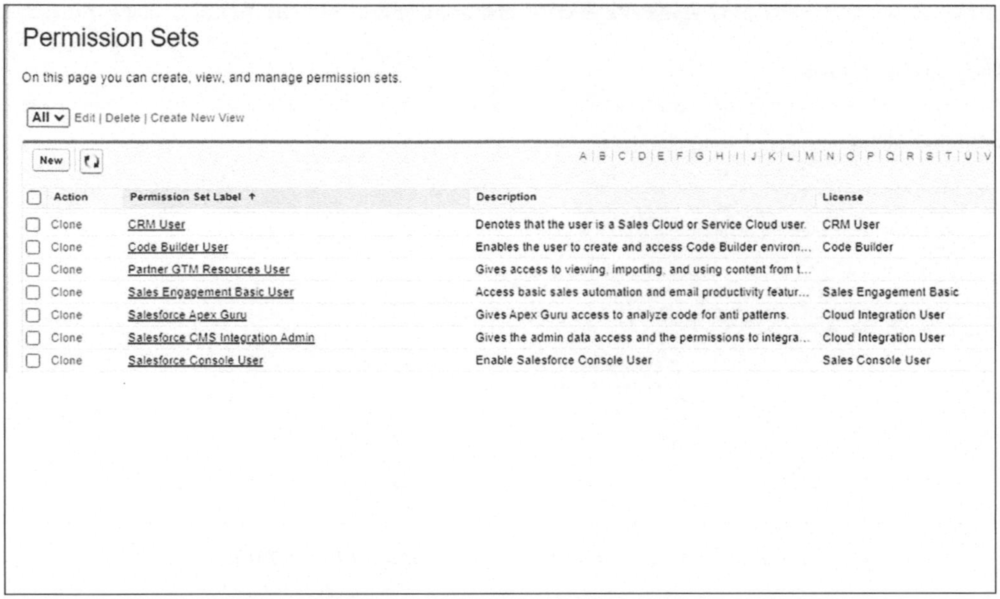

***Figure 1.20**: Permission sets in Salesforce*

Record-level Security

Record-level security refers to object records the users have access to on the basis of their profiles. As records are rows of data in Salesforce, record-level security essentially controls what data a user can view in Salesforce.

There are multiple ways access to records can be granted or restricted to users. By default, if a user has CRUD (Create, Read, Update, and Delete) permission on an object, they can perform CRUD operations on the record they create. Restrictions can be imposed to prevent users from taking action on records created by other users.

There are four different ways in Salesforce through which we can control record access. They are listed below in top-down order. Salesforce recommends setting the most restrictive access through org-wide defaults and then gradually increasing access through record security tools.

- **Org-wide default:** It specifies the default level of access that the user will have in that Salesforce org

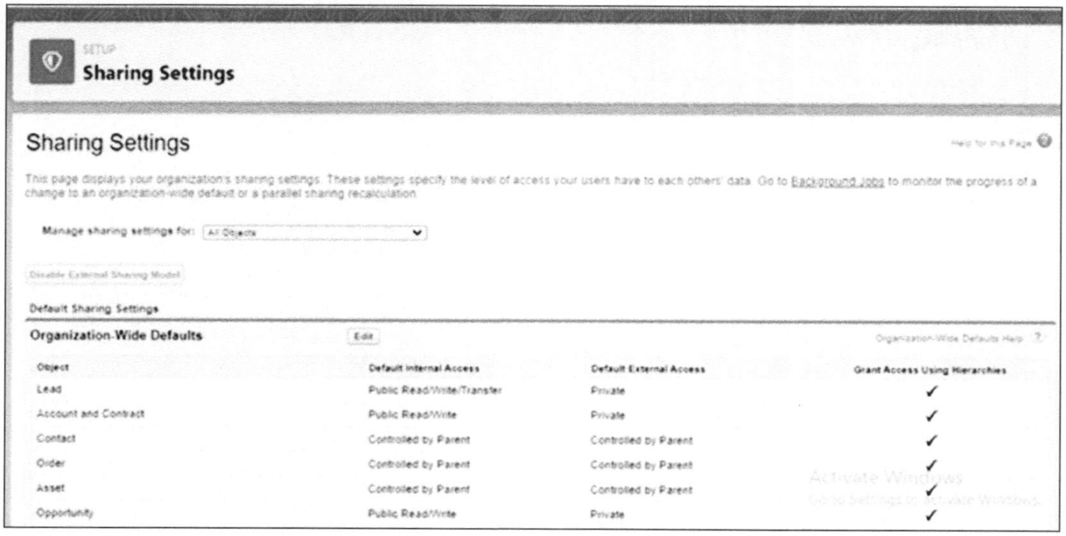

Figure 1.21: *Salesforce Org-wide default settings*

There are four options to choose from for each object: private, public read-only, public read/write, and public read/write/transfer. The most restrictive is private, and the most access is given by public read/write/transfer. Access to records for child objects is determined by the access levels of the parent object.

- **Role Hierarchies**: Through role hierarchies, you can give access to users based on their role hierarchy. This means that managers have access to all records that are owned by their subordinates. Subordinates will not be able to access records that are owned by the managers.
- **Sharing rules**: If you want to give access to certain records to users, and if it is restricted by the two methods mentioned here, then you can use sharing rules. Sharing rules are like permission sets, except sharing rules give access to records, whereas sharing rules are for giving access to records. For example, if you want the marketing department to have access to those opportunity records where the lead is generated from email marketing, then you can create a sharing rule that will give the marketing team access to those records.
- **Manual sharing**: Manual sharing is used to give access to a user based on ad-hoc requirements. It is generally done by the owner of the record, but admins can also do it on their behalf.

Field-level Security

Field-level security controls whether a user has access to certain fields in an object. So even if a user has access to an object and access to the record, certain fields can be hidden from the user. So if a company wants to hide the sales quota of sales agents from other fellow sales agents, they can use field-level security to restrict access to the field. Restrict access to data in Salesforce means that the user won't be able to see the field on the page layout or in reports. It is as if the fields don't exist.

Field-level security helps in protecting sensitive fields from users without restricting complete access to the object. Field-level security is also controlled by profiles and permission sets.

Salesforce Customer 360

If you read Salesforce's marketing collaterals, you will often hear the term *Customer* 360 . What exactly is customer 360, and why should you care?

Customer 360 refers to the complete view of a customer, right from the lead stage to the stage of product/service delivery and beyond. It means you will be able to know exactly where the customer is in their customer journey. The ultimate vision of Salesforce is to provide a complete view of customers to enterprises.

Customer 360 helps to connect marketing, sales, commerce, IT service, and order management for every customer. The connection will lead to improved productivity, increased profitability, and reduced friction and costs.

Customer 360 is thus a collection of tools that connect different Salesforce applications and create a unified view of the customer. Salesforce Customer 360 is an integrated CRM platform that connects your departments and customer data. So, you would have your customer sales data from Sales Cloud, service data from Service Cloud, marketing data from Marketing cloud, and commerce data from Commerce cloud and then use this to create a unified user profile.

Customer 360 means an integrated CRM platform. It is not to be confused with a single product. It is the collection of all Salesforce products, integrated together that forms the Salesforce Customer 360. So it is more like a vision or a concept that Salesforce has, rather than it being a Salesforce product.

When you have Salesforce Customer 360, you will be able to create a unified profile of your customer. That means when a customer comes to your company for any service-related query, you need not ask for details regarding their purchase. You will be able to see all the data in a central place: the integrated CRM. After a successful service experience, you may send the customer a few marketing collaterals for a new offer and thereby increase cross-sell and upsell opportunities. That is the goal of Customer 360.

Figure 1.22: *Salesforce Customer 360 (Source:* **https://craftware.com/customer-360-degree-view-in-salesforce-service-cloud/**)

Benefits of Customer 360

Some benefits of Customer 360 are explained here:

- **Consistent experience for customers:** When you have an integrated CRM, then you get all the customer data in one place. So whether you are providing service to your customers or marketing to them, you have relevant customer data with you. You should not provide a new offer to a customer who is facing issues with one of their purchases. Likewise, customers won't have to explain what they bought and their other details again and again to your service team in order to get service. Your service agents will have that information on their screens all in one place.

- **Increase the productivity of employees:** Your employees get a single, unified view of the customer, so they don't have to spend time collecting information.
- **Improve marketing spending:** Running and optimizing marketing spending is easier with the correct data. You can track which customers are responding to which marketing assets and optimize accordingly
- **Easier Collaborations**: Collaborations among sales, service, marketing, and so on become easier with a unified customer profile.

Salesforce Data Cloud

We have discussed almost all the important products from Salesforce. But we haven't yet touched upon Salesforce Data Cloud. Where does Salesforce Data Cloud fit in?

So far, we have talked about Sales Cloud, Service Cloud, marketing cloud, Tableau, and so on. We also talked about an integrated CRM called Salesforce Customer 360, which aims to bring together the customer data from different Salesforce or third-party applications and then create a unified customer profile. We also said that Salesforce Customer 360 is not a product but rather a vision: to have Salesforce as a single source of truth for customer data.

To understand Data Cloud, we need to understand another Salesforce product, which we haven't yet talked about: Salesforce CDP, or Data Cloud for Marketing as it is known now. Salesforce CDP refers to the customer data platform product from Salesforce. The birth of Salesforce CDP started with a product known as Customer Audience 360 (CA360). CA360 was created with the initial vision of collecting data from different sources and making it available for marketing for user activations. Data collected from different systems would be collected from different sources, and then used to power the connected and personalized marketing experience. However, in the industry, the application that did this was called the customer data platform. Salesforce decided to change the name of the product to adhere to industry standards. SO CA360 was rebranded as Salesforce Customer Data Platform (CDP) without any meaningful change to the functionalities.

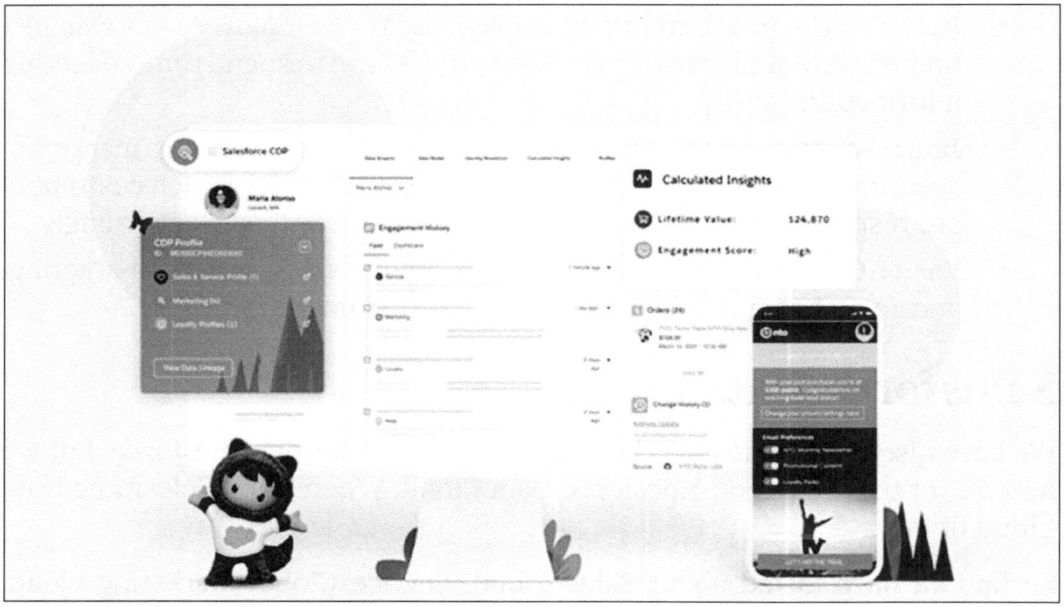

***Figure 1.23**: Salesforce CDP (source- **https://www.salesforce.com/resources/articles/what-is-a-customer-data-platform/**)*

Salesforce again rebranded the Salesforce CDP to Salesforce Data Cloud for Marketing to specify that the product has a use case for marketing. The major features were still the same.

However, there is still a gap that needed to be addressed. Even though Salesforce was helping enterprises capture data from different sources and bring it all in one place, the data was not real-time. In today's fast-paced digital world, data becomes stale very quickly. People check out a product on their mobile phone, later they again check in their tab and might make a purchase from their laptop later. All of this might happen over a period of a few hours. Companies need to make sure that they provide a consistent experience to users shifting devices or channels. For that, we need data in real-time or near real-time rather than data that is refreshed once a week or even once a day.

Here comes Salesforce Data Cloud. Salesforce Data Cloud was launched to power the customer 360 experience by making data in the Salesforce CDP product available to not just other products of the C360 suite of applications but also to other applications, in real-time. The keyword here is real-time. The data to which enterprises will take access will be real-time data. Salesforce Data Cloud is not only built for marketing but also for other use cases like product analytics, customer service, engagement, and so on.

Salesforce Data Cloud is supposed to revolutionize the customer data platform industry by making decisions accurate based on real-time data. We will delve into the details of the technology in the later chapters.

Figure 1.24: *Salesforce Data Cloud (Source-* **https://www.avasoft.com/how-salesforce-Data Cloud-empowers-customer-360/**)

So if we have to sum it up in an equation, it will be something like this:

```
SF CDP + SF Data Cloud = Real-time Customer 360
```

Conclusion

We are excited to understand in more detail, and we hope you are too. But before we go to the topic of Salesforce Data Cloud, we would like to introduce and understand the working of a customer data platform. That is what comes in the next chapter.

Before moving on to the next chapter, let us summarize what we learned here:

- A CRM is a technology for managing all your company's relationships and interactions with customers and potential customers
- Salesforce is a cloud-based CRM platform that helps businesses manage customer relationships effortlessly
- Salesforce has different products catering to different business use cases, like Sales cloud for sales, service cloud for service, marketing

cloud for marketing, and Salesforce Data Cloud for customer data management, among others

- Salesforce is easy to use and customize for business users using its point and click based development tools. Although custom coding is also available for Salesforce developers
- Salesforce provides industry best practices when it comes to data security and data storage
- Salesforce Data Cloud Customer Data Cloud or commonly known as Salesforce Data Cloud, is a cloud-based CDP platform that helps to unify customer data

Questions

If you can answer the following questions and explain them to someone who has not read the book, consider yourself knowledgeable enough to proceed to the next chapter:

1. What is meant by a CRM platform, and why do businesses depend on it?
2. Which is the most popular CRM platform today?
3. What are the different Salesforce products that are meant for business enterprises?
4. Explain the Salesforce architecture.
5. What data model does Salesforce have?
6. How does Salesforce ensure data security and data privacy?
7. What is the need for a product like Salesforce Data Cloud?

Further Readings

If you wish to read more about Salesforce than what we could cover here, please go to the following links or resources:

- **https://trailhead.salesforce.com/**
- **https://developer.salesforce.com/signup**
- **https://www.salesforceben.com/**
- **https://www.salesforce.com/**

CHAPTER 2
Introduction to Customer Data Platform

Introduction

This chapter introduces the reader to the concept of Customer Data Platform (CDP) and its importance today. Readers will be able to understand the challenges faced by companies in delivering a great customer experience.

In this chapter, we will understand what a CDP is and why it is important for all companies to invest in one. We will discuss the challenges faced by companies that don't use a CDP and, hence, don't have a single source of truth for their customer data. We will also discuss in theory how a CDP platform solves customer data problems for companies. Next, we will learn the concepts behind the working of a CDP before discussing the different types of CDPs.

Understanding the high-level workflow of a CDP will help the readers to conceptualize an abstract model of a CDP and what it brings to the table. After this, we will delve into a detailed discussion on different concepts required for implementing a CDP for your organization. Lastly, we will finish this chapter by understanding the challenges faced by customer data platforms today. In the later chapters, we will learn how to solve those challenges.

Structure

In this chapter, the following topics will be covered:

- Introducing the Customer Data Platform (CDP)
- Challenges faced by Companies due to the L ack of a Single Source of Truth
- How a CDP solves Customer Data Problems for Companies
- Data Types handled by CDPs
- Identity Resolution
- Types of CDP
- The High-Level Workflow of a CDP Platform
- Tracking Plan, Event Tracking, and Event Streaming
- Challenges faced by CDP Platforms

Introducing the Customer Data Platform (CDP)

Customer data platforms, or CDPs are among the most important yet confusing technology. It means different things to different people. It does not help that technology keeps changing every year and that makes it very difficult to put into words what it means. We will attempt to define it and then explain what it means.

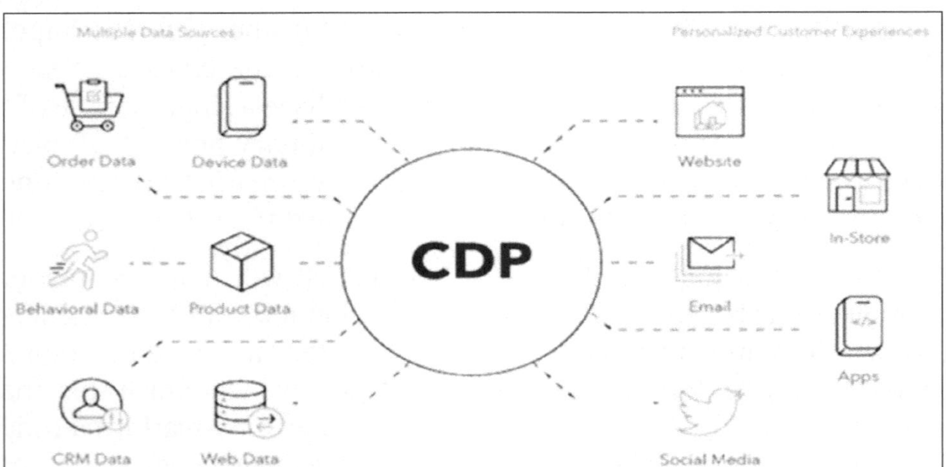

Figure 2.1: *Customer Data Platform takes data from different sources and creates a unified customer profile*

According to the CDP Institute (source **https://www.cdpinstitute.org/cdp-basics/**), the definition of a CDP is "A *Customer Data Platform is packaged software that creates a persistent, unified customer database that is accessible to other systems.*"

It is called packaged software as a majority of the components you require to run a CDP are provided within the package itself, requiring less effort for setup and maintenance. It helps to create a unified customer database, which means it helps to bring customer data from different sources and store it in one place. *Accessible to other systems* means that the data stored in the CDP can be sent to other platforms for business initiatives like marketing, user engagement, personalization, and so on.

A relatively newer concept in CDP is to leave out the database part. So, a CDP can refer to a software package that helps you connect your different sources of data (input) to your chosen destination (where your data needs to reside, usually a data warehouse). These are leaner CDP tools that do not include a database with the CDP. They just help you to bring the data from different sources to a single platform and then re-direct that data to your chosen data warehouse. You can then unify the data and make it available to different platforms from the data warehouse (*Figure* 2.2).

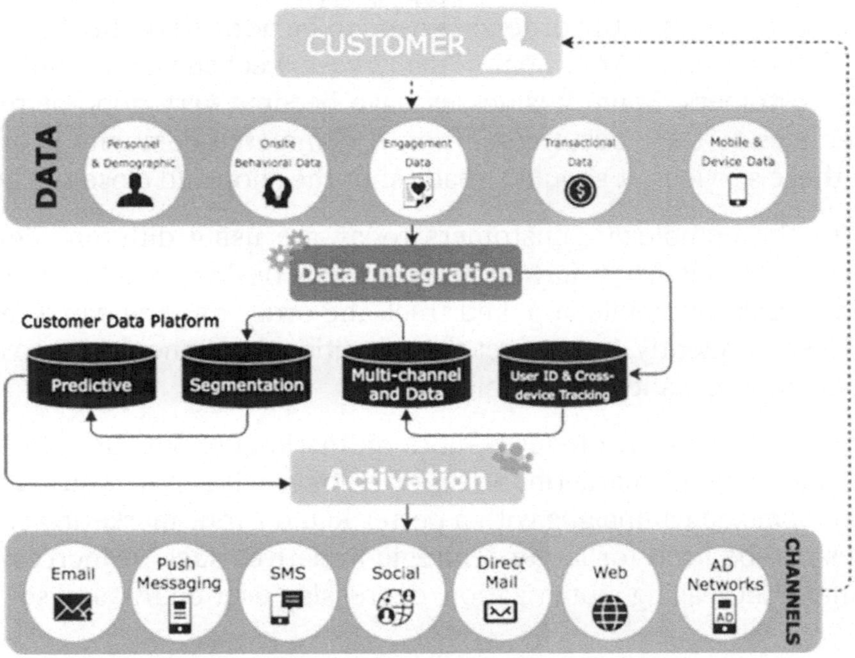

Figure 2.2: *CDP makes data available for different platforms*
(**Source: https://infotrust.com/articles/what-is-a-customer-data-platform-cdp/**)

Whether the CDP includes a database or gives the flexibility to choose the database of your choice, the important thing to note is that any CDP helps you bring customer data from different channels and then merge it all together to create a unified customer profile. If you understand this core principle of CDP software, you are good to go ahead.

So, in *Figure* 2.2, you can see data coming from different sources into the CDP and the data that is coming out of the CDP helps to create personalized customer experiences.

Challenges Faced by Companies due to the Lack of a Single Source of Truth

In this digital world we are living in, customers expect a lot from businesses. If you are in the B2C business, customers expect great buying as well as after-sales experiences. 20 years ago, this was not the case.

As more and more companies became customer-centric, it's set a benchmark for all the other companies to follow suit or perish. For example, when we order a product from an e-commerce store, we expect a confirmation mail immediately. Then we expect the shipping details to be shared with us. We need the ability to track the order. We need to be notified of the day when the order will be delivered to our home. Finally, we expect some discount coupons for loyal customers. Some businesses have become very good at providing these services to their customers. If an e-commerce company is unable to provide these services, it should already shut the shop and close the business.

To add to the complexity, customers today are using different devices to connect with brands. They may place an order on desktop machines, make the payment through a mobile app, and track the order on their tab. Customers shift devices frequently, but expect the transition from one device to another to happen smoothly and without hiccups.

A lot of literature on CDP focuses more on marketing. But the role CDP has to play goes beyond marketing. Yes, of course, with CDP, you can create more personalized campaigns with a better ROI on your marketing spending. But CDPs can be used for larger strategic initiatives such as increasing user engagement, increasing monetization, decreasing user churn, and so on.

Figure 2.3: *Survey results on top challenges to customer experience delivery* (*Source:* **https://www.marketingcharts.com/customer-centric/customer-experience-115587**)

Based on a survey conducted by Gartner, among the top challenges to customer experience delivery are issues related to collecting, managing, and storing customer data. It is only second to the lack of an appropriate customer experience strategy.

Collecting and storing customer data is a difficult task that prevents companies from creating a single source of truth, due to which they face the following challenges:

- **Fragmented customer data**: If there are challenges to collecting and unifying customer data, then companies have fragmented customer data in different systems. The data is useless and cannot be used for decision-making or any other business initiatives. It defeats the purpose of collecting the data in the first place.
- **Ineffective marketing:** Lack of proper data results in ineffective marketing efforts. Companies may send a discount voucher to a customer who is not happy with the service instead of solving the customer's problem first. Or they will send the same marketing artifact to that customer who has already bought the product. The lack of a single source of truth reduces marketing effectiveness.

- **Inconsistent experience for customers**: Lack of a unified customer profile across different platforms means that customers will not have a consistent experience across different channels or mediums. This will increase customer churn.
- **Incorrect metrics**: Due to the lack of a single source of truth, the data becomes unreliable. So, calculating business metrics using unreliable data can provide incorrect business metrics. Decision-making is affected as often there will be conflicts regarding the veracity of the data.
- **Adhering to data protection and privacy laws**: Without proper storage and collection of data, adhering to strict data protection and privacy laws becomes a challenge for organizations.

How a CDP solves Customer Data Problems for Companies

Now that we appreciate the problems faced by enterprises due to the lack of a single repository of customer data; let us see how CDPs solve customer data problems for companies.

Problem: Different sources for customer data

Solution: Connect different sources of customer data easily using a CDP

Explanation: CDPs solve the business problem of having different sources for customer data. The customer data may come from an iOS app, an Android app, a FireTV app, a website, a physical point of sale, Salesforce, WordPress, and so on. CDPs come with connectors, using which you can easily integrate with different sources cost-effectively. Using APIs or using SDKs, you can connect your sources to your CDP to bring the data from different sources into one single database. You can also send the data after transformation, or as it is, to different destinations. For example, after building customer profiles, you can send the data for analytics to Mixpanel, or marketing systems like Blaze.

Problem: Lack of unique customer profile

Solution: Connect different sources of customer data and built a unique customer profile

Explanation: In today's phydigital world, customer interactions with brands have become complex. Customers may interact with a digital ad on one channel and then may purchase from a physical store. Without the ability to combine the data from different sources, getting a complete picture of the customer journey is impossible. CDPs offer identity resolution or identity stitching capabilities, where CDPs correctly attribute multiple data points to the same person and assign each profile a permanent customer ID. With the use of AI and machine learning, it is now possible to evaluate thousands of touchpoints and assign the correct customer ID. Imagine doing it manually!

The customer profile created is called persistent customer ID and can now be utilized for different business use cases. A persistent Id is an identifier that can provide a single view of an individual across numerous devices, including desktop, mobile web, and in-app, without duplication.

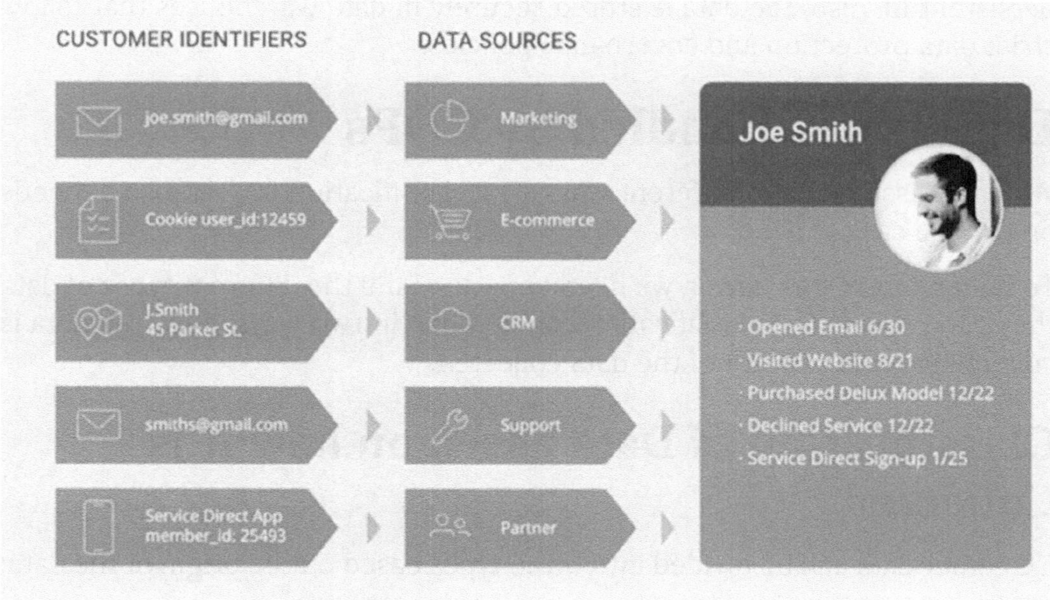

***Figure 2.4**: CDPs help in unifying data from different sources*
(*source*: **https://www.treasuredata.com/cdp-academy/customer-data-unification/**)

Problem: Ineffective marketing

Solution: Using persistent Id, marketers can avoid targeting certain users with low or zero interest and improve marketing effectiveness.

Explanation: After you create persistent IDs, it is possible to recognize customers as individuals rather than just disconnected data points from different sources. This information can be used to improve the accuracy of attribution models, which will help you understand which channels are working the best in sales. Based on the complete set of data, you can optimize the campaigns more effectively. You can avoid sending ads for products to people who have already bought the product or are actively pursuing a support ticket related to a purchase. You can deploy cross-channel frequency capping to prevent oversaturating your audience with too many ads.

Problem: Adhering to strict data protection and privacy laws

Solution: CDPs are designed to handle data protection regulations and privacy laws.

Explanation: CDPs use persistent Ids due to which it is easier to follow regulations such as the *right to be forgotten* . If any user wants their data erased, an enterprise can do so if all the collected information is recognizable using a persistent Id. Also, the data is stored securely in data warehouses that follow strict data protection and governance policies.

Data types handled by CDPs

We can classify data in different ways. The classification of data also depends on the use case at hand.

To understand CDPs better, we need to understand the different types of data they can collect. The classification can be done in two ways: h ow the data is collected and the nature of the data collected.

Classification of Data based on how it is Collected

Customer data can be divided into three types based on the origin of the data:

- **First-Party Data**: First-party data refers to the data brands collect when users interact with their websites, apps, retail stores, and so on. The data is collected with consent, and user identification is possible. Most of the collected data is supplied by the user, like email IDs and phone numbers. Others are collected when users interact with the brands, like purchase history, membership details, loyalty program info, and so on. First-party data is highly reliable and accurate, and the most useful data for brands.
- **Second-Party Data**: Second-Party data is the data that brands collect from trusted partners. The agreement with partners can be based on a data-sharing agreement, or brands may purchase the data from a third-party partner. As the partner is a trusted one, second-party data is also

accurate and reliable, but less so than first-party data. It is important to be cognizant of privacy regulations like GDPR and CCPA before you buy data from partners. Second-party data is merged with first-party data to create more accurate data models.

- **Third-party Data**: Third-party data is the data that brands acquire from data aggregators. Data aggregators are companies that collect data from different sources and compile them into datasets to sell to other companies. The data aggregators do not themselves interact with the customers. They maintain and build datasets. As the data is obtained from different sources, they are less reliable and accurate than first-party and second-party data. Also, one has no clue whether data regulations were followed while obtaining the data. So brands have to be careful while using third-party data. But if properly used, third-party data can be stitched together with other first-party to improve targeting. Examples of third-party data include data collected from Google advertising.

In the following table, we have summarized the differences between the three data types:

First-party Data	Second-party Data	Third-party Data
Direct relationship with the customer	Indirect customer relationship	Indirect customer relationship
Collected with consent	Collected with consent	Unknown if it's collected with consent (depends on the data provider)
Individual data	Individual data	Aggregate Data
High accuracy and reliability	High accuracy and reliability	Low accuracy and reliability
Not shared	Shared only with trusted partners	Shared with many companies
Examples: Customer Email	Examples: Website Activity	Examples: Income
- Customer email	- Website activity	- Income

***Table 2.1**: Classification of Data based on how it is collected*

Classification of Data based on the Nature of the Data Collected

Based on the nature of the data collected, data can be divided into four major types:

- **Identity Data** refers to data that helps to identify a user. For example, First and last names, age, gender, email id, social media ids, and so on
- **Descriptive data** refers to data that reveals more information about the person and their lifestyle, for example, their income, hobbies, type of house, type of car, relationship status, nature of the job, and so on.
- **Behavioral data** refers to the data that reveals how a person behaves with brands, for example, purchase history, cart abandonment, ads liked, ads clicked, interaction on the app and website, and so on.
- **Qualitative data** refers to the data that provides more information about customer preferences and opinions, for example, product rating, service rating, reasons for a particular brand preference, and so on.

These four types of data can come from first-party, second-party, or third-party sources. Identity data comes from a first-party or second-party source, the rest can come from any source.

The job of a CDP is to take the different sources of data and their different data types and bring them to a single platform where we can stitch the data. Next, we will discuss the concept of data stitching and focus on identity stitching which is used to create unique customer profiles.

Identity Resolution

Now that we know that CDPs bring in different types of data, we need to understand how they manage to make sense of it. Customer data comes from different devices, user ids, session ids, and so on. To create unique customer profiles, we need to uniquely identify the user irrespective of the device, IP addresses, and so on. We also need to consider privacy regulations like the GDPR. The job is easier said than done, but we will try to understand the challenges here and propose solutions later in the book.

To put it simply, identity resolution is the process of uniquely identifying the user who is using different channels to interact with the brand. For example, you may visit the website of a brand, and add a product to the cart. But to checkout, you need to log in. After you log in to that website, you would still want that product to be in your cart, rather than having to again add the product to the cart. Now it is the job of the identity resolution system to identify the previously not logged-in user as the same as the logged-in user. Once it does that, you will be able to see that the cart already has the product which you added when you were browsing without logging in. This provides a better customer experience.

The preceding example was a relatively easy scenario. Let us look at another scenario. Let's say you are browsing an e-commerce website without logging in from your laptop. Then you add a few products to the cart. But you don't check out from the laptop. Later, you open the same website on your mobile. There, you log in and can see the products in your cart. This was possible because of identity resolution.

Identity resolution is the ability to persistently recognize a unique entity across all digital and physical channels to build a rich profile to personalize the customer journey.

Identity resolution makes sense of the distributed customer data and turns it into a concrete data point useful for business use cases. It is a challenging process when you have to also consider privacy restrictions. For users who don't give consent to use the data for personalization, we need to make sure we are not storing any data that can be used to uniquely identify that user.

Identity resolution is done using identity stitching, also called user stitching. It is a process through which we collate and tie or stitch together matching identifier data, such as email ids, and device ids, to create a single customer profile. We use the word *stitched* as normally if one user is using different devices then it will be counted as different users as they will be given different user IDs. But a CDP will try to stitch the different user Ids to a single profile. Identity stitching takes the help of identity graphs.

An identity graph is a type of database that stores all identifiers that correlate with individual users.

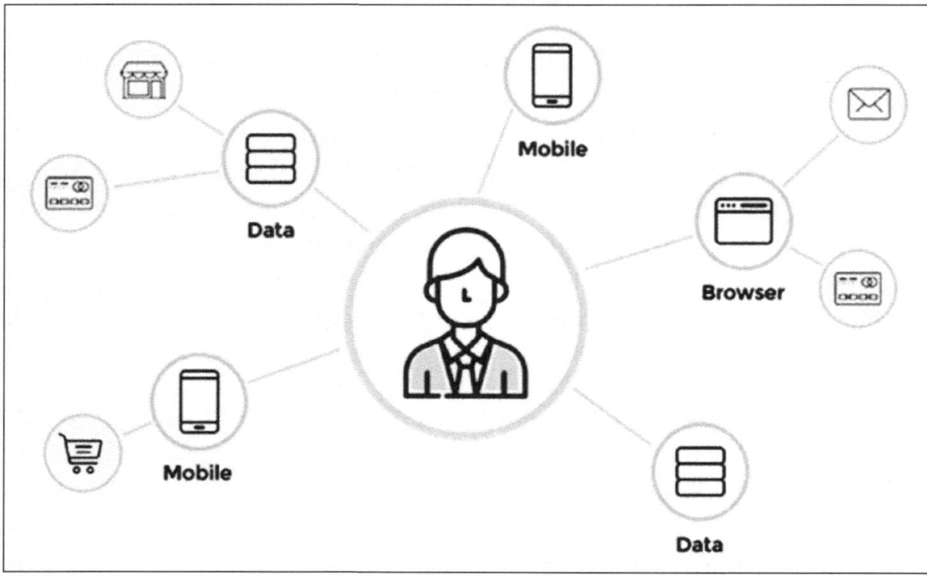

***Figure 2.5**: Identity graph*
(*source:* **https://www.richpanel.com/blog/what-is-an-identity-graph**)

Identity graph focuses on the connection between nodes. The relationship is based on different data points connected via nodes. The nodes can be generated for an anonymous session (user browning without logging in) or an authenticated session where the user has logged in. When a new data point is added, the graph database determines where the new node fits. As more and more data points are fed, it matches those points to a customer identifier.

Identities are stitched using three types of matches:

- **Fuzzy matching**: Fuzzy matching is an approximate string-matching technique. It helps to identify two elements of text, string, or entries that are similar but not identical. For example, Joe Smith can be matched to Joseph Smith if the device ids are the same.
- **Deterministic**: If there is a clear connection between two data points, like a matching device id or a credit card number, then the data point can be attributed to a relevant user node. This method is called a deterministic match. We can conclusively say that we have matched the data point with the correct user.
- **Probabilistic**: For data points where we are less certain of finding a match, we create a model based on predictive algorithms. For example, when we use identifiers like IP address, device type, browser ids, and so on , to find a match. In one house, many users can use the same device

or IP address, so this match comes with a certain probability, which is less than 100%.

Table 2.2 shows the differences between these three types of matches:

	Fuzzy Matching	**Deterministic**	**Probabilistic**
Definition	Relationship created based on approximate string matching	Relationship created based on clear connection	Relationships created based on predictive algorithms
Examples	Match PII data (for example Name, home address, and so on)	Match Cookies ID to email when a user logs into a browser Cookie123=smith@gmail.com	Match Cokie ID and MAID based on common characteristics Cookie123=IDFA413
Use Case	• CRM • Customer Support	• Email Marketing • Social activation	• Scale and reach on the open web

Table 2.2: *Differences between different methods of identity stitching*

So far, we have just scratched the surface of identity resolution. There is a lot to understand here. Data engineers who work to resolve identity resolution face a lot of challenges in attributing a user behavior to a particular user as the user journey becomes more and more complicated with the advancements of technology. The idea was to introduce the topic of identity resolution to the reader so that they are aware of the concept. We will get into more details in the later chapters.

Types of CDP

Since the origin of data platforms, there have been many developments in this field. Different platforms have come and gone. Some stayed back, modified to fit the latest requirements. It is difficult to categorize the different types of CDPs that are available in the market today, and there are quite a number of them. The CDP market is fragmented, with more than 100 players. However, we have identified the most important ones among those.

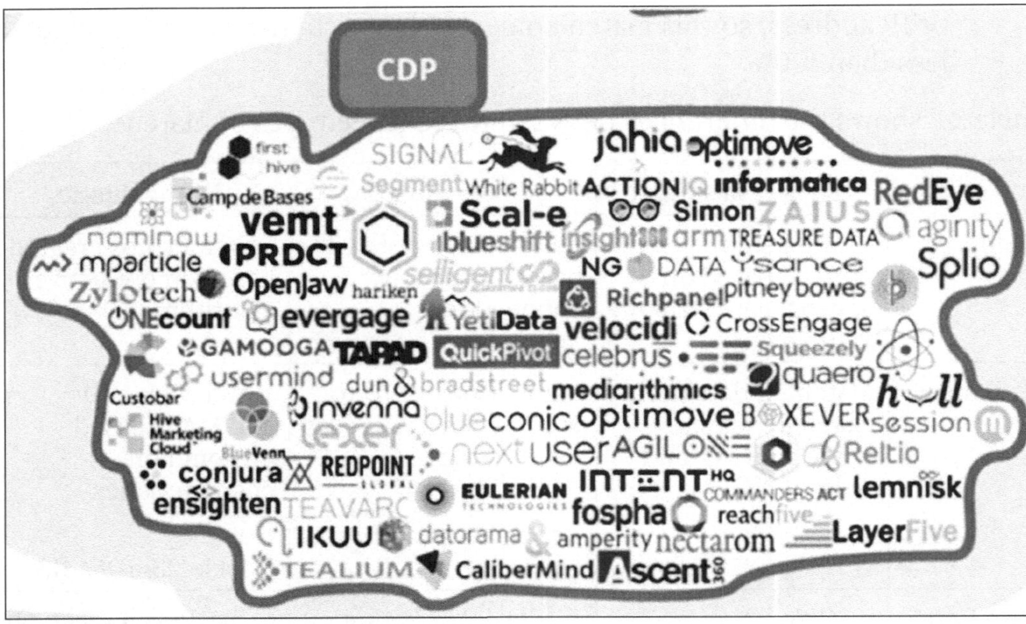

Figure 2.6: *The CDP market is very fragmented with more than 100 players (source:* **https://chiefmartec.com/2020/04/marketing-technology-landscape-2020-martech-5000/***)*

CDPs can be classified as follows:

- **MarTech Suites**: These are CDP offerings from MarTech vendors. They are integrated with other tools from the same vendor. These are more engagement or data management oriented with the former more prevalent. Example: Salesforce Data cloud for marketers (previously Salesforce CDP), Adobe real-time customer data platform, and so on.
- **Engagement-oriented CDP**: These are pure play CDPs focusing more on engagement and offering self-service capabilities like self-service segmentation, journey orchestration, audience builder, and so on. Example: Segment, Tealium, Blueshift, and so on . They are the preferred choice for marketers as they are powerful marketing solutions. User Activation is the main goal.
- **Data Management oriented CDP**: These types of CDPs focus more on data management like ingestion, profile unification, data cleansing, identity resolution, and so on. The main job is to connect different sources of data and unify and transform customer data. These are not

activation tools and require other third-party tools for activation. Data management CDPs are further classified based on where the data is stored. Some CDPs act as data storehouses where the customer data is stored. Whereas others are data warehouse-agnostic CDPs where you are free to use the data warehouse of your choice to store the data. Your data, your Warehouse. These offer the most flexibility and you are not locked in for a particular data storage partner. Examples are RudderStack, Treasure Data, mparticle, and so on.

The High-Level Workflow of a CDP Platform

Now that you understand the basic concepts of the workings of a CDP platform, it is time to introduce the high-level workflow of a CDP platform. This will help to create a roadmap for a CDP implementation although we will not be getting into the details of the implementation here.

The high-level workflow of a CDP platform looks as follows:

Step 1: Setting up source systems to send data to the CDP

The first step is to make sure the source system is ready to send data to the CDP. How exactly you make this happens depends on what type of CDP vendor you have chosen and what is your use case.

We will tackle a common scenario here. Most CDPs come with prebuilt connectors, which you can use to connect to different systems. All you need to do is to set up authentication between the two systems and set the criteria for ingesting the data. Then you will be able to ingest data into your CDP. You can also ingest data into CDP from any data lake or data warehouse.

CDPs simplify the process of data ingestion by automating the data connection using pre-built connectors. Alternatively, one can write the code to ingest data from different systems.

For sending event data from apps and websites, one can use SDKs. Client-side systems push data to CDP through SDK implementation.

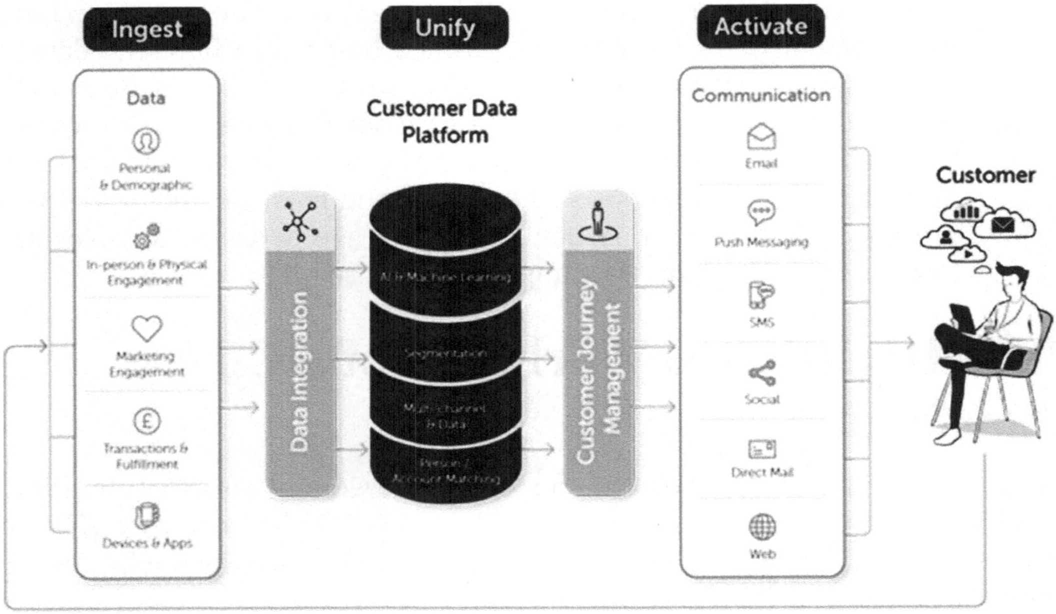

***Figure* 2.7**: *We need to set up different systems to send data to CDP (source:* **https://clever-touch.com/learn/what-makes-a-customer-data-platform-a-customer-data-platform**)

Step 2: Data Ingestion

There are different methods by which CDP ingests data from different sources. It also depends on whether you are doing batch ingestion or streaming ingestion.

- **Batch ingestion**: In batch ingestion, you ingest data as batch files. Batches are units of data that contain one or more files to be ingested as a single unit. Once the data is ingested, batches provide metadata that describes the number of records successfully ingested as well as provide messages for failed records. CSV files are ingested by this method.
- **Streaming ingestion**: Streaming ingestion allows you to send data from client-and server-side sources to the CDP platform in real-time. The incoming data is instantly made available for use. Stream ingestion is useful for tracking real-time events like website metrics, event data, and so on.

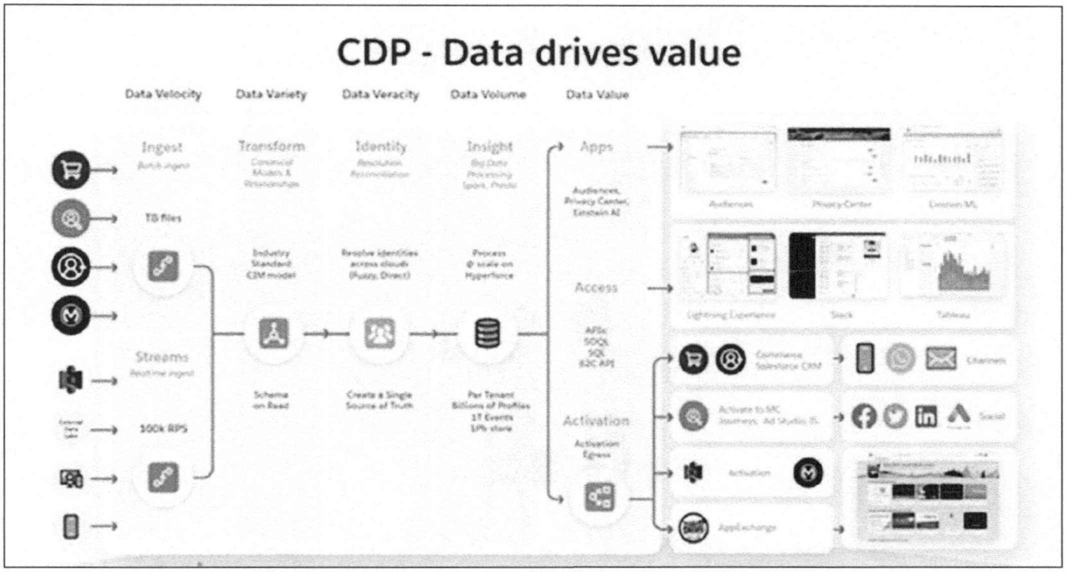

Figure 2.8: *You can ingest data in batches or in real-time*
(*source:* **https://medium.com/salesforce-architects/4-considerations-for-salesforce-cdp-data-ingestion-c00af75167bc**)

Step 3: Data Processing and Transformation

The next step is to process and transform the data that we ingested. Based on the end use case, the data needs to be processed and transformed. First and foremost, the data needs to be cleaned and duplicated. Most CDPs have built-in data processing and transformation workflows, which you can choose to simplify the task. You can alternatively write your code to clean and transform the data.

Step 4: Identity Resolution

After making sure that we have clean data in our database, the next step is to perform identity stitching for identity resolution. As explained in the identity resolution section, we use identity graphs to attribute data to a particular user id based on fuzzy matching, deterministic or probabilistic matching.

Most CDPs provide services that help with identity resolution. You can create identity resolution rules to create unique customer profiles. These customer profiles will be useful when you move to the next step.

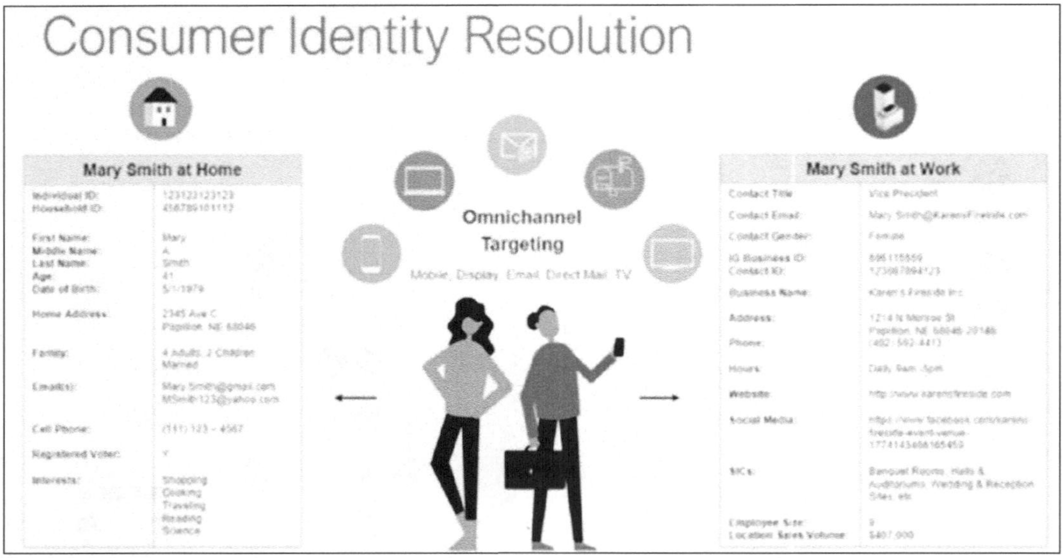

***Figure* 2.9**: *Identity resolution*
(*source*: **https://www.data-axle.com/resources/blog/solving-the-identity-graph-gap-through-robust-identity-resolution/**)

Step 5: Segmentation and Activation

Now, this is the time for marketers to segment the customer profiles created through identity resolution. Marketers segment customers based on certain business criteria. After you are done with segmentation, the next step is to publish and activate the segment. Publishing and activating the segment is done through marketing platforms like Google ad manager, Facebook ads manager, or other third-party tools like Blaze. This ensures your marketing campaigns are always targeted toward the right audience. Segmentation and activation are continuous tasks for marketers.

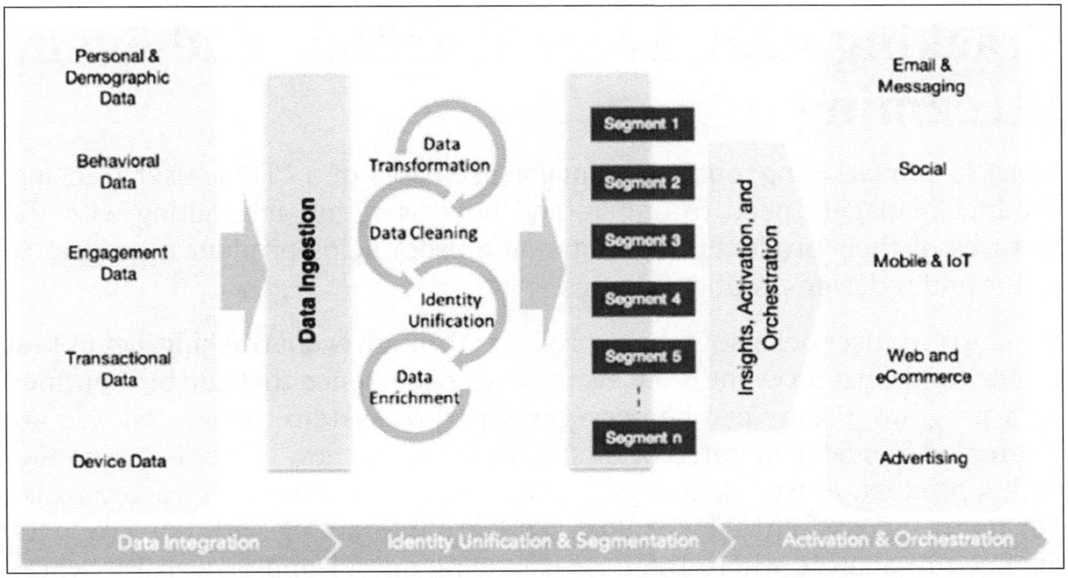

Figure 2.10: *Marketers create different segments before activation (source:* **https://quadrant-solutions.com/market_research/market-outlook-customer-data-platforms-cdp-2019-2024-worldwide/**)

The unique customer profiles can also be used for other use cases like product analytics, personalization, and so on. Earlier CDPs were mostly used by marketers to market to the right audience. However, now the customer data is used to push relevant notifications in Android and iOS apps. It is used to personalize the app and web experience based on the user. It is also used to analyze how users are interacting with the product. The use cases are one and many once we get the unique customer profile.

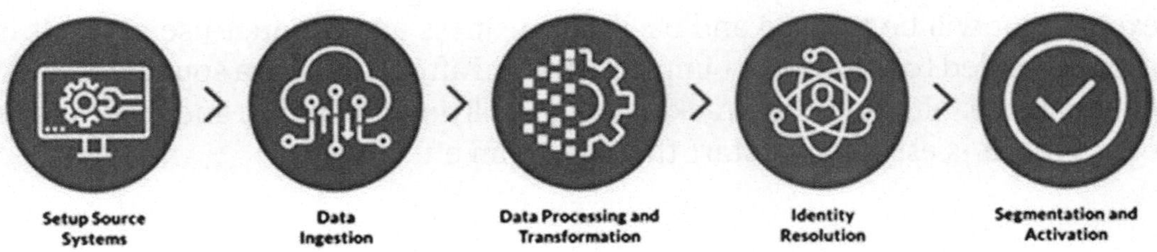

Figure 2.11: *CDP workflow*

Tracking Plan, Event Tracking, and Event Streaming

Apart from marketing, one of the major use cases of a CDP is user tracking. Product managers need to understand how users are interacting with the features of their products. Understanding users helps product managers to refine and redesign product features.

We can track user behavior for our products through event tracking. Let us first understand what an event is. An event is any occurrence that can be identified by a program. Events can be user-generated or system- generated. We are interested in user-generated events, as those reveal how a user is interacting with a product. A user-generated event can be click a button or a keystroke. For us to successfully analyze how users are interacting with our products, we need to analyze where the user is landing on our app or website, where are they visiting, which features are most used by them and which are seldom used, and so on.

Before we start tracking events, we need to come up with a list of events that should be tracked. That list is called the tracking plan. Creating a tracking plan is strategic work where inputs from different stakeholders are required. So generally, different teams provide their tracking plans (usually spreadsheets, but there are tools available that help to create tracking plans) along with business justification for the same. After discussions, the list is consolidated, and then a final company-wide tracking plan is created.

The final tracking plan provides a codified single source of truth for the events that will be tracked and used for business and product use cases. It is recommended to always start implementation after you have a sound-tracking plan in place. Although the tracking plan is a living document and can change over time, it is essential to start the basic plan effectively.

EVENTS

Indicative Event	Definition	Event Properties	Source	Location	Code	Unique Identifier	Timestamp	Status
App Installed	User installed the app on their device	osType	App (frontend)	/app-installed	Indicative.buildEvent('App Installed,' 'user_id');	user_id	_timestamputc	Done
Intro Landing Screen	User viewed landing screen	deviceType	Website (frontend)	/landing-screen	Indicative.buildEvent('Intro Landing Screen,' 'user_id');	user_id	_timestamputc	Done
Sign Up Selected	User started the account creation process by selecting 'sign up'	emailAddress firstName lastName	Website (frontend)	/sign-up	Indicative.buildEvent('Sign Up', 'user_id', { emailAddress: 'petlover@address.com', firstName: 'Kitty', lastName: 'Cat' });	user_id	_timestamputc	Done
Details Confirmed	User completed personal information	petAge petGender petDiet	Website (frontend)	/profile-complete	Indicative.setUniqueID('user_id'); Indicative.buildEvent('Personal Information Added', { petAge: 7, petGender: 'Female', petDiet: 'Vegan' });	user_id	_timestamputc	Done
Account Created	User finalized account creation by submitting necessary information	accountUsername createProfile	Backend	backend	Indicative.buildEvent('Account Created', 'user_id', { "account username": 'CatLuver', "create profile": true });	user_id	_timestamputc	In Progress
Open PetCam	User opened PetCam	deviceType	App (frontend)	PetCam app screen open	Indicative.setUniqueID('user_id'); Indicative.buildEvent('Open PetCam', { deviceType: 'Android' });	user_id	_timestamputc	In Progress
Apply PetCam Filter	User applied PetCam Filter	filterType	App (frontend)	Apply Filter button	Indicative.buildEvent('Apply PetCam Filter', 'user_id', { "filterType": 'CatEars' });	user_id	_timestamputc	Open

Figure 2.12: *A sample tracking plan*

Here are the entities you can track:

Events: Events include any actions the user takes- like *submit form* , *account created* , and *add to cart* .

Event Properties: Event properties are also known as parameters. These describe the event and provide more contextual information about the tracked event. These are captured and passed as parameters. Examples of event properties are browser id, previous screen, device type, and so on.

User properties: These are also called attributes. They provide more contextual information about the user, for example, contact information, payment information, and so on.

https://www.indicative.com/resource/data-tracking-plan/

Next, let's talk briefly about how you can set up these events to stream the data to a CDP.

We need to stream event data to the CDP. Streaming data is the constant flow of data each containing information about an event or a change of state. Streaming data is processed in real-time.

Once you set up the CDP with different sources of customer data, the CDP will allow you to stream event data from the source to the destination. This is one of the main benefits of using a CDP platform.

Challenges faced by CDP Platforms

Although CDPs solve a lot of challenges around creating a unique customer profile, they still suffer from different challenges. There are a multitude of CDP vendors today, along with some customer build CDPs that companies use.

These have been able to solve some of the issues, but no one solution solves all the challenges. We will cover solving some of the challenges in the later chapters, but first, we need to understand the challenges.

Companies need to understand and analyze the following challenges before they start implementing CDP:

- **Challenge 1: Inability to Scale**

  Every company starts with a few use cases when implementing a CDP, as should be the case. But selecting a CDP is as much a strategic decision as a technical one. So even if the company is small now, it is important to choose a CDP that can scale. Most CDPs available in the market today can handle small datasets well. Some can handle even hundreds of gigabytes of data. But most CDPs fall short when your organization's data needs become very large.

  Migrating to a new solution to tackle the scale challenge becomes too difficult a task. Therefore, it is important to assess how easily your CDP can scale with the growth of your company and your customer data. Event data can grow exponentially, and it is important to prepare for the future. Scalability remains a big challenge for most of the CDP tools available on the market today.

- **Challenge 2: Not User-friendly**

  CDPs need to be user-friendly in the sense that non-technical users should be able to use the data inside the CDP to create segments and activate the data through marketing campaigns, product analytics, and so on. If, for creating a segment or generating a report, a CDP requires the help of a data engineer, then end-user adoption will suffer. All the hard work of implementing the CDP will go to waste as end-users like the marketing folks or the product analysts will be unable to independently use the product. A CDP has to be user-friendly for non-technical people as well as have provisions where technical talent can make changes according to business needs. It needs to be customizable as well as user-friendly.

- **Challenge 3: Difficult to get data in real-time**

  For certain use cases, like personalized push messages, and marketing emails, we need data to flow from source to destination in real-time. However, most CDP players out there struggle to make the data available for usage in real-time. Where time is a crucial factor, data becomes stale very quickly, and underscores the customer experience. Most CDP players in the market do not have the capabilities to handle gigabytes of data being streamed in real-time, processed in real-time, and activated in real-time.

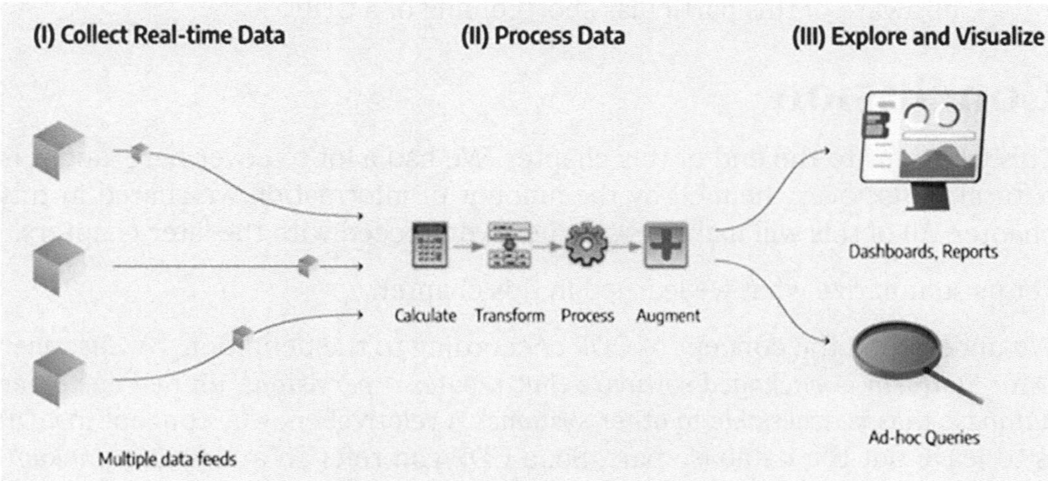

Figure 2.13: *Real-time data*
(*source*: **https://memgraph.com/blog/guide-to-real-time-analytics**)

- **Challenge 4: Difficult to demonstrate quickly the value to the business**

  Ask any CDP implementation consultants, and they will say that it is very difficult to demonstrate quickly the value of a CDP to business leaders. CDP project sponsors want to see early wins and upticks in business metrics once they start implementation of the CDP. But most CDPs are complex and require a long gestation period before they can demonstrate value to the business. In today's agile-driven technology world, the long gestation period can be a project killer for most CDP projects.

  Many companies start implementing CDP with the hope that they will be able to do personalization, user analytics, and so on within a few months. But the chosen CDP tool might take a year of implementation to deliver value. It results in a loss of trust in the project, and more often than not, the project get shelved. Most CDPs in the market today are complicated and time-consuming to implement.

  The problem is further complicated by the lack of end-to-end CDP solutions. Some CDPs might be good only at getting data from different sources. Some CDPs might be good at activating the data, provided you have collected the data correctly. Some may be good at only cost-effectively storing the data. So, if you have purchased a CDP which does one thing and your business use cases are meant to do another, then you are in a soup. As we said earlier, it is more difficult to migrate from one CDP to another than it is to implement a fresh one. So, we need to be aware of this particular shortcoming of a CDP.

Conclusion

This brings us to the end of this chapter. We had a lot to cover here, and it is natural to get overwhelmed by the amount of information we shared in this chapter. All of this will make sense when we proceed with the later chapters.

Let us summarize what we learned in this chapter.

We understood the concept of CDP . According to the definition, "A *Customer Data Platform is packaged software that creates a persistent, unified customer database that is accessible to other systems*". A relatively newer concept in CDP is to leave out the database part. So, a CDP can refer to a software package that helps you connect your different sources of data (input) to your chosen destination.

One of the top challenges to great customer experience delivery is related to collecting, managing, and storing customer data. CDPs solve the challenge of collecting customer data from different sources and storing it in one place to create a unified customer profile.

We learned that a persistent Id is an identifier that can provide a single view of an individual across numerous devices, including desktop, mobile web, and in-app, without duplication.

Customer data can be divided into three types depending on the data origin: first-party, second-party, and third-party. Customer data can be classified into three types based on the nature of the data collected: identity data, descriptive data, behavioral data, and qualitative data.

Identity resolution is the process of uniquely identifying the user who is using different channels to interact with the brand. It is the ability to persistently recognize a unique entity across all digital and physical channels to build a rich profile to personalize the customer journey. Identity resolution is done using identity stitching.

There are mainly three types of CDP: MarTech Suites, engagement-oriented CDP, and data management-oriented CDP. The list of events that should be tracked is called the tracking plan. Events include any actions the user takes- like submit form , account created , and add to cart . The CDPs available today in the market suffer from some challenges, mainly the inability to scale, and difficulty getting data in real-time, among other challenges.

In the next chapter, we are going to discuss the main topic of this book: Salesforce Data Cloud. We will understand how Data Cloud solves common challenges that plague the modern CDP and how to best utilize it. Are you excited? If you have come this far in the book, we are sure you are!

Questions

If you can answer the following questions and explain them to someone who has not read the book, consider yourself knowledgeable enough to proceed to the next chapter:

1. Explain what a CDP is and how it works?
2. What business challenges do companies face while managing customer experience delivery?
3. How does a CDP solve challenges faced by companies dealing with customer data?
4. At a high level, how does a CDP work? What is the typical workflow for a CDP?
5. What is a persistent ID?
6. What are the different data types CDPs need to handle?
7. What is identity resolution, and how is it done?
8. What do you mean by a Tracking plan?
9. What are events, event properties, and user properties?
10. What are the challenges that the current generation of CDPs faces?

Further Readings

If you wish to read more about SalesForce than what we could cover here, please go to the following links or resources:

- **https://www.cdpinstitute.org/**
- **https://www.gartner.com/reviews/market/customer-data-platforms**
- **https://www.forrester.com/report/now-tech-customer-data-platforms-q1-2022/RES177030**

CHAPTER 3

Going beyond CDP: Salesforce Data Cloud

Introduction

This chapter introduces the reader to Salesforce Data Cloud. Readers will be able to understand the value Salesforce Data Cloud brings to the table. They will be able to appreciate how Data Cloud solves the challenges faced by modern CDP tools.

In this chapter, we will explain Salesforce Data Cloud and why Salesforce introduced the product. We will take a look at the challenges resolved by Salesforce Data Cloud that plagues modern customer data platforms. We will talk about the business use cases for it and discuss in theory the concepts important for understanding how Salesforce Data Cloud works. Next, we will understand the high-level workflow of Salesforce Data Cloud. This will help the readers to conceptualize an abstract model of Data Cloud and what it brings to the table. Lastly, we will see how Salesforce Data Cloud fulfills Salesforce's Customer 360 promise, and understand why Data Cloud plays a crucial role in creating a real-time single source of truth for customer data.

Structure

In this chapter, the following topics will be covered:

- Introduction to Salesforce Data Cloud
- Problems solved by Salesforce Data Cloud addition to the Salesforce Ecosystem
- Business use cases for Salesforce Data Cloud
- Key Benefits offered by Salesforce Data Cloud
- Key Concepts for understanding how Salesforce Data Cloud works
- A high-level view of how Salesforce Data Cloud works
- Making Customer 360 Real-time through Salesforce Data Cloud

Introducing Salesforce Data Cloud

In the earlier chapters, we discussed Salesforce and the Customer Data Platform (CDP). We have even briefly discussed Salesforce Data Cloud. So, now is the best time to introduce the main protagonist of our story, The Salesforce Data Cloud, and give it the screen time it deserves. No, we are not writing a screenplay. Nonetheless, Salesforce Data Cloud is the hero of the book, and we have done enough homework to introduce and understand it.

Figure 3.1: *Salesforce Data Cloud*
(*Source:* **https://www.salesforceben.com/salesforce-announce-the-Data Cloud-platform/**)

We want to highlight that Salesforce Data Cloud is also called Data Cloud, Data Cloud Data Cloud, or Customer Data Cloud. All of these refer to the same product. Please do not get confused with the different names. We have used Salesforce Data Cloud or Data Cloud to refer to the product, whereas in different materials you might encounter different names. Nonetheless, it refers to the same product.

Essentially, Salesforce Data Cloud is a CDP with a twist. Hence the title of the book is "*Going Beyond CDP: Salesforce Data Cloud*". Salesforce Data Cloud helps to bring all your customer data from different sources in real-time and store it in a central repository to create and activate unified customer profiles.

As we have already discussed in *Chapter 1: Introducing the Salesforce platform*, to understand Data Cloud, we need to understand another Salesforce product, Salesforce CDP or Data Cloud for Marketing, as it is known now. Salesforce CDP refers to the customer data platform product from Salesforce. Salesforce CDP was created with the initial vision of collecting data from different sources and making it available for marketing for user activations. Data collected from different sources are brought to a central repository and used to power the personalized marketing experience.

However, there was still a gap that needed to be addressed. Even though Salesforce was helping enterprises capture data from different sources and bring it all in one place, the data was not real-time. In today's fast-paced digital world, data becomes stale very quickly. People check out a product in a retail store and check the price on a mobile app, later they again check on their iPad/tablet and later might make a purchase from their laptop. All of this might happen over a few hours. Companies need to make sure that they provide a consistent experience to users shifting devices or channels. For that, we need data in real-time or near real-time rather than data that is refreshed once a week or even once a day.

Here comes Salesforce Data Cloud. Salesforce Data Cloud was launched to power the customer 360 experience by making data in the Salesforce CDP product available to not just other products of the C360 suite of applications but also to other applications in real-time. The keyword here is real-time. The data to which enterprises will take access will be real-time data. Salesforce Data Cloud powers the Salesforce CDP by making it real-time.

A simplified version looks like this: Salesforce Data Cloud is a real-time customer data platform. In an equation, it would look like:

CDP+Real-time data capabilities= Salesforce Data Cloud

Figure 3.2: *Salesforce Data Cloud brings all the customer data to create a unified customer profile*

Salesforce Data Cloud provides two innovations:

The first is real-time data. That means it collects and unifies data in milliseconds. Brands can react to customer choices better with real-time customer data.

The second is that it enables all your teams- across sales, service, marketing, commerce, and more-to alter the customer experience in real-time based on the customer's actions.

Unlike other CDPs on the market, Salesforce Data Cloud is not solely focused on marketing or commerce. It goes beyond that. Salesforce Data Cloud brings data from all the customer interactions with the brand. Customers feel the difference when they don't need to repeatedly tell the different customer service reps what they bought, what issues they face, and what resolution they want. We all have faced this frustration when we had to tell the different customer service reps our problems time and again as they don't have the information we provided yesterday to a different agent. Salesforce Data Cloud aims to solve this and other such problems for customers.

Problems solved by the addition of Salesforce Data Cloud to the Salesforce Ecosystem

Let us again discuss the different challenges faced by modern CDP tools and how Salesforce Data Cloud solves them.

Challenge 1: Inability to Scale

Solution: Salesforce Data Cloud is based on the Hyperforce platform. Hyperforce is a public cloud infrastructure as a service offering from Salesforce. It is highly scalable and suited for big enterprises. As Salesforce Data Cloud is based on the platform, it can scale to billions and trillions of records each day. So companies can focus on growing their user base, letting Salesforce take care of scalability. According to a Salesforce press release dated December 8, 2022, "Data Cloud Customer Data Cloud now processes more than 100 billion customer records on average daily across the entire Salesforce Customer 360, enabling every company to use data and become a customer company." (Source-**https://investor.salesforce.com/press-releases/press-release-details/2022/Salesforce-Data Cloud-Customer-Data-Cloud-Now-Powered-by-Tableau-Processes-More-Than-100-Billion-Customer-Records-on-Average-Daily-Making-It-Easy-for-Every-Company-to-Become-a-Customer-Company/default.aspx**)

Challenge 2: Not User-friendly

Solution: One of the major complaints with CDPs is that they are not user-friendly. If marketer needs to go to the data engineer every time they need to create a new audience segment, then it defeats the purpose of speed to market. Salesforce Data Cloud is intuitive and easy to use. Salesforce's philosophy of clicks, not code, makes it the perfect tool for end users. Marketers and business users do not need to depend on the technical team for their work. With many drag-and-drop tools, users can perform analysis, create segments, model data, and do much more without the need to learn to code.

Challenge 3: Difficult to get data in real-time

Solution: Getting data in real-time from different sources is one of the major challenges. As we have already discussed, one of the USPs of Salesforce Data Cloud is that it can get data in real-time from different customer touchpoints, thus hyper-charging the personalized customer experience. It enables all your teams: across sales, service, marketing, commerce, and more-to alter the customer experience in real-time based on the customer's actions.

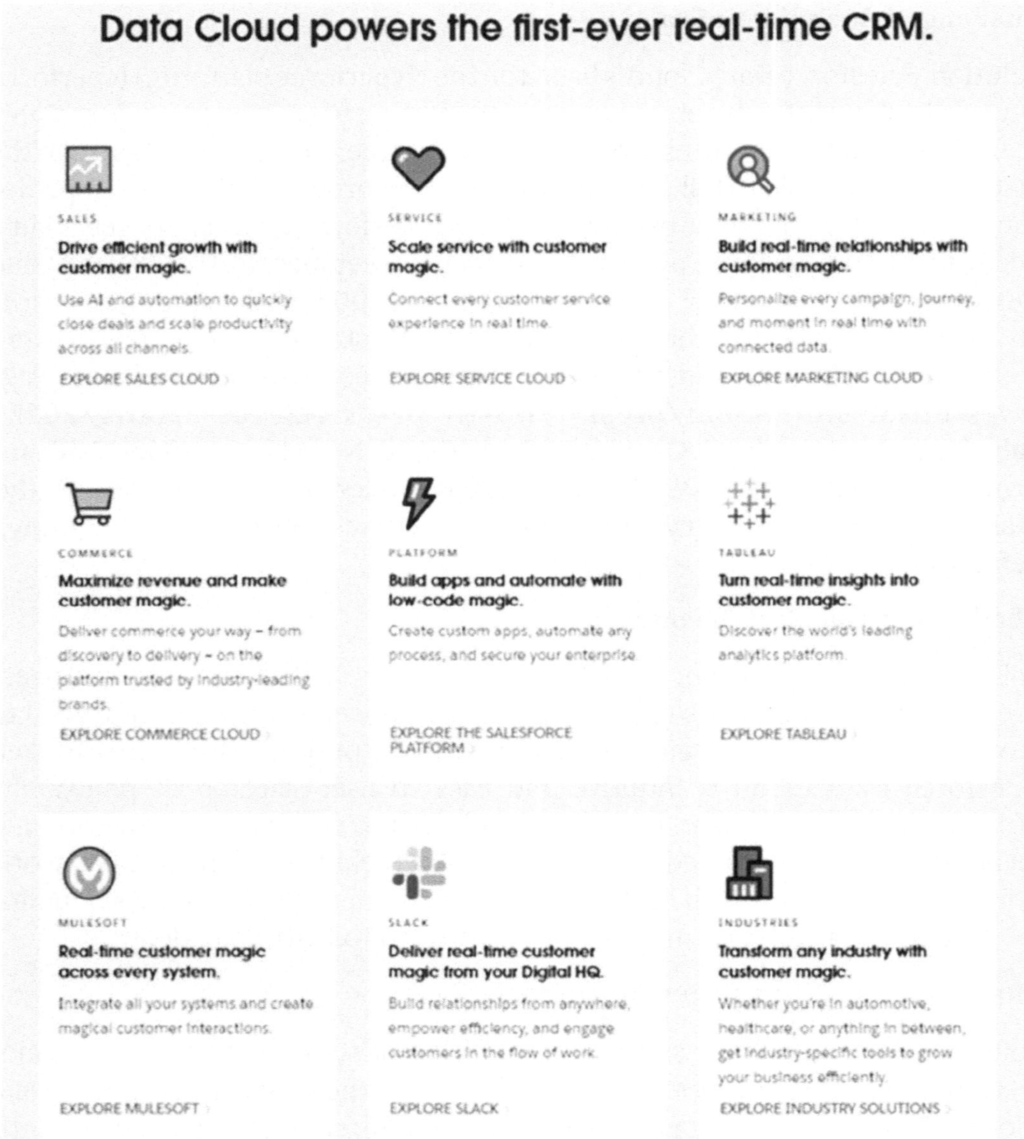

Figure 3.3: *Salesforce Data Cloud powers the customer 360 (source-* **https://www.salesforce.com/products/Data Cloud/overview/?d=cta-body-promo-4&_gl=1*1x6do25*_ga*MTQ5NjIyOTA5My4xNjI3MTE0MTk5*_ga_3VHBZ2DJWP*MTY4MTMwOTU3NS41MC4wLjE2ODEzMDk1NzUuMC4wLjA.**)

Challenge 4: Difficult to demonstrate quickly the value to the business

Solution: Implementing a CDP for your business is a challenging task. There are more stories of failures than successes. Demonstrating value to the business is crucial, where budget is always a concern for businesses. If the project team is not able to demonstrate to the management that the investment is worth it, it can kill the project. Salesforce Data Cloud aims to solve the problem by being easier to implement than most CDPs. It claims to reduce the time to market significantly compared to other competing vendors and, hence, provide value to the business. On top of it, the ease of use means business users will be happy to use and provide positive feedback to management regarding the tool.

Data Cloud addition to the Salesforce ecosystem

To achieve the vision of a real-time 360-degree view of the customers, Salesforce Data Cloud plays a crucial role. Although the different Salesforce products shared the same or similar data model and had a lot of synergies between them, there was one missing link. The missing link was the ability to bring the data from different Salesforce products into a single repository. Customer 360 aimed to solve that. But companies do not keep all their business information in Salesforce alone. They have different systems to store different information. A company can use SAP for ERP solutions, Adobe for marketing, and Salesforce for CRM and Commerce. It was necessary to bring data from different systems into a single platform. Apart from these systems, data on the client side, like event streaming data, product analytics data, and so on also needed to be part of the holistic customer view. Thus the idea of Salesforce CDP was born. Salesforce Data Cloud made Salesforce CDP in real-time. Salesforce Data Cloud was the missing link in connecting all the customer data points. It helps to achieve the vision of Customer 360.

Figure 3.4: *Salesforce Data Cloud connecting all the different Salesforce platforms*

In the preceding diagram, the rabbit is the mascot for Salesforce Data Cloud, connecting all of the Salesforce products. So, it does not matter whether you are using Sales Cloud, Service Cloud, Salesforce Industry solutions, Slack, Salesforce platform, and so on. All your systems are interconnected through Data Cloud.

Business use cases for Salesforce Data Cloud

We have talked about Salesforce Data Cloud and how it solves some of the challenges faced by CDPs. But we are yet to discuss what possibilities Salesforce Data Cloud brings to businesses. We will now discuss some of the business use cases that can be solved by Salesforce Data Cloud.

- **Business use case 1: Increase the customer lifetime value by personalizing the experience for each customer**

  Acquiring customers is not an easy task. Ask any D2C brand and they will talk about how expensive it has become to acquire a customer. Once you acquire a customer, it is important to increase the Customer Lifetime Value (CLV), which is the total amount that the customer spends with the brand. To generate repeat purchases, brands have to personalize the experience for each customer. Doing this in real-time and at scale is no easy task. This is where Salesforce Data Cloud can come to the rescue. Using Data Cloud, it is possible to build individual consumer journeys, delivered through preferred channels, such as email and social media, from real-time and historical data. This allows brands to send consumers tailored product recommendations, and special offers automatically – wherever they prefer to engage with the brand.

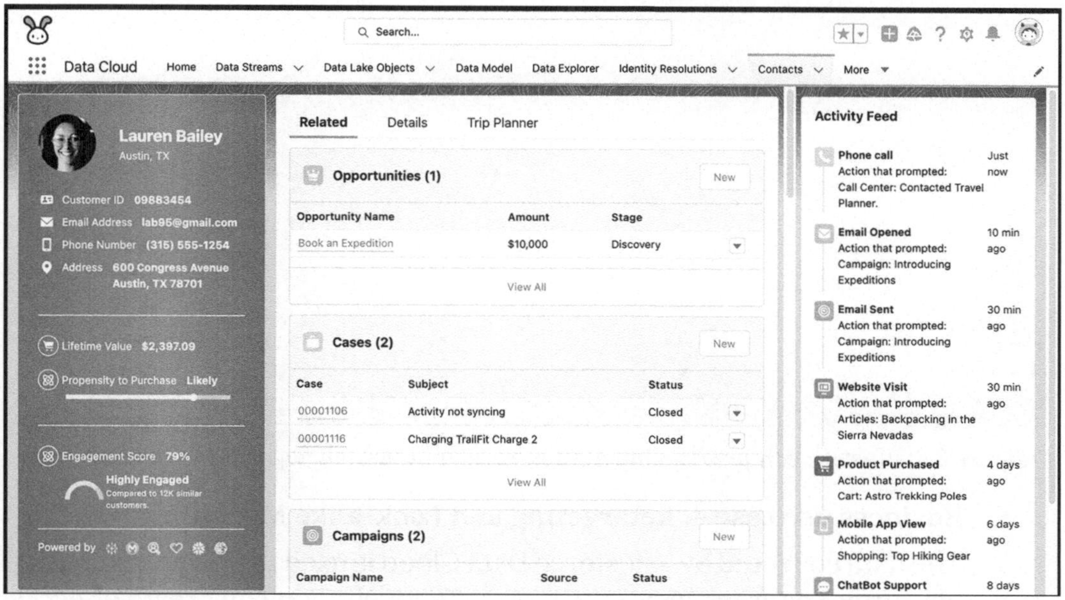

Figure 3.5: *Salesforce Data Cloud helps in creating personalized experiences for customers*

- **Business use case 2: Actionable insights from telemetry data**

  Telemetry automatically collects, transmits, and measures data from remote sources, using sensors and other devices to collect data. The data can be fed to Salesforce Data Cloud to generate real-time insights which can be used for different purposes. One of the use cases is to utilize the telemetry data from vehicles to provide vehicle owners with real-time updates about their cars.

- **Business use case 3: Reduce customer attrition by identifying customers most likely to churn**

  Unique customer profiles allow marketers to monitor individual customers. Another Salesforce product called Einstein Discovery can help to predict and identify which customers are more likely to churn. Based on the analysis, marketers can send personalized offers to retain the said customers.

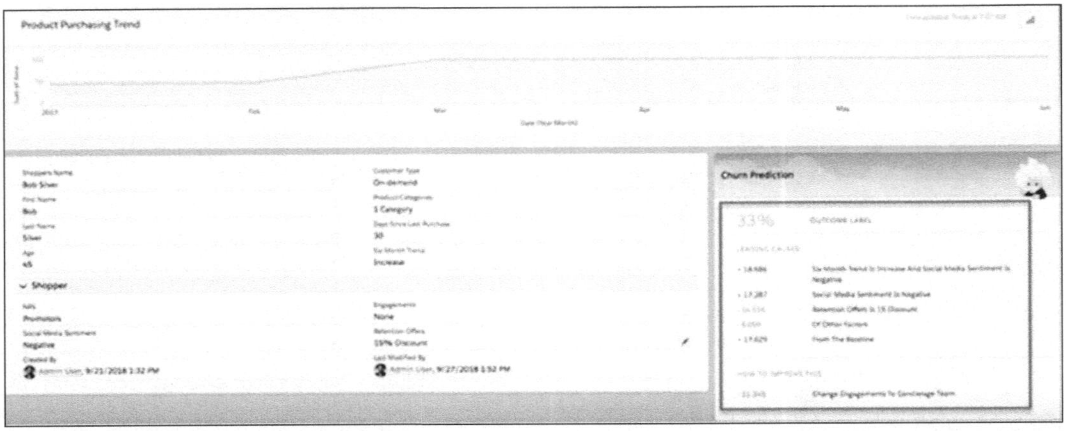

Figure 3.6: *Einstein can predict churn rates based on users' engagement with the brand*

- **Business use case 4: Retargeting and Look-alike Modelling**

  The data collected by Salesforce Data Cloud is used to power advertising platforms to target segments more effectively. You can create effective retargeting campaigns and attract new customers with similar preferences as your current customers via look-alike modeling.

- **Business use case 5: Data Privacy and Governance**

  Consumers demand more control over their data and expect companies to provide them with the ability to manage consent. Additionally, there is the right to be forgotten (RTBF), which is the right to have private information about a person removed from Internet searches and other directories under some circumstances. Companies find it challenging to comply with data privacy rules.

Salesforce Data Cloud gives IT and data teams more control over data management, with the ability to manage access controls and permissions across teams. Salesforce Data Cloud helps to streamline customer consent with Preference Manager, which helps businesses stay compliant with regulations.

Key Benefits offered by Salesforce Data Cloud

Before diving into the concepts and high-level overview of Salesforce Data Cloud, let us understand the key benefits offered by it. As more and more companies use Salesforce Data Cloud to transform their businesses, we will get more such benefits. For a reasonably new product on the market, here are the key benefits offered by Salesforce Data Cloud:

- **Benefit 1: Salesforce Data Cloud offers real-time data**

  We know we have said this a lot in the book but we cannot put emphasis enough on what a game-changing impact real-time data can have on businesses. On top of that, Salesforce allows Data Cloud to directly access the data in Snowflake, which is a data warehouse. There is no need to store the data in Salesforce. You can store the data in Snowflake and access it in real-time with the help of Salesforce-Snowflake integration. The open data sharing between Salesforce and Snowflake allows Data Cloud to directly access data stored in Snowflake, and vice-versa, enabling a real-time customer 360 view across the two platforms without moving or duplicating data.

  Salesforce Data Cloud is also faster than Salesforce CDP with its zero *data copy* architecture. This means that Data Cloud can *read* data sources without having to migrate (or duplicate) the data into Salesforce. With this level of *integration*, Data Cloud can perform the required action in a matter of milliseconds.

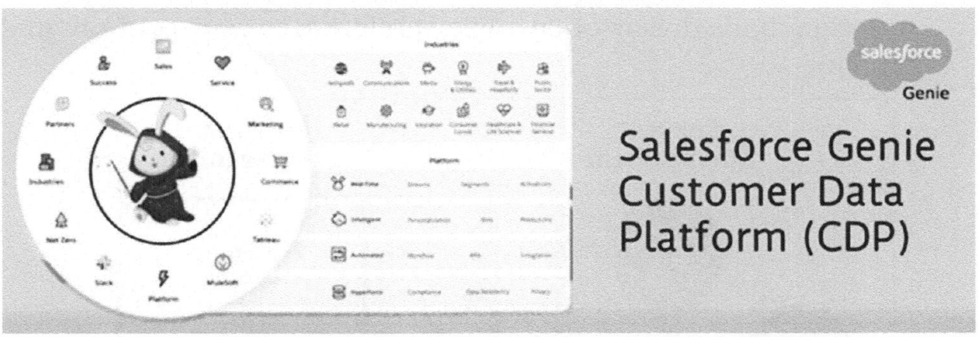

Figure 3.7: *Salesforce Data Cloud CDP can access data directly from Snowflake*

- **Benefit 2: Separate data by business units with Data Spaces**

  Data Cloud helps to partition real-time Data Cloud data by business units enabling different teams or brands within an organization to use the same Data Cloud instance, but only access the data they need to do their work. This is done using Data Spaces. This helps utilize the same Data Cloud instance at the same time protecting the data across departments.

- **Benefit 3: Advertising with first-party data with partners such as Amazon, Google ads, and Meta**

  You can use your Salesforce Data Cloud first-party data for privacy-safe advertising activation and aggregated insights for more personalized and effective marketing campaigns.

Figure 3.8: *You can use your first-party data with advertising platforms like Amazon, Meta, and Google*

- **Benefit 4: Streamline customer consent with Preference Manager**

  As stated earlier, Data Cloud helps to resolve challenges related to consent management. A new, simplified customer consent and preference management capability through Salesforce's Privacy Center solution helps businesses build trust and stay ahead of privacy and compliance requirements. This streamlines requirements like the Right to Be Forgotten and Data Portability across multiple interactions to form a unified view of customer preferences as part of the unified profile.

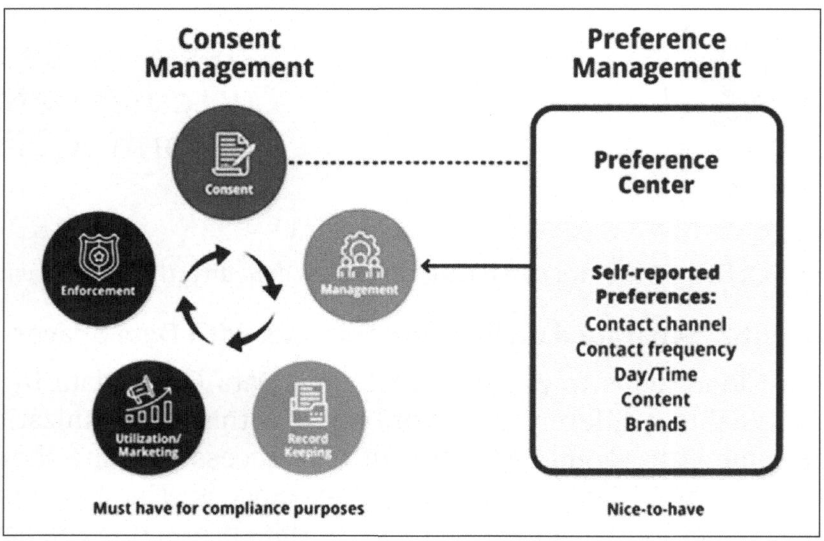

Figure 3.9: *Companies need to have a consent management system to take care of privacy regulations*

- **Benefit 5: Real-time analytics**

  Modern analytics tools are unable to provide real-time analytics. Data Cloud along with Tableau and CRM analytics is changing the way organizations use customer analytics. With one-click access to live analytics across all data in Data Cloud from any data source, companies can build a single source of truth – bringing in Data Cloud data alongside third-party data sources and accelerating time to insight.

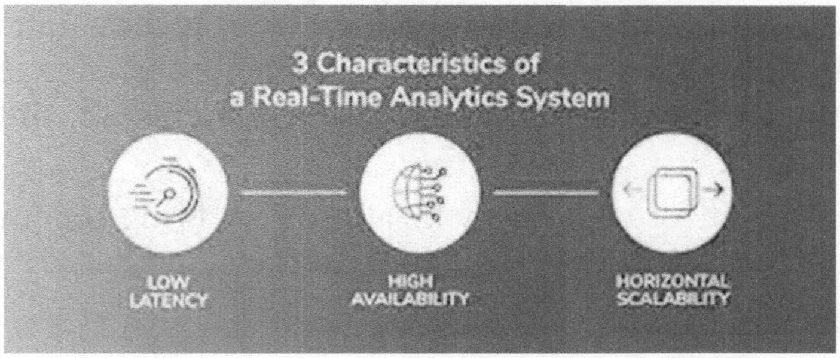

Figure 3.10: *Characteristics of real-time analytics system*

In the preceding figure, we can see the three characteristics of a real-time analytics system:

- Low latency
- High availability
- Horizontal scaling

Low latency ensures that changes in the data are reflected quickly in the downstream applications.

High availability means that the analytics system has low downtime and is available more than 99.95% of the time.

Horizontal scaling refers to the ability to distribute loads across multiple nodes.

Salesforce Data Cloud, along with Tableau and CRM analytics, has these three characteristics to make it a real-time analytics system.

Key Concepts for understanding how Salesforce Data Cloud works

We understand now that Data Cloud is a powerful CDP tool. To better understand the high-level overview of Data Cloud, we need to understand a few concepts that we haven't yet talked about in the book so far. Along with the concepts we already discussed in *chapters 1 and 2*, we will discuss a few more concepts, specific to Data Cloud.

- **Harmonization of data**

  Data harmonization refers to combining data from different sources and providing users with a comparable view of data from different sources. Data harmonization improves the quality and utility of the data. In this context, it would mean bringing the customer data from different sources along with unification, enrichment, and validation in one place.

  The net result of data harmonization is to bring together data from different sources into one place so that they function as if they are from a single source.

- **Customer graph**

  Also called an identity graph, refers to a database that stitches customer records from different data sources to create a single unified customer profile. After the process of identity resolution, we create a customer graph.

  A customer graph is a framework by which a company determines what type of customers they have, how they are interacting, how the company should interact with the customers, and so on. It enables companies to understand their customers better. Siloed customer channels get unified into one after creating the customer graph (*Figure* 3.11).

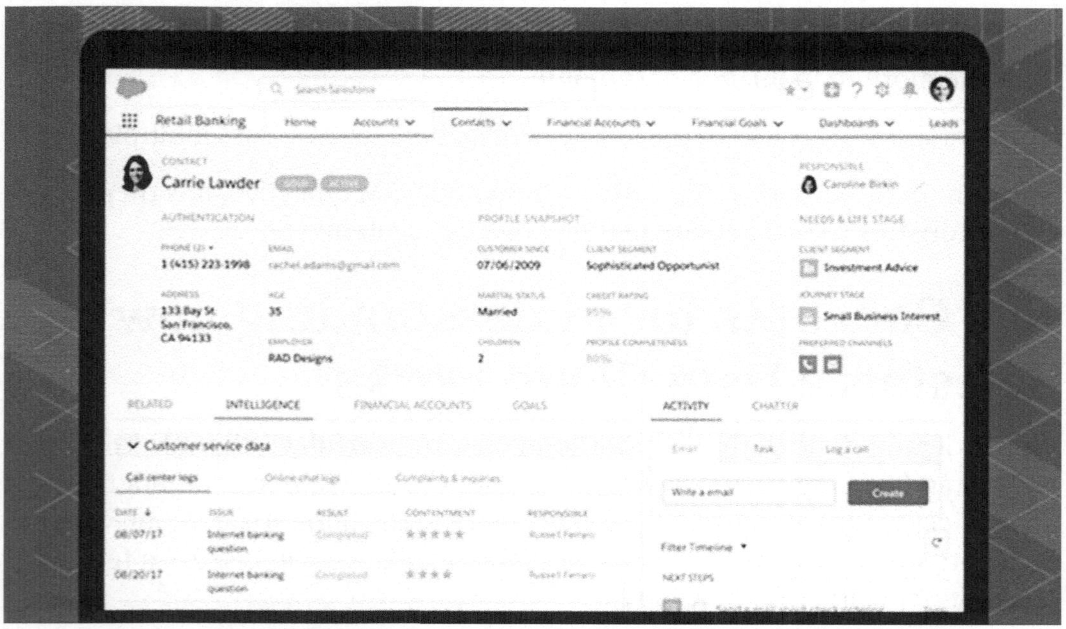

Figure 3.11: *Customer graphs help to understand how customers are interacting across channels*

In Salesforce Data Cloud, customer graphs are created based on data models derived from their 20 plus year of business experience. Data from different sources are harmonized in a single customer profile.

- **Lakehouse architecture**

  Salesforce Data Cloud stores data using a lakehouse architecture. Lakehouse architecture refers to data lakehouse, which is a new open data management architecture that combines the flexibility, cost-efficiency, and scale of data lakes with the data management and ACID transactions of data warehouses. Thus, it is a combination of the best features of a data lake and a data warehouse. The best of both worlds.

  Merging the two into a single system means that customer data teams can move faster as they can use data without needing to access multiple systems. Data Lakehouse is fast becoming an industry best practice for storing customer data (*Figure* 3.12).

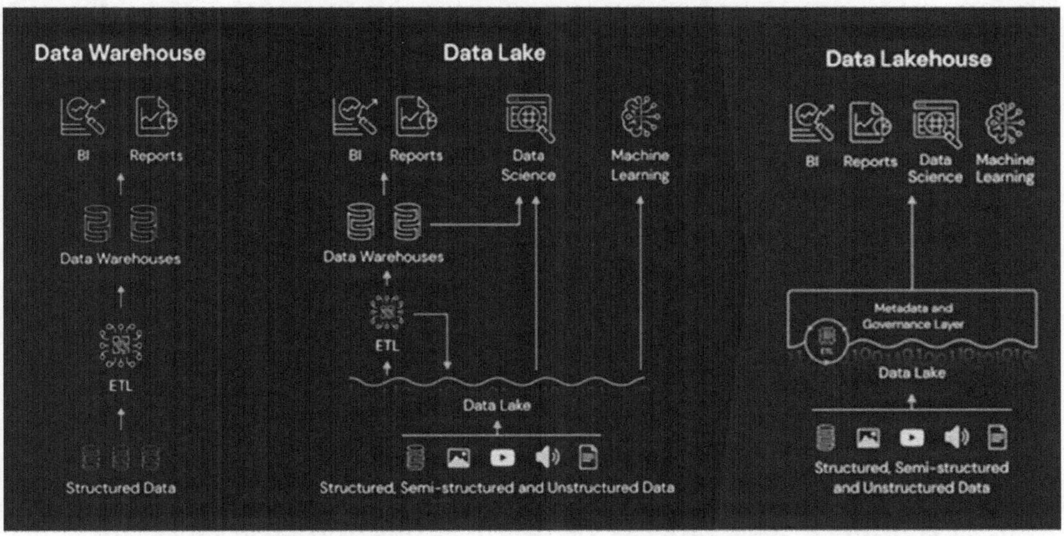

Figure 3.12: *Data Lakehouse packs the best of Data Warehouse and Data Lake* (*source*-**https://www.databricks.com/glossary/data-lakehouse#:~:text=A%20data%20lakehouse%20is%20a,(ML)%20on%20all%20data.**)

A High-level view of how Salesforce Data Cloud works

Now we will understand the high-level working of Salesforce Data Cloud. We have already introduced you to the concepts required for understanding the high-level overview, so let us directly jump into it (*Figure* 3.13).

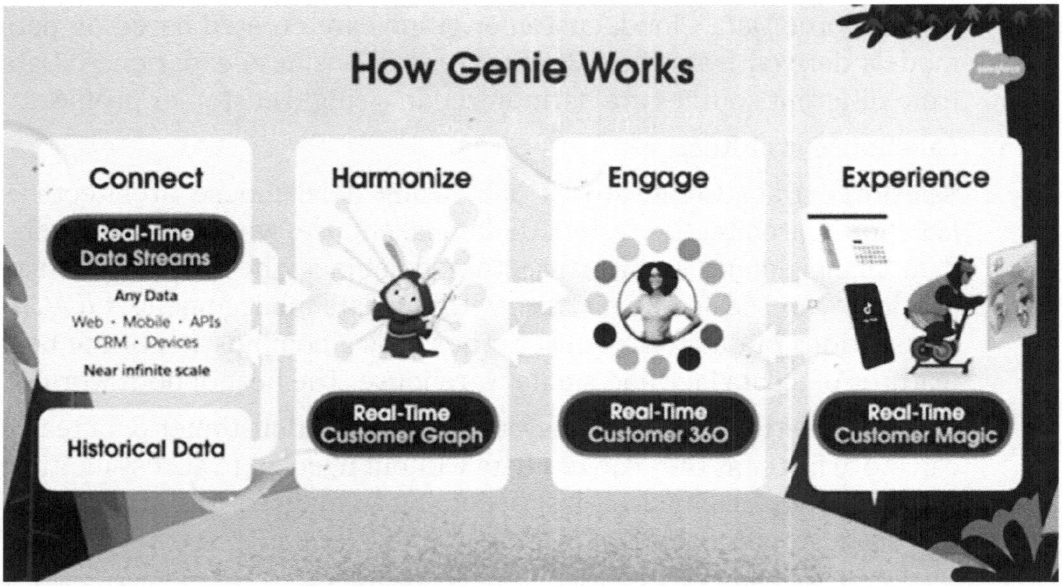

Figure 3.13: *Building blocks for Salesforce Data Cloud*

Salesforce Data Cloud has four building blocks:

- **Connect**: Refers to connecting the different sources of data from web, mobile, APIs, CRM, and real-time streaming data. Salesforce Data Cloud can receive data and scale up based on the need.
- **Harmonize**: Refers to harmonizing the incoming data to form a real-time customer graph.
- **Engage**: This is the process of creating unified customer profiles through identity resolution and customer segments. We can also create predictive models to help us engage with customers in a more effective way.
- **Experience**: The process of personalizing the customer experience with the data we have in Data Cloud. The customer segments can be activated through different systems, such as mobile apps, web, ad platforms, and so on. Data Cloud provides real-time personalization at an immense scale.

Next, we will discuss the high-level overview of Salesforce Data Cloud.

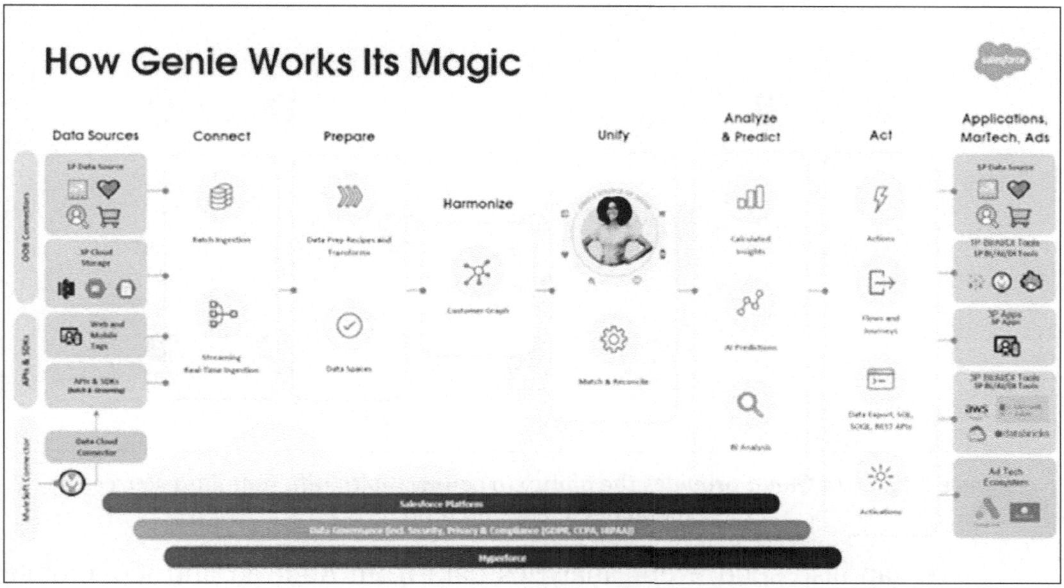

Figure 3.14: *Salesforce Data Cloud high-level workflow diagram*

In *Figure* 3.14, you can see the high-level diagram for Salesforce Data Cloud. Let us understand how data moves from one stage to another to finally provide the real-time personalized experience that customers want.

- **Setting up the data sources**

  Salesforce Data Cloud supports several data sources (*Figure* 3.15). It has some out-of-the-box connectors, which are pre-built integrations that companies can use to quickly set up the connection between two systems. This not only includes the connectors to different Salesforce Applications like Sales Cloud, Service Cloud, and Marketing Cloud but also other popular tools like AWS, Adobe, Google Cloud Studio, and so on. Data Cloud also supports a variety of third-party cloud storage services like data warehouses, databases, and data lakes from AWS, Microsoft, Snowflake, and Google among others. We will discuss later in detail how to set up the connections, but for now, we just need to keep in mind that Data Cloud allows us to easily connect to our data sources.

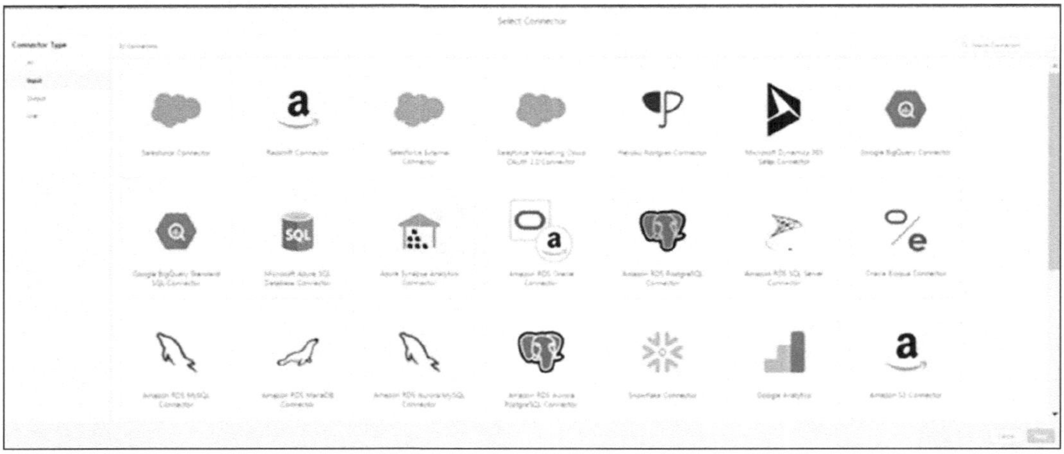

Figure 3.15: *Data Cloud provides the ability to connect with different data sources by following a few simple steps*

We can also send event analytics data from Android and iOS mobile devices through API connections or SDKs. There are options to send data in batches or stream data to the data cloud platform. Additionally, Mulesoft allows you to connect different data sources to Data Cloud. We will have a detailed discussion on how it can be done in a later chapter.

- **Connecting the data sources**

  After setting up the data sources, the next step is to start ingesting the data, either through batch processing or streaming.

- **Prepare the data**

  The next step is to prepare the data through data cleaning and data transformation. Data Cloud provides an easy-to-use interface to perform data transformation (refer to *Figure* 3.16), but developers can also write code to perform complex data transformation functions. Most common data transformations are available out of the box and can be used with clicks. Owing to these functionalities, it is easy to perform these transformations even if someone is not a data engineer.

Figure 3.16: *Salesforce provides a user-friendly UI for data transformation*

Data spaces help to separate customer data from different business units logically. Data Spaces allow Admins to organize their real-time Data Cloud data into secure, logical spaces. So, different departments, with their different sets of customer data and use cases, can use the same Data Cloud instance (*Figure* 3.17).

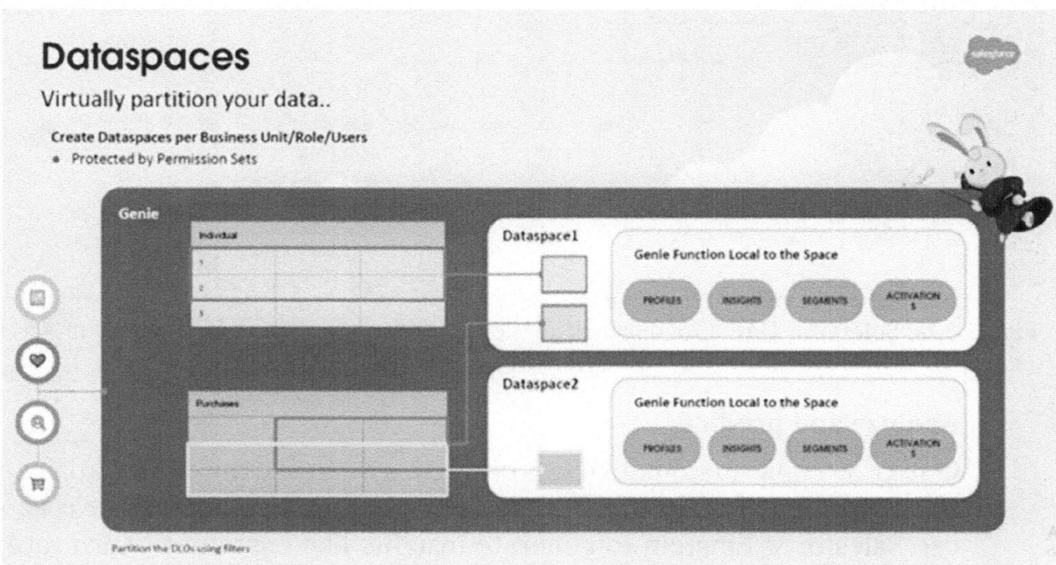

Figure 3.17: *Dataspaces enable virtual partition of data for different business units, users, and roles*

- **Harmonize**

  The next step is to harmonize the data to create a single repository of data and create customer graphs. Harmonization is required before stitching the different identities and creating a unique customer profile.

- **Unify**

  Using matching rules and criteria, the different identities of a single customer are stitched together to create unique customer profiles. Each customer is then uniquely identified and all their interactions with the brand are consolidated in one consolidated view.

  Salesforce helps to bring all the different customer interactions with a brand in a single view.

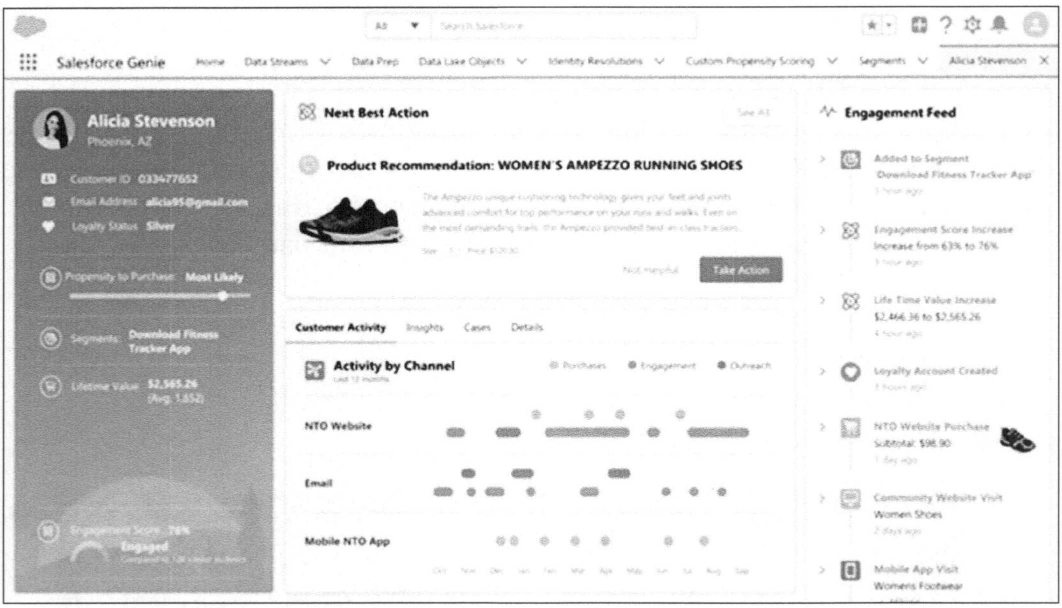

Figure 3.18: *Salesforce Data Cloud brings all the customer interactions for a profile under one roof*

- **Analyze and predict**

  Once the single customer view is created, we can use the data to analyze the customer interactions and undertake predictive analysis. We can use Salesforce Einstein to generate insights like customer churn rate, likelihood to purchase, and so on. using built-in models. We can use the data in a BI tool to create reports and dashboards for analysis. With real-time data, you can create real-time predictions and analyses for your customer data. Understanding how your users are using your product or service is easier with real-time analytical data.

- **Act**

  You can take actions on the real-time customer data by using it in Lightning actions, using the data inflows and journey maps, and so on. You can also use the data to enrich your first-party data sources. You can create audience segments and use the data on ad platforms like Meta, Google, and so on for efficient targeting and better ROI. Salesforce Data Cloud helps to connect with different outbound applications for marketing, advertising, analytics, and so on. You can export the data to different sources, like Databricks, for building your AI models.

  In a nutshell, Data Cloud helps to bring all the customer data from different sources in real-time and create a single unique profile for each customer, which can then be used for marketing, analytics, data enrichment, and other business use cases.

Making Customer 360 Real-time through Salesforce Data Cloud

As discussed earlier, Salesforce Data Cloud brings together the real-time customer 360 vision for Salesforce (*Figure* 3.19).

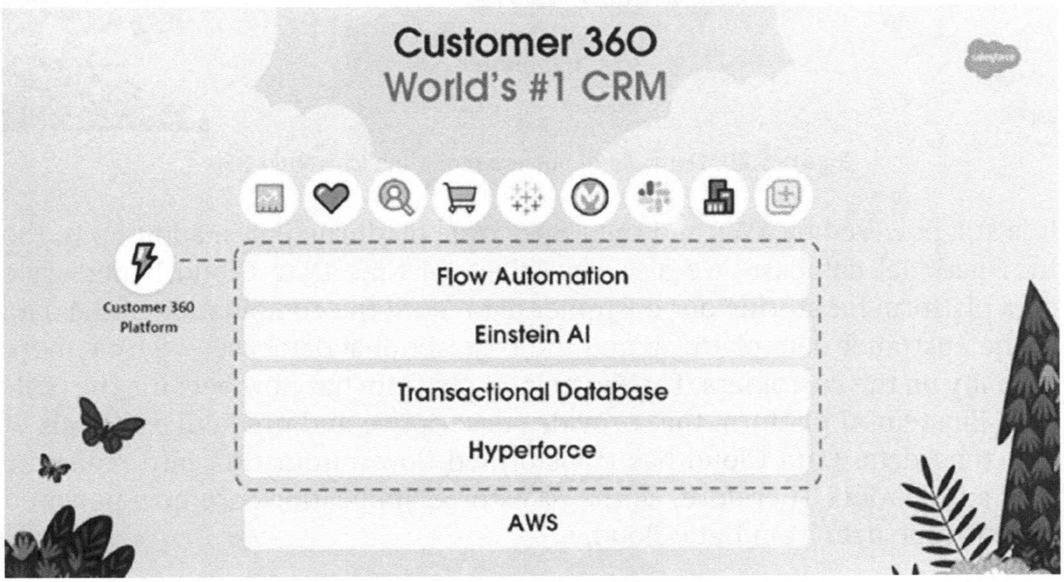

Figure 3.19: *Salesforce 360 vision*

Powered by AWS, the Salesforce Customer 360 platform provided the hyper-scale platform Hyperforce, on top of which we had the transactional database which stored our Salesforce data. Einstein AI provided descriptive and predictive analytics, and flow automation enabled businesses to automate certain business processes. The different Salesforce applications run like Sales Cloud, Service Cloud, Salesforce Industries, and so on ran on this customer 360 platform.

But with the onset of Data Cloud, the platform changed, as depicted in *Figure 3.20*:

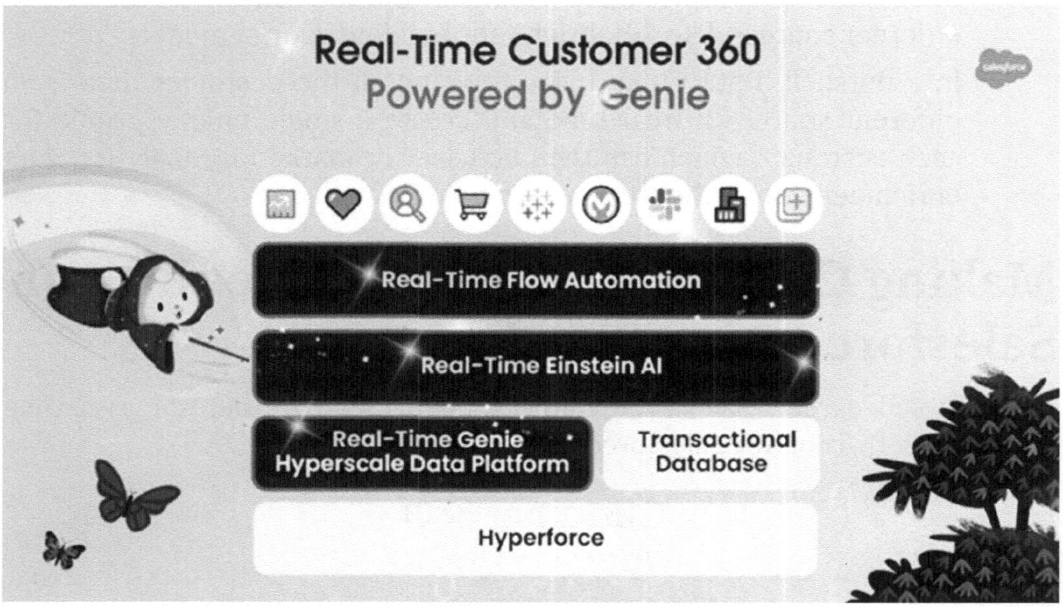

Figure 3.20: *Data Cloud powers real-time Customer 360*

It is still powered by AWS and the Hyperforce platform. But in addition to the transnational database, we also have the real-time Data Cloud hyper-scale data platform for storing our customer data. With the combination of the data in the customer data platform and the transactional database, we have more visibility on the customers. The Einstein AI platform has now become the real-time Einstein AI platform that provides descriptive and predictive analysis of real-time data. Data Cloud has transformed flow automation into real-time flow automation. Therefore, all the Salesforce applications are now powered by real-time data from Data Cloud.

Conclusion

Salesforce Data Cloud was introduced to help businesses bring data from different systems in real-time and store in a consolidated place and enable user profile creation. It's real-time data capabilities solved several challenges faced by CDP tools. The unique user profiles help businesses to deliver superior customer experiences.

In the next chapter, we will talk in more detail about Salesforce Data Cloud architecture. We are going to study in detail the key building blocks of Salesforce Data Cloud and understand how they interact with each other. We will also talk about the benefits of Salesforce Data Cloud and learn how to drive productivity, efficiency, and value with Salesforce Data Cloud.

Points to Remember

- Salesforce Data Cloud was launched to power the customer 360 experience by making data in the Salesforce CDP product available to not just other products of the C360 suite of applications but also to other applications in real-time.

  In an equation, it looks something like this:

  ```
  CDP + Real-time data capabilities = Salesforce Data Cloud
  ```

- Salesforce Data Cloud solves many challenges that modern CDP applications face, like the inability to scale, the interface not being user-friendly, difficulty getting data in real-time, and difficulty demonstrating the value to the business quickly.

  With the addition of Data Cloud to the Salesforce ecosystem, real-time customer 360 is possible in Salesforce.

- The key benefits offered by Salesforce Data Cloud are:
  - Salesforce Data Cloud offers real-time data
  - Separate data by business units with Data Spaces
  - Advertising with first-party data with partners, such as Amazon, Google ads, and Meta
  - Streamline customer consent with Preference Manager
  - Real-time analytics
- Data harmonization refers to combining data from different sources and providing users with a comparable view of data from different sources. Data harmonization improves the quality and utility of the data.
- Customer graph, also called identity graph, refers to a database that stitches customer records from different data sources to create a single unified customer profile.

- Lakehouse architecture refers to data lakehouse, which is a new open data management architecture that combines the flexibility, cost-efficiency, and scale of data lakes with the data management and ACID transactions of data warehouses.
- At a high level, Salesforce Data Cloud has a 7-step process for setup and run. It starts with preparing the data sources to send data to Data Cloud, connecting the data sources, preparing the data that comes to Data Cloud, then performing harmonization and unification of the data. Next comes analyzing and predicting outcomes based on the available data. Finally, we can take action using the unified customer data in Data Cloud.

Questions

1. What is Salesforce Data Cloud?
2. What are the challenges that were solved by the addition of Salesforce Data Cloud to the Salesforce ecosystem?
3. Explain some of the business use cases that are relevant for Salesforce Data Cloud.
4. What are the key benefits offered by Salesforce Data Cloud to businesses?
5. What do you mean by harmonization of data?
6. What is a customer graph?
7. What kind of architecture does Salesforce Data Cloud have? Explain.
8. Describe how Salesforce Data Cloud works at a high level.
9. How did Salesforce Data Cloud make Customer 360 in real-time a possibility for Salesforce?

Further Readings

If you wish to read more about Salesforce than what we could cover here, please go to the following links or resources:

- **https://www.salesforceben.com/salesforce-Data Cloud/**
- **https://www.salesforceben.com/the-drip/how-salesforce-uses-salesforce-cdp-Data Cloud/**
- **https://www.salesforce.com/products/Data Cloud/overview/**

CHAPTER 4
Salesforce Data Cloud Architecture

Introduction

This chapter introduces the reader to the Salesforce Data Cloud architecture. We will delve into a detailed examination of the key building blocks of Salesforce Data Cloud and understand how they interact with each other.

We will start our discussion with the Salesforce Data Cloud architecture, followed by a deeper examination of its various components. This will allow us to understand and appreciate how Salesforce Data Cloud gets its power from. Next, we will distinguish between Salesforce and the Salesforce Data Cloud technical architecture.

Furthermore, we will discuss the technical benefits of Salesforce Data Cloud and learn how to drive productivity, efficiency, and value with it. In the end, we will discuss about the integration of different capabilities into Commerce, Sales, Service, and Marketing Cloud with the addition of Salesforce Data Cloud.

Structure

In this chapter, the following topics will be covered:

- Salesforce Data Cloud Architecture
- Difference Between Salesforce Architecture and Salesforce Data Cloud Architecture
- Key Technical Benefits Offered by the Salesforce Data Cloud Platform
- Salesforce Applications Powered by Salesforce Data Cloud

Salesforce Data Cloud Architecture

The architecture of Salesforce Data Cloud consists of several key components, including:

- **Data Sources**: The data sources component is responsible for collecting and ingesting data from various sources, such as social media platforms, data providers, and customer relationship management (CRM) systems. The platform supports both batch and real-time data ingestion, which allows businesses to access the most up-to-date data.
- **Data Storage**: The data storage component is responsible for storing the ingested data in a centralized data warehouse. The platform uses a variety of data storage technologies, such as Hadoop, Amazon S3, and Microsoft Azure, to store and manage the data. The data storage component provides scalable and flexible data storage, which allows businesses to store large amounts of data and retrieve it quickly and efficiently.
- **Data Management**: The data management component is responsible for cleaning, transforming, and enriching the data. The platform uses a variety of data management techniques, such as data normalization, data standardization, and data enrichment, to ensure that the data is accurate, consistent, and actionable.
- **Data APIs**: The data APIs component is responsible for exposing the data to other applications and services. The platform provides a range of APIs, such as REST APIs and SOAP APIs, that enable businesses to access the data and integrate it into their existing workflows and applications.
- **Data Analytics and Insights**: The data analytics and insights component is responsible for providing insights into the data and helping businesses

make better decisions. The platform provides a range of data analytics and reporting tools, such as dashboards, charts, and reports, that enable businesses to visualize and analyze the data.

- **Data Security and Privacy**: The data security and privacy component is responsible for ensuring that the data is secure and protected. The platform uses a range of security and privacy features, such as encryption, access controls, and data governance policies, to protect the data from unauthorized access and to ensure compliance with data privacy regulations.

Figure 4.1 shows the architecture of Salesforce Data Cloud.

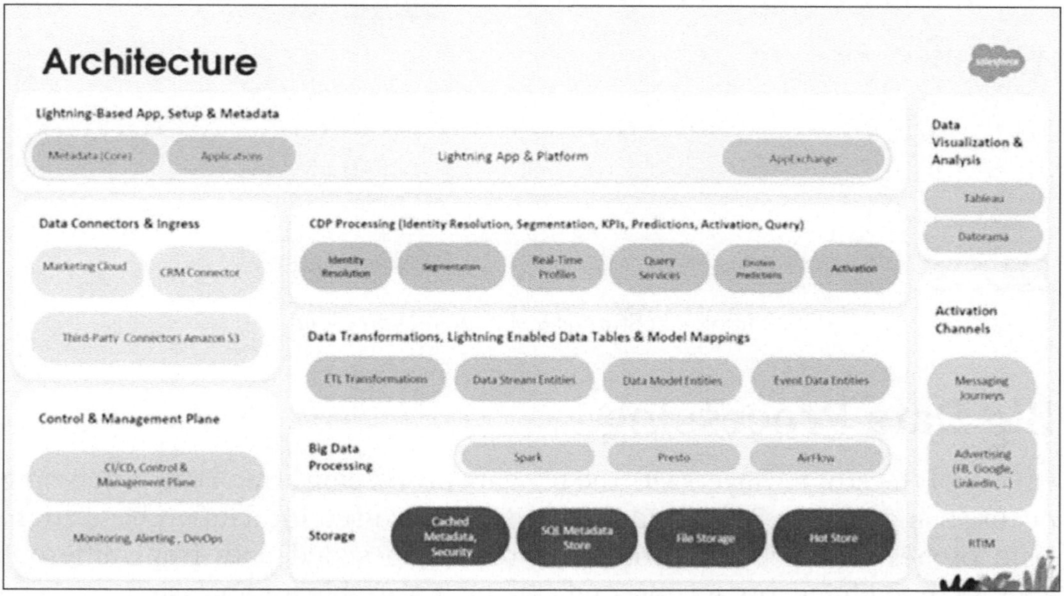

Figure 4.1: *Salesforce Data Cloud Architecture Diagram*

Salesforce Data Cloud is built on AWS. It uses many services offered by AWS for storage, data processing, data transformation, and the like. Let us now examine the architecture diagram.

There are different building blocks in the architecture diagram, and we will look at them one by one.

Storage

Starting with the storage block, data is stored in Data Cloud in the Parquet file format in Amazon S3. Parquet is a columnar storage that provides warehouse-type columnar access. There are three layers of storage: cold, warm, and hot. For hot storage, it uses Amazon DynamoDB. Additionally, it has an SQL metadata store and cached metadata security (see *Figure* 4.2).

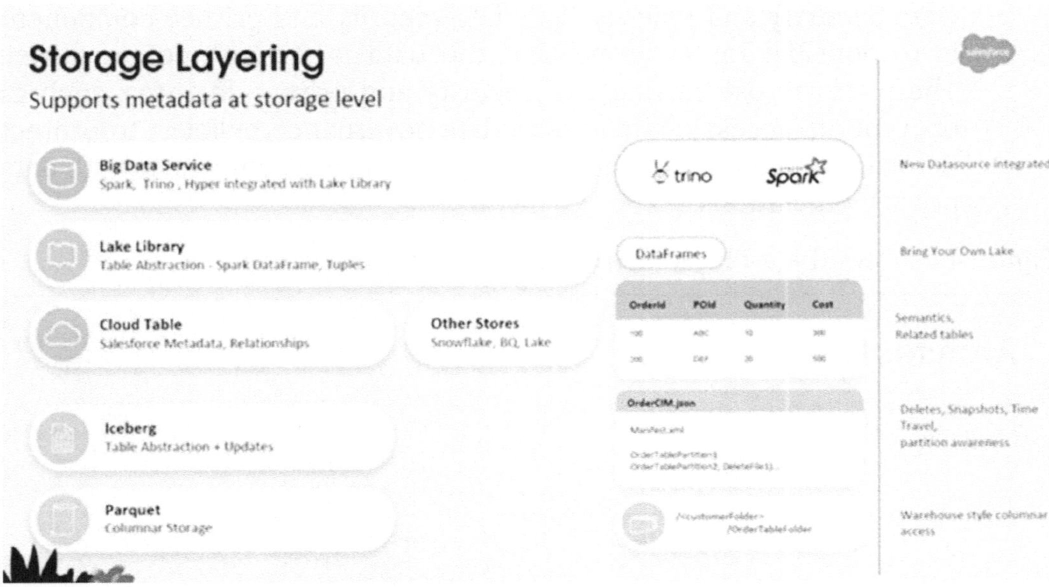

Figure 4.2: *Storage layering in Data Cloud*

Big Data Processing

On top of the storage layers sits the big data processing layer. Data processing occurs using Apache Spark and Presto. Airflow is used for data orchestration. Data orchestration is the process of retrieving siloed data from different sources, combining, organizing, and making it available for analysis.

Data Transformation, Lighting-enabled Data Tables, and Model Mappings

On top of the big data processing layer sits the data transformation layer. Salesforce has a table abstraction feature called Iceberg. In Salesforce, an **iceberg** is a term used to describe a complex data model where most of the data is hidden or not easily visible on the surface. It refers to the idea that, like an iceberg, the majority of the data is below the surface and not immediately visible.

In Salesforce Data Cloud, data transformation, lightning-enabled data tables, and model mappings are all related to the process of data management and analysis. Here is an overview of each feature:

- **Data Transformation**: Data transformation refers to the process of converting data from one format to another. In Data Cloud, data transformation is performed using a data mapping tool that allows users to map source data fields to target data fields.

  With data transformation, users can perform various data operations, such as filtering, aggregation, and enrichment. This allows them to standardize and normalize data, making it easier to analyze and use for personalized experiences.

- **Lightning-enabled Data Tables**: Lightning-enabled data tables are a feature of Salesforce that allows users to view and interact with large datasets. These tables provide a user-friendly interface for browsing, searching, and filtering data.

  In Salesforce Data Cloud, lightning-enabled data tables can be used to analyze customer data and create personalized experiences. Users can apply filters, group data, and perform calculations, allowing them to identify trends and insights that can inform marketing and engagement strategies.

- **Model Mappings**: Model mappings are a way of connecting data sources and targets in Salesforce Data Cloud. They provide a standardized way of defining how data should be transformed and delivered to different systems.

With model mappings, users can define data mappings between different systems and data models, such as Salesforce objects, external databases, or marketing automation platforms. This allows them to maintain a consistent view of customer data across different systems, improving data quality and reducing errors.

For data flow architecture in Salesforce Data Cloud, please refer to *Figure* 4.3.

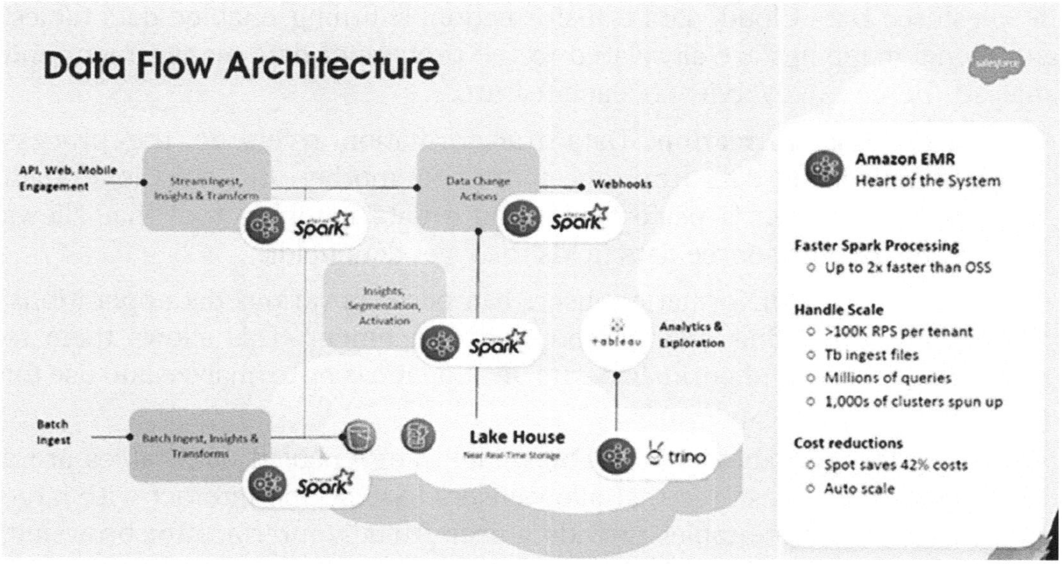

Figure 4.3: *Data Flow Architecture in Salesforce Data Cloud*

CDP Processing

CDP processing enables Data Cloud to perform many CDP functions like identity resolution, segmentation, real-time profiles, query services, Einstein predictions, and activations.

Activation Channels

Salesforce Data Cloud can be connected with several activation channels, such as Salesforce Marketing Cloud, Facebook, Google AdSense, LinkedIn, and more, to reach the right audience at the right time.

Control and Management Plane

In Salesforce Data Cloud, the Control Plane and the Management Plane refer to two distinct components of the platform:

- **Control Plane**: The Control Plane is responsible for managing access to the Data Cloud platform and its resources. It includes features such as authentication, authorization, and access control, ensuring that users have the appropriate permissions to access and modify data.

  The Control Plane provides a centralized location for managing security policies, user access, and other governance controls. It also supports integration with third-party identity providers and authentication protocols, such as Single Sign-On (SSO).

- **Management Plane**: The Management Plane is responsible for managing and configuring the CDP platform itself. It includes features such as data ingestion, data mapping, data transformation, and data delivery.

  The Management Plane provides a user-friendly interface for managing data workflows, creating data pipelines, and configuring integrations with external systems. It also includes tools for data quality management, data lineage tracking, and data governance.

Data Connectors and Ingress

In Salesforce Data Cloud, data connectors and ingress are used to bring customer data into the platform.

- **Data Connectors**: Data connectors are pre-built integrations that allow Salesforce Data Cloud to connect to a variety of external data sources, such as CRM systems, marketing automation platforms, and social media channels. These connectors simplify the process of bringing data into the platform, allowing organizations to quickly ingest and use customer data from a range of sources.

  Salesforce Data Cloud provides a range of pre-built data connectors, including connectors for Salesforce CRM, Salesforce Marketing Cloud, Marketo, Eloqua, Google Analytics, and Facebook. Additionally, the platform supports custom data connectors, enabling organizations to build their own integrations with external systems.

- **Ingress**: Ingress refers to bringing data into Salesforce Data Cloud, whether through data connectors, file uploads, or other means. The platform provides a range of ingress options, including batch file uploads, real-time API integrations, and streaming data ingestion.

Data Visualization and Analysis

Salesforce Data Cloud provides a data visualization and analysis layer. It can connect with different BI tools and enable users to analyze customer data in the form of charts, tables, graphs, and more. Tableau and CRM analytics are some of the in-house analytics tools. However, it can also connect with other BI tools like Power BI.

The data in Data Cloud can be connected to Datorama, which helps to visualize and present campaign performance data to stakeholders. It is used by companies to share the performance of marketing campaigns with their clients.

The Lightning-based App, Setup, and Metadata

The topmost layer is the all-familiar lightning UI, which Salesforce users are familiar with. It contains all Salesforce applications, connecting to AppExchange products, metadata, data model, and more. Users can create custom pages, components, and workflows using the Lightning App Builder, a drag-and-drop interface that allows users to create custom interfaces without writing code.

Metadata refers to the configuration and customization data that defines how Salesforce CDP is configured and used. This includes objects, fields, workflows, and other elements that define the platform's data model and user interface.

Metadata in Salesforce Data Cloud is managed using the Metadata API, which allows users to retrieve, modify, and deploy metadata components across different environments. This enables organizations to manage the configuration of Salesforce Data Cloud across multiple instances, such as development, testing, and production environments.

Salesforce Data Cloud uses Amazon AWS services for most of its needs (refer to *Figure 4.4*).

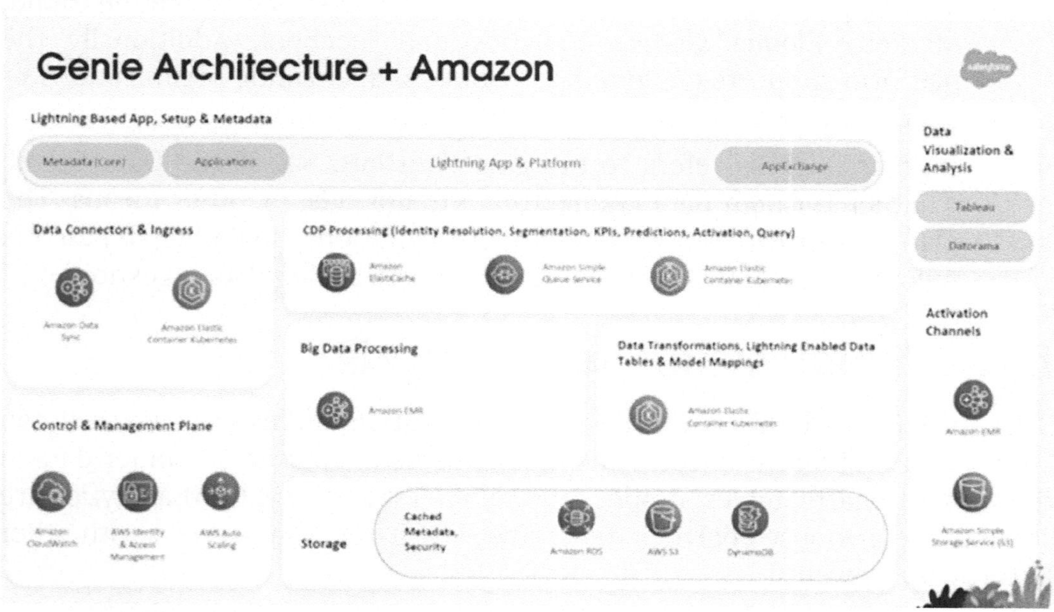

Figure 4.4: *Salesforce Data Cloud architecture is dependent on AWS service*

The storage is managed by Amazon RDS, AWS S3, and DynamoDB. Big data processing is performed using Amazon EMR. Data transformation, lighting-enabled data tables, and model mappings are handled by Amazon Elastic Container Kubernetes. CDP processing is done using Amazon ElastiCache, Amazon Simple Queue Service, and Amazon Elastic Container Kubernetes. Activation channels use Amazon EMR and Amazon Simple Storage Service (S3). Data connectors and ingress are managed by Amazon Data Sync and Amazon Elastic Container Kubernetes. Control and management planning is conducted using Amazon CloudWatch, AWS Identity and Access Management, and AWS Autoscaling.

Difference Between Salesforce Architecture and Salesforce Data Cloud Architecture

Salesforce Architecture and Salesforce Data Cloud architecture are related to the Salesforce platform, but they have different purposes and components.

- **Salesforce Architecture**

  Salesforce Architecture refers to the underlying infrastructure and components that make up the Salesforce platform. This includes the Salesforce database, servers, APIs, and user interface. It is designed to provide a scalable, secure, and reliable platform for businesses to manage their customer data and operations. It includes features such as Salesforce Lightning, which provides a modern user interface, and Salesforce Einstein, which provides artificial intelligence capabilities for the platform.

  Let us look at the high-level Salesforce architecture diagram in *Figure* 4.5.

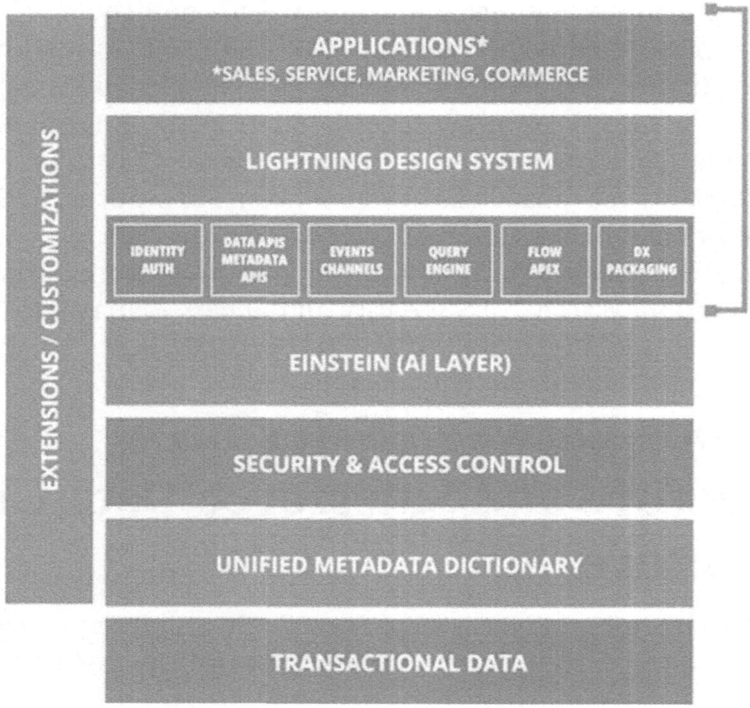

Figure 4.5: *Salesforce Architecture*

In the preceding diagram, at the bottom is the transaction database, which stores transaction data. Transaction data includes data related to Leads, Opportunities, Accounts, and other objects used in daily operations. It is a traditional relational database that every Salesforce org shares with all the tenants of the instance. Both standard and custom objects are physically stored here, making the data easily accessible for all queries, triggers, flows, and process automation.

The unified metadata dictionary describes the data structures to enforce integrity when saving records. The security and access control layer ensures that data is only visible to relevant users in a specific org.

The Einstein layer is the artificial intelligence layer of Salesforce that provides machine learning and AI capabilities to Salesforce. The AI can train on the data residing in Salesforce and provide analysis or predictions to users. The end users interact with the top three layers, which contain the lighting design system, applications, and other features. These layers enable users to interact with the Salesforce system. Salesforce is extensible and customizable, which is denoted by the left-hand side block. You can connect various applications from the AppExchange or build your own on top of the Salesforce platform, leveraging its architecture.

- **Salesforce Data Cloud Architecture**

  Salesforce Data Cloud Architecture, on the other hand, is specifically focused on managing data from various sources to drive better business decisions. It includes several components such as data sources, data storage, data management, data APIs, data analytics and insights, and data security and privacy. These components work together to provide businesses with access to a wide range of data sets, including third-party data, customer data, and social media data.

  The Salesforce Data Cloud Architecture enables businesses to collect and ingest data from various sources, clean, transform, and enrich the data, store it in a centralized data warehouse, expose the data to other applications and services, and provide insights into the data through data analytics and reporting tools. The platform also includes security and privacy features to protect the data from unauthorized access and ensure compliance with data privacy regulations.

  Now, let us examine the high-level Salesforce Data Cloud architecture diagram (see *Figure* 4.6).

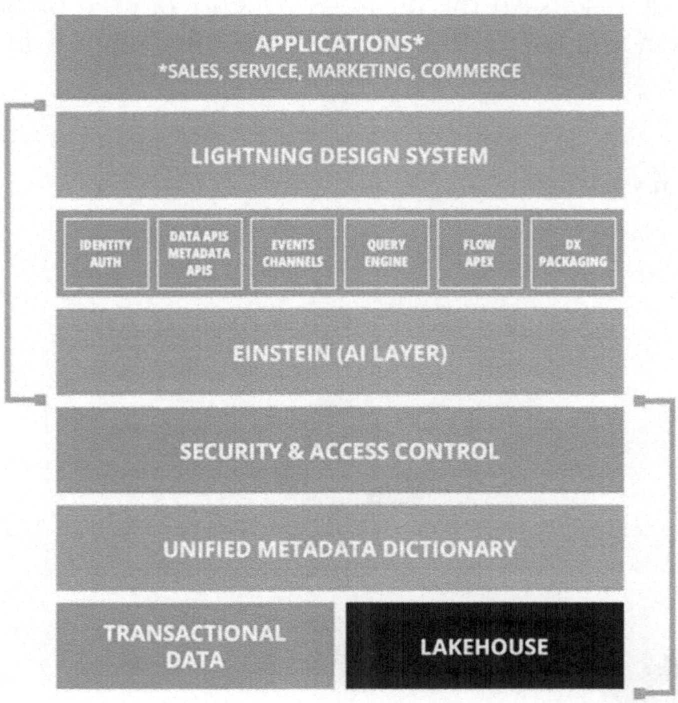

Figure 4.6: *Salesforce Data Cloud Architecture diagram*

As you can see, there is an addition of a Lakehouse to the Salesforce architecture. Data Cloud essentially brings this Lakehouse to the Salesforce platform and the data that resides in it.

The rest of the architecture remains the same. The difference is that the Lakehouse data is incorporated in the transaction data, unified metadata dictionary, and security and access control layers. The Einstein layer also gets a boost from the data in the Lakehouse. It gets more data to train on and can be used to solve more AI use cases. The applications on the top layer can operate on Lakehouse data. You can also build customizations with it.

While both architectures are related to the Salesforce platform and similar, they serve different purposes. Salesforce Architecture is focused on providing a platform for managing customer data and operations, while Salesforce Data Cloud Architecture is focused on managing data from various sources to drive better business decisions.

Key Technical Benefits Offered by the Salesforce Data Cloud Platform

We have already discussed the business benefits offered by Salesforce Data Cloud. Let us now look at the technical benefits offered by the platform (see *Figure* 4.7):

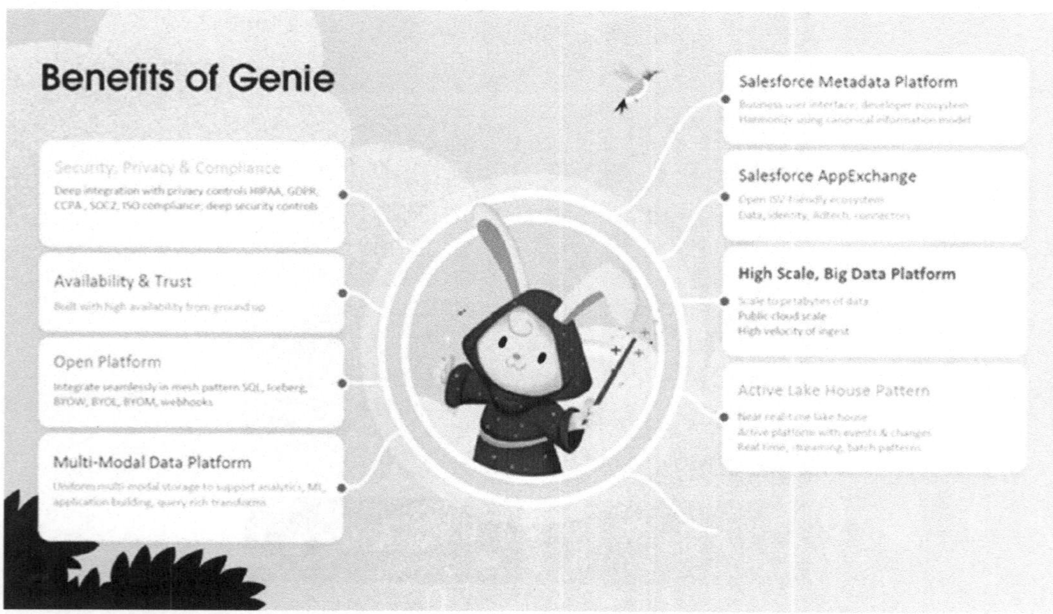

Figure 4.7: *Technical Benefits of the Salesforce Data Cloud Platform*

- **Security, Privacy, and Compliance**: With increasing data privacy regulations, businesses need to prioritize data compliance and governance. Salesforce Data Cloud helps organizations meet these requirements by providing tools for data consent management, data transparency, and data subject rights. It enables businesses to maintain data privacy and security, build customer trust, and mitigate regulatory risks. Data Cloud provides deep integration with privacy controls HIPAA, GDPR, CCPA, SOC2, ISO compliance, and deep security controls. Salesforce is compliant with various data privacy and security regulations, such as the General Data Protection Regulation (GDPR) and the California Consumer Privacy Act (CCPA). They prioritize data governance and provide tools to help businesses ensure compliance with relevant regulations.
- **Availability and Trust**: Salesforce Data Cloud is known for providing a highly available platform to its customers. They have implemented robust infrastructure and operational practices to ensure the availability and reliability of their services. Here are some key aspects that contribute to the high availability of the Salesforce platform:
    - **Data Centers**: Salesforce operates multiple data centers across different regions, ensuring redundancy and failover capabilities.
    - **Redundancy and Resilience**: Salesforce utilizes redundant hardware and network configurations to minimize single points of failure. They employ redundant storage systems, load balancers, and network equipment to ensure seamless failover and uninterrupted service in case of hardware or network failures.
    - **Disaster Recovery**: Salesforce has disaster recovery plans and processes in place to handle unforeseen events and natural disasters. They regularly replicate customer data across geographically dispersed data centers, ensuring data integrity and allowing for a swift recovery in case of any disruptions.
    - **Performance Monitoring and Optimization**: Salesforce continuously monitors the performance and availability of its platform to identify and address any potential issues proactively. They employ real-time monitoring tools and perform regular performance optimizations to ensure optimal system performance and availability.
    - **Regular Updates and Maintenance**: Salesforce performs regular updates, patches, and maintenance activities on its platform to enhance security, performance, and reliability. These updates

are often rolled out seamlessly with minimal impact on service availability.

- **Open Platform**: Unlike other CDP tools which are closed applications, Salesforce offers an open platform for you to integrate different applications your business uses. Salesforce Data Cloud can integrate seamlessly with various technologies and patterns, including SQL, Iceberg, BYOW (Bring Your Own Workflow), BYOL (Bring Your Own Language), BYOM (Bring Your Own Model), and webhooks. Here's a brief explanation of each integration:
    - **SQL Integration**: Salesforce Data Cloud supports SQL-based integrations, allowing you to query and retrieve customer data using standard SQL syntax. This integration enables you to leverage your existing SQL skills and tools to interact with the CDP platform.
    - **Iceberg Integration**: Iceberg is an open-source table format for large-scale data processing. Salesforce Data Cloud can integrate with Iceberg, allowing you to store and process customer data using the Iceberg table format. This integration provides scalability, performance, and data management capabilities for handling large volumes of customer data. Iceberg enables you to use SQL for accessing big data tables.
    - **BYOW (Bring Your Own Workflow)**: BYOW refers to the flexibility of Salesforce Data Cloud to integrate with external workflow systems or tools that you bring to the platform. This integration allows you to incorporate your own custom workflows, automation, or business processes into the CDP environment, enabling seamless end-to-end data operations.
    - **BYOL (Bring Your Own Language)**: Salesforce Data Cloud supports BYOL, which means you can use your preferred programming or scripting language to interact with the platform. Whether it's Python, Java, JavaScript, or any other language, you can leverage your existing expertise and coding practices to interact with the CDP and perform data operations.
    - **BYOM (Bring Your Own Model)**: Salesforce Data Cloud enables you to bring your own machine-learning models into the platform for advanced analytics and data-driven insights. You can integrate your custom models, algorithms, or predictive analytics into the CDP ecosystem, leveraging the power of your own models to drive personalized customer experiences and decision-making.

- o **Webhooks Integration**: Webhooks are a way to receive real-time notifications or data updates from external systems. Salesforce Data Cloud supports webhooks, allowing you to set up event-based triggers or notifications that can be sent to external applications or services. This integration enables you to react to specific events or changes in customer data, facilitating real-time actions and integrations with other systems.

These integration options offered by Salesforce Data Cloud ensure flexibility, customization, and interoperability with other technologies and workflows, enabling you to leverage your existing tools and frameworks seamlessly within the CDP environment.

- **Multi-modal data platform**: To support analytics, machine learning, application building, and query-rich transformations for multi-modal data, a uniform multi-modal storage system is essential. Such a system provides a cohesive and integrated infrastructure to store, process, and analyze diverse types of data within a single platform. Multi-modal refers to a flexible data model that can represent and store different data types in a coherent and structured manner. This may involve using a schema-on-read approach, where the schema is applied during the query or analysis phase, allowing for the dynamic handling of diverse data structures. Salesforce Data Cloud provides multi-modal storage for various use cases like analytics, machine learning, query-rich transformation, and more. You can also consider integrating external solutions or platforms to achieve this goal as Salesforce Data Cloud is an open platform.
- **Salesforce Metadata Platform**: Salesforce Metadata Platform is a powerful tool that enables developers and administrators to manage, migrate, and deploy Salesforce application configurations and customizations across different Salesforce environments. It provides a programmatic interface for accessing and manipulating metadata components, such as objects, fields, workflows, layouts, and more. You can keep different instances for Salesforce Data Cloud like dev, QA, pre-production, and production, and move metadata changes from one org to another easily using different tools. The Salesforce metadata platform makes development easier.
- **Salesforce AppExchange**: As discussed earlier, Salesforce AppExchange is the marketplace for applications that work with Salesforce. You can get secured applications that work with Salesforce Data Cloud like data connectors, AdTech connectors, and other applications. It is always

better to check AppExchange for applications to solve a business need before trying to build it in-house. It is faster, cheaper, and easier to maintain.

- **High-scale, big data platform**: Salesforce Data Cloud is built on a cloud-based infrastructure, offering scalability and flexibility to accommodate the growing needs of businesses. It can handle large volumes of data and support the increasing demands of customer data processing and analysis. Data Cloud can scale to petabytes of data with a high velocity of ingest.
- **Active Lakehouse pattern:** Salesforce Data Cloud supports the active Lakehouse pattern, which is an emerging data architecture pattern that combines the strengths of data lakes and data warehouses to provide a unified and scalable platform for data storage, processing, and analytics.

Figure 4.8 shows the diagrammatic representation of Data Lakehouse storage.

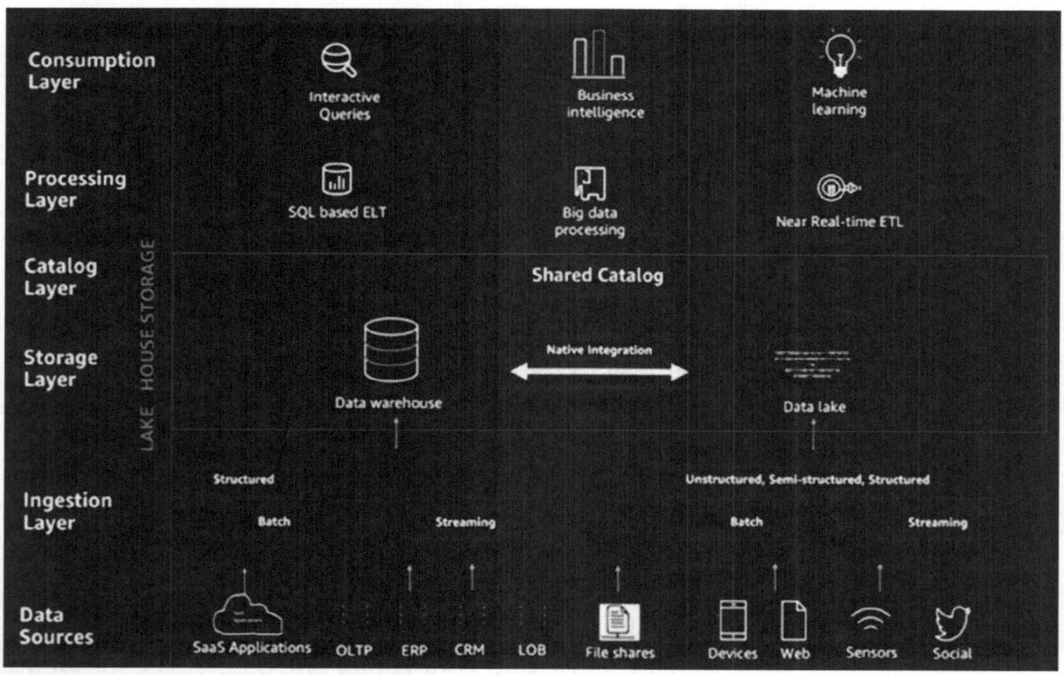

Figure 4.8: *Data Lakehouse storage*
(*Source:* **https://aws.amazon.com/blogs/big-data/build-a-lake-house-architecture-on-aws/**)

The key characteristics and principles of the Active Lakehouse pattern include:

- **Data lake storage**: The pattern leverages a data lake as the central storage layer, which allows for the ingestion and storage of diverse and raw data in its original format. This provides flexibility and agility in handling different types of data, including structured, semi-structured, and unstructured data.
- **ACID transactions**: Unlike traditional data lakes, the Active Lakehouse pattern supports atomicity, consistency, isolation, and durability (ACID) transactions on the data stored in the lake. This ensures data integrity and allows for reliable data updates and modifications.
- **Schema enforcement**: The Active Lakehouse pattern introduces schema enforcement on the data lake, which means that a schema or structure is enforced on the ingested data, ensuring data quality and consistency. This allows for better control over the data and facilitates query optimization and performance improvements.
- **Unified processing engine**: The pattern utilizes a unified processing engine, such as Apache Spark, that can operate directly on the data lake. This eliminates the need for data movement between different systems and enables efficient data processing and analytics across diverse data types.
- **Incremental data processing**: With the Active Lakehouse pattern, incremental data processing is emphasized, enabling near real-time analytics and insights. This means that as new data is ingested into the lake, only the incremental changes are processed, reducing processing overhead and enabling faster time-to-insights.
- **SQL-based analytics**: The pattern supports SQL-based analytics, making it accessible to many users with SQL skills. This simplifies the data exploration and analysis process and allows for seamless integration with existing analytics tools and workflows.

These key benefits make Salesforce Data Cloud a valuable tool for businesses aiming to leverage customer data to enhance marketing efforts, drive customer satisfaction, and achieve business growth.

Salesforce Applications Powered by Salesforce Data Cloud

Once you have set up Data Cloud or Data Cloud and it is up and running, Data Cloud is going to provide a lot of value to other Salesforce products like Sales Cloud, Service Cloud, Marketing Cloud, and more. There is no use in getting customer data from different sources if we cannot use the data to improve the customer experience.

We can use the data available to us in different Salesforce products. Let us now look at them one by one.

Data Cloud for Sales

The Sales Console, integrated with Salesforce Data Cloud, offers sales representatives a comprehensive view of the customer, including important information, recommended actions, optimal contact timing, and a history of engagements. This consolidated view, constantly refreshed with real-time updates from multiple data sources, simplifies the sales process and enhances efficiency. It's the seamless connection between the Sales Console and Salesforce Data Cloud that brings together all the necessary details on a single screen, providing sales reps with a powerful tool for managing customer interactions (see *Figure* 4.9).

Figure 4.9: *Sales Cloud Data Cloud can supercharge your sales agents to deliver better sales experience to your customers*

As of now, there are two functions from Salesforce to support Salesforce Cloud Data Cloud:

- Sales Cloud Enablement
- Einstein Bots for Sales

Let's understand these two functions:

- **Sales Cloud Enablement**: "*Enhance voice and video conversations through instant guidance.*"

  Using Sales Cloud Enablement, utilize data-driven coaching to support sales managers in enhancing critical skills. Enablement automatically monitors and tracks key milestones, delivering training programs seamlessly within the workflow. This ensures that sales representatives can quickly develop and improve their skills, maximizing their effectiveness in their role. With Data Cloud, Sales Cloud Enablement is powered with real-time feedback.

- **Einstein Bots for Sales**: "*Increase the efficiency of every sales representative with the use of bots.*"

  We understand that chatbots can assist customers in finding answers to common questions and completing tasks, reducing the need for direct assistance from a sales representative. Now, Einstein Bots are not limited to the service team and have been extended to Sales Cloud. When sales reps receive messages through the chat window, they have access to comprehensive customer information, including key details, engagement history, and the recommended next action. For example, if a customer shows interest in upgrading based on their in-app behavior, the sales rep will see a prompt such as `Upgrade this fan`, as shown in *Figure 4.10*. This enables sales reps to provide personalized assistance while leveraging the capabilities of chatbots.

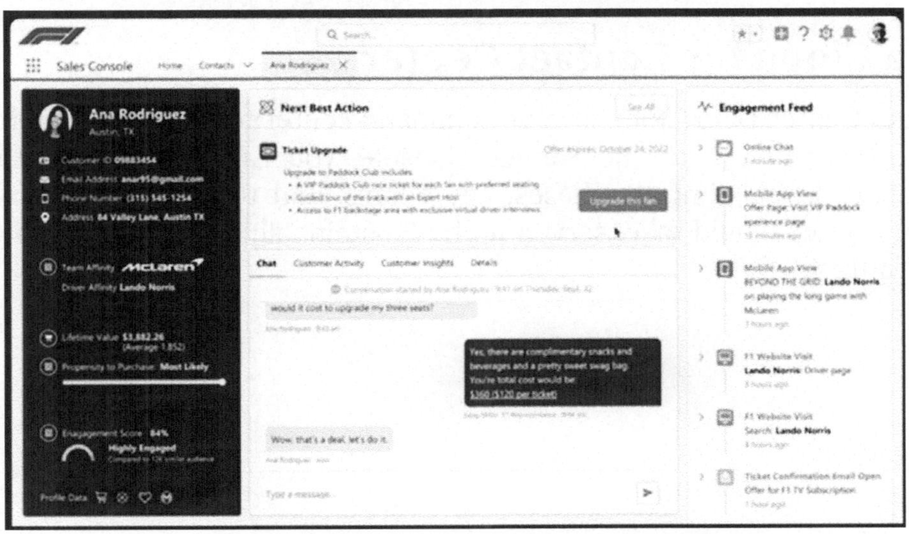

Figure 4.10: *Einstein Bot Chat window from the sales rep's view, Sales Console connected to Data Cloud*

Data Cloud for Service

Service Cloud is now powered by Data Cloud's real-time data. Contact Center Data Cloud serves as your central hub for all customer-related activities. Through the Service Console, you can access the customer's interactions, live purchases, important information, and Einstein's recommendations on the best course of action for agents to take (see *Figure* 4.11).

Figure 4.11: *Service Cloud Data Cloud makes customer service representatives more productive*

There are currently three services generally available that work with Data Cloud:

- Contact Center Data Cloud
- Frontline Service
- WhatsApp-First Business Messaging

Data Cloud for Contact Center

Contact Center Data Cloud is your command center for all the things related to the customer. With the Service Console, you can view the customer's interactions, real-time purchases, key details, and the predicted next best action agents should take, served up by Einstein, all powered by Data Cloud (see *Figure* 4.12).

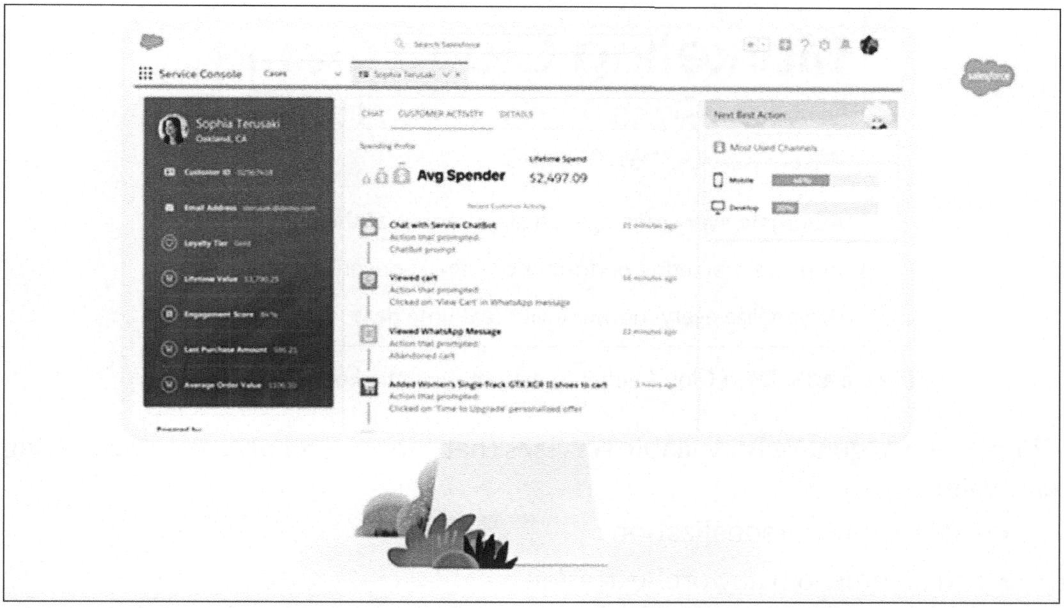

Figure 4.12: *Get insights for each individual customer, served in real-time by Data Cloud*

Frontline Service

Real-time data from Data Cloud is geared towards Field Service, specifically frontline service teams who are physically present in the field to serve customers. With Data Cloud's assistance, these teams can enhance the operational efficiency of assets and improve customer satisfaction by adopting a proactive approach to frontline service.

WhatsApp-First Business Messaging

Salesforce Customer 360 and WhatsApp are joining forces to enable organizations to seamlessly engage with their customers and streamline communication using the WhatsApp Business Platform API. This integration will facilitate efficient and effective customer interactions for businesses.

Data Cloud for Marketing

Traditionally, CDPs are used to support marketing activities, so it is a no-brainer that Data Cloud will supercharge your marketing efforts with the real-time data available at your disposal. Perhaps the biggest benefit from Salesforce Data Cloud comes in the form of more personalized marketing to customers (see *Figure 4.13*). Here, Data Cloud does not disappoint.

Figure 4.13: *Data Cloud helps to personalize marketing in real-time*

There are two generally available services that can supercharge your marketing campaigns:

- Real-time personalization
- Real-time journey orchestration
- **Real-time personalization**

  Delivering personalized and meaningful experiences relies on the availability of accurate and timely data within unified customer profiles. To achieve this, the Marketing Cloud and Data Cloud have enhanced their integration, enabling marketing teams to leverage Data Cloud data and the real-time customer graph. This integration empowers marketers to provide AI-driven personalized recommendations in real-time, adapting these offers as the customer's unified profile is updated with the latest data.

- **Real-time journey orchestration**

  Real-time journey orchestration in Salesforce refers to the capability of orchestrating and managing customer journeys in real-time. It involves leveraging customer data, interactions, and triggers to dynamically guide customers through personalized journeys across various touchpoints and channels.

  With the help of Data Cloud, real-time journey orchestration is now possible. The real-time journey orchestration in Salesforce involves automating and optimizing customer interactions based on real-time data, such as customer actions, events, or changes in their profile. This enables businesses to deliver seamless and consistent experiences across channels, ensuring that customers receive the most relevant and timely messaging or offers.

Data Cloud for Commerce

If there is one place where real-time data matters, it is in e-commerce. Real-time data can be the difference between someone buying a product or going to a competitor. With Data Cloud, Salesforce Commerce Cloud gets the best personalized offers and recommendations in real-time, thus tilting the scales in favor of your company (see *Figure* 4.14).

***Figure 4.14**: Salesforce Data Cloud helps Commerce Cloud deliver personalization in the e-commerce experience*

Commerce Cloud Data Cloud is a highly agile and efficient platform that encompasses the entire customer journey from initial discovery to final product delivery. It employs advanced technologies, such as AI-powered merchandising, to make fulfillment decisions based on the customer's unique profile. Additionally, it leverages real-time browsing behavior to personalize and customize shopping experiences for each individual customer. With its speed and flexibility, Commerce Cloud Data Cloud ensures seamless and tailored interactions throughout the customer's shopping journey.

You get the following benefits:

- Automate fulfillment based on your customer profile
- Maximize every cart with AI-powered merchandising
- Tailor every shopping experience with real-time activity data

Conclusion

In this chapter, we examined the architecture of Salesforce Data Cloud, discussing in detail its key building blocks and their interactions with each other.

We started our discussion with the Salesforce Data Cloud architecture and then explored the various components of Data Cloud. Then, we differentiated between the Salesforce architecture and the Salesforce Data Cloud architecture.

Next, we outlined the benefits of Salesforce Data Cloud and learned how to drive productivity, efficiency, and value with Salesforce Data Cloud. Finally, we examined how Data Cloud helps increase the capabilities of Commerce, Sales, Service, and Marketing Cloud products from Salesforce.

In the upcoming chapter, we will delve into the implementation of a CDP and the steps involved in it.

Points to Remember

- The architecture of Salesforce Data Cloud consists of several key components, namely, data sources, data storage, data management, data APIs, data analytics and insights, and data security and privacy.
- The difference between Salesforce and Salesforce Data Cloud architecture is the addition of a Lakehouse to the Data Cloud architecture. The data stored in the Lakehouse can be utilized by Salesforce to create a 360 view of the customer.
- Key technical benefits of the Salesforce Data Cloud platform include:
    - Security, Privacy, and Compliance
    - Availability and Trust
    - Open Platform
    - Multi-Modal Data Platform
    - Salesforce Metadata Platform
    - Salesforce AppExchange
    - High-Scale, big-data platform
    - Active Lakehouse pattern
- Salesforce Data Cloud enhances the capabilities of other Salesforce products, such as Sales Cloud, Service Cloud, Marketing Cloud, Commerce Cloud, and more, by providing real-time data access to these applications. This helps to increase productivity as well as power the users to provide superior customer experience.

Questions

1. Explain the different components of the Salesforce Data Cloud architecture.
2. What are the different layers in the Salesforce Data Cloud architecture?
3. Explain the difference between Salesforce and Salesforce Data Cloud architecture.
4. What are the key technical benefits offered by Salesforce Data Cloud?
5. How does Salesforce Data Cloud help the Sales Cloud?
6. How does Salesforce Data Cloud enhance the Service Cloud?
7. How does Salesforce Data Cloud power the Marketing Cloud?
8. How does Salesforce Data Cloud transform the Commerce Cloud?

Chapter 5

Implementing a Customer Data Platform

Introduction

This chapter discusses the steps involved in implementing a Customer Data Platform (CDP) solution. We will understand the step-by-step approach for implementing a CDP solution, covering topics such as choosing a CDP vendor, creating business use cases to get traction from business leaders for your CDP project, creating a steering team, tracking plan, and implementing the tracking plan among other steps.

This chapter will prepare you for managing a CDP implementation project from the lens of a project manager or a business analyst. You will gain insights into the high-level steps involved in such a project, enabling you to steer a team toward a successful CDP implementation.

For the sake of generalization, we have remained vendor-agnostic here, which means that these steps can be applied irrespective of which CDP vendor you have chosen for your implementation. This chapter is not specific to any CDP vendor or Salesforce Data Cloud. A detailed discussion on the implementation of Salesforce Data Cloud will be provided in a later chapter.

Structure

In this chapter, the following topics will be covered:

- Prepare for Implementing a CDP Solution
- Discovery Phase
- Define and Design Phase
- Build Phase
- Deployment

Prepare for Implementing a CDP Solution

If you are planning to implement a Customer Data Platform (CDP) for your company or are involved in such a project, you need to make sure that the team has completed the pre-implementation steps first. Before you can begin the implementation, you need to prepare for it. An initial analysis can help to avoid unwanted complications later in the implementation phase.

Implementing a CDP requires careful planning and execution to ensure its success. Here's a step-by-step guide to help you prepare for the same:

- **Define your objectives**: Clearly define your goals and objectives for implementing a CDP. Identify the problems you want to solve, such as improving customer insights, personalization, or marketing efficiency.
- **Assess your data infrastructure**: Evaluate your existing data infrastructure, including data sources, storage systems, data quality, and integration capabilities. Identify any gaps or limitations that may impact the implementation of a CDP.
- **Identify data sources**: Identify all the relevant data sources within your organization that you want to integrate into the CDP. This may include customer databases, transactional systems, website analytics, CRM, social media, and more.
- **Data mapping and schema design**: Map out the data elements from different sources and design a unified data schema for your CDP (see *Figure* 5.1). Determine how the data will be structured, organized, and standardized to ensure compatibility and consistency.

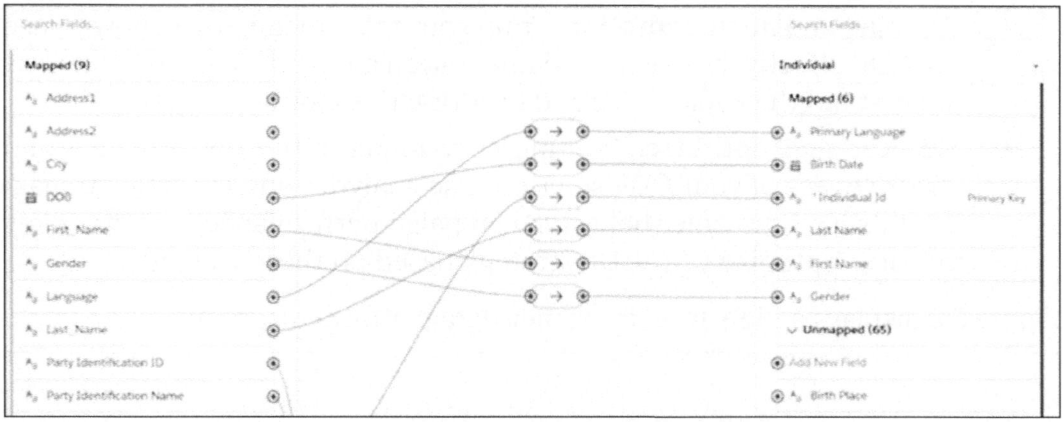

***Figure 5.1:** Data schema design*

- **Data privacy and compliance**: Ensure that you comply with data privacy regulations, such as GDPR or CCPA. Review your data handling practices, consent management, and security measures to protect customer data and maintain compliance.
- **Select a CDP solution**: Research and evaluate various CDP vendors based on your requirements and objectives. Consider factors such as scalability, flexibility, integration capabilities, data security, and vendor support. Request demos and engage in discussions with vendors to make an informed decision.
- **Develop an implementation plan**: Create a detailed implementation plan that outlines the steps, timelines, and responsibilities for deploying the CDP. Consider factors such as data migration, integration with existing systems, testing, and training.
- **Data integration and migration**: Implement the necessary integrations with your existing systems to feed data into the CDP. Ensure that the data is cleansed, transformed, and migrated properly, maintaining data integrity and consistency.
- **Data governance and quality**: Establish data governance policies and processes to ensure the ongoing quality, accuracy, and consistency of the data within the CDP. Implement data validation, monitoring, and cleansing mechanisms to maintain data hygiene.
- **Testing and validation**: Conduct rigorous testing to ensure that the CDP is functioning as expected. Validate the data integration, segmentation, personalization, and other features to verify that the CDP meets your objectives.

- **Training and documentation**: Train your team members on how to use the CDP effectively. Create documentation and guidelines to help users understand the capabilities and best practices for utilizing the CDP.
- **Monitor and optimize**: Continuously monitor the performance and effectiveness of your CDP solution. Use analytics and reporting to gain insights into customer behavior, campaign performance, and other key metrics. Optimize your CDP strategy based on these insights.

Figure 5.2 displays a high-level customer data platform diagram:

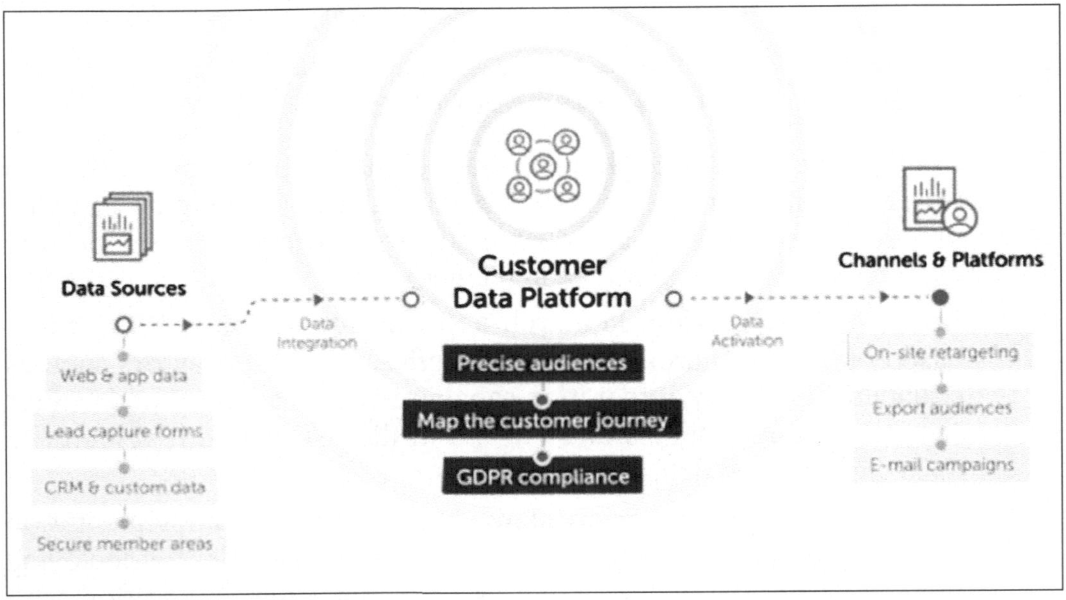

***Figure* 5.2:** *High-level customer data platform diagram*

The first step in preparing for implementation is to define your objectives. Ideally, you would want the CDP to do everything, but that is not a foolproof plan. You need to clearly state what you want to achieve using the CDP in a 6-month, 12-month, and 24-month goal sheet. The team needs to be realistic in their assumptions. The objectives should take into account your current state of data infrastructure and comply with security and privacy standards.

Some of the objectives to consider are as follows:

- **Unified customer view**: Create a comprehensive, unified view of each customer by integrating data from various sources such as CRM, website interactions, social media, and customer support. The objective is to have a holistic understanding of each customer's preferences, behaviors, and interactions with your business.

- **Improved personalization**: Enhance your ability to deliver personalized experiences to customers across various touchpoints. This may involve segmenting customers based on their attributes and behaviors and using this information to tailor marketing messages, product recommendations, and offers.
- **Enhanced customer journey analysis**: Gain deeper insights into the customer journey by tracking and analyzing customer interactions and touchpoints. Understand how customers move through different stages of the buying process, identify bottlenecks or areas for improvement, and optimize the customer journey accordingly.
- **Advanced analytics and reporting**: Leverage the data within the CDP to generate meaningful analytics and reports. Identify key performance indicators (KPIs) that align with your business objectives and track them over time. Use these insights to make data-driven decisions and optimize marketing strategies.
- **Improved marketing efficiency**: Streamline your marketing operations by automating repetitive tasks, such as data extraction and segmentation. Reduce manual effort and human error while improving the speed and accuracy of marketing campaigns.
- **Increased customer engagement and loyalty**: Use the insights derived from the CDP to engage customers more effectively and build long-term loyalty. By delivering personalized, relevant experiences and offers, you can increase customer satisfaction, retention, and advocacy.
- **Data-driven decision-making**: Establish a culture of data-driven decision-making within your organization. Enable various teams, such as marketing, sales, and customer service, to leverage the CDP's insights and make informed decisions that align with customer needs and preferences.
- **Compliance and data security**: Ensure compliance with relevant data privacy regulations, such as GDPR or CCPA. Implement robust data security measures and consent management processes to protect customer data and maintain their trust.

From a project management perspective, there are four main phases to a CDP implementation, as shown in *Figure* 5.3:

***Figure* 5.3:** *Phases in a CDP implementation project*

Discovery Phase

The discovery phase of CDP implementation is a crucial step where you gather information, analyze requirements, and assess your organization's readiness for implementing a Customer Data Platform. If we had to pick a phase that is the most important for a successful CDP implementation, it would be the discovery phase. The decisions taken in this phase will determine whether the implementation will go well or fall below expectations. We will go through the different activities you need to do to ensure a smooth discovery phase and subsequently a successful CDP implementation.

The discovery phase sets the foundation for a successful CDP implementation by gathering the necessary information, aligning stakeholders, and establishing clear objectives. It helps you identify any gaps or challenges upfront, enabling you to plan and execute the implementation more effectively.

Before you can get started on a CDP project, you need to get the buy-in from different departments in your organization. For that purpose, you should create a steering team for the CDP project. Let us take a look at the details next.

Formulate a Steering Team

The first step in a CDP implementation project is to create the steering team. The team is responsible for the current state analysis, prioritizing the business use cases, creating business KPIs, overseeing the implementation of the CDP, as well as operating the CDP once implemented. A CDP does not restrict itself to a single department or a use case; it is used by multiple departments in a company ranging from marketing, insights, customer service, product analytics, and more. CDP affects all departments, including finance, so, it is crucial to have members from all the departments who are affected by the implementation of the CDP. We need to assemble a cross-functional team comprising stakeholders from departments such as marketing, IT, data analytics, customer service, and compliance, among others. This team will be responsible for driving the discovery phase and representing different perspectives and requirements (see *Figure* 5.4).

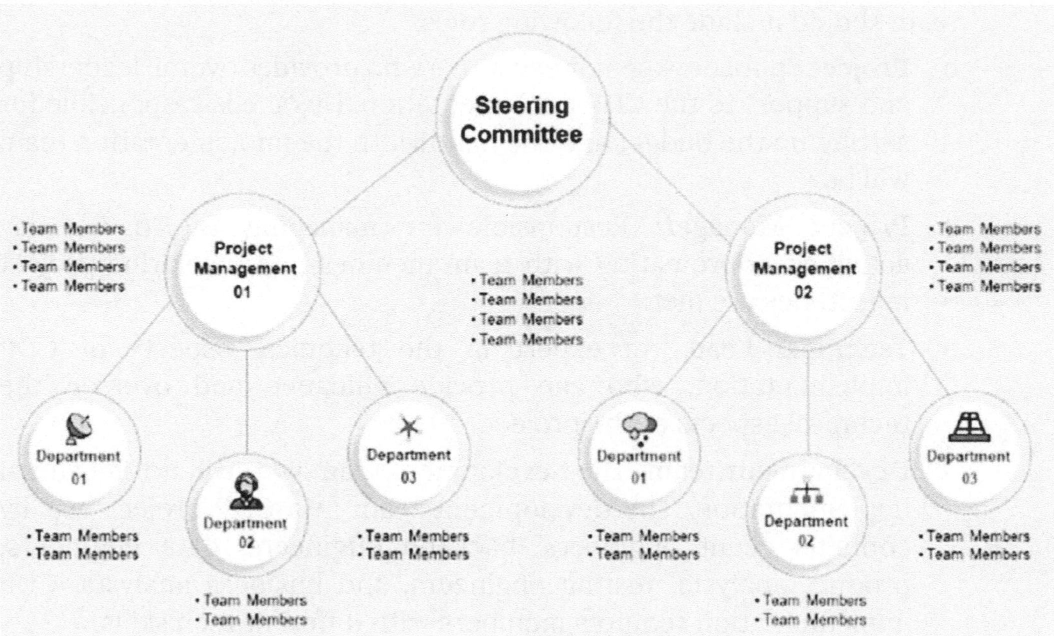

Figure 5.4: *Create a steering committee and project teams across different departments*

Some of the tasks that should be performed by this team are as follows:

- **Define the purpose, objectives, and set expectations**: Clearly articulate the purpose and objectives of implementing a CDP within your organization. Determine the specific outcomes and goals you want to achieve through the implementation. Set reasonable expectations for the implementation. Ideally, you would want all your use cases to get implemented in the first go, but that is never going to happen. The team should set 6, 12, and 24-month goals that are reasonable to achieve given the current state of customer data.

- **Identify stakeholders and their needs**: Identify the key stakeholders within your organization who will be impacted by the CDP implementation. This may include representatives from marketing, IT, sales, customer service, data governance, and other relevant departments. Ensure that the stakeholders have a vested interest in the success of the project. Engage in discussions with these stakeholders to understand their needs, pain points, and expectations from a CDP solution. This will help you prioritize requirements and align the implementation strategy accordingly.
- **Determine roles and responsibilities**: Define the roles and responsibilities of the steering team members. Typically, the steering team should include the following roles:
  - **Project Sponsor**: A senior executive who provides overall leadership and support to the CDP implementation. He/she is responsible for setting up the budget and the bandwidth the implementation team will have.
  - **Project Manager**: Responsible for managing the day-to-day activities, coordinating with team members, and ensuring project milestones are met.
  - **Technical Lead**: An expert in the technical aspects of CDP implementation, who can provide guidance and oversee the technical aspects of the project.
  - **Development team**: The development team who will do the actual implementation. The development team in a CDP project usually contains client engineers, backend engineers, data engineers, product analysts, testing engineers, and business analysts. CDP implementation requires members with different tech skills.
  - **Data Governance Lead**: Responsible for ensuring compliance, data quality, and privacy considerations are addressed throughout the implementation.
  - **Business Representatives**: Representatives from different business units who can provide insights, requirements, and feedback on how the CDP should align with their needs.
- **Define meeting cadence and structure:** Establish a regular meeting cadence for the steering team. Determine the frequency and duration of the meetings, and ensure that all members can commit to attending.

Define the structure of the meetings, including agenda items, decision-making processes, and any supporting documentation needed.

- **Provide resources and support**: Ensure that the steering team has access to the necessary resources, such as budget, technology infrastructure, and support from relevant departments. Assign dedicated resources to assist the team members in their respective roles.
- **Communicate and engage**: Regularly communicate updates, progress, and challenges to the broader organization. Keep stakeholders informed about the benefits of the CDP implementation and address any concerns they may have. Encourage open dialogue and engagement from all team members.
- **Monitor and evaluate**: Continuously monitor the progress of the CDP implementation against the defined objectives. Regularly assess the performance of the steering team and address any issues or roadblocks promptly. Evaluate the outcomes achieved and make necessary adjustments as needed.

Document Business Use Cases

After the steering team is successfully created, the next step is to use the expertise of the steering team to document business use cases, KPIs, metrics, and more. Use cases can be across departments. For example, a use case can involve marketing, product analytics, and the UI team. So, it is essential to involve all business representatives from different business units, as well as project sponsors, project managers, and more. You may or may not involve the development team at this stage, but it is usually a good idea to involve the business analyst or the CDP product owner in these sessions.

So, how to document the business use cases, and what are the best practices for it? We will discuss that next.

The process of getting buy-in and alignment across an organization cannot be understated in importance. Having the right executives involved in the early stages of customer data use case development ensures you can develop a proof-of-concept (PoC) pilot program. So, make sure you complete the first step (creating the steering team) properly.

Here are some of the methods that can be used to get business use cases.

Schedule workshops with the larger group

Scheduling workshops with a larger group is an effective way to gather input, collaborate, and ensure alignment when documenting business use cases for CDP implementation. Initial workshop sessions are crucial for bringing alignment to the project and understanding the group's expectations from the implementation. Different business units can discuss their pain points and explore possible resolutions. Do not restrict ideas at this stage based on budget, technical constraints, and more. Allow everyone to speak freely about their Wishlist. Further tuning can be done later. Document all the use cases that are being discussed, irrespective of their feasibility.

Keep in mind the following while scheduling and conducting workshop sessions:

- Determine Workshop Objectives
- Identify the key stakeholders and subject matter experts
- Set Workshop Dates and Duration
- Define Workshop Agenda
- Share Pre-Workshop Materials
- Document Workshop Outputs
- Review and Refine
- Communicate Progress
- Follow-up and Action Items

Schedule workshops with individual business units

Once the workshops with the larger group are wrapped up, schedule workshops with individual business units to fine-tune requirements. One-on-one discussions with each group reveal more detailed information about their needs, which is not always revealed in a joint session. Few use cases might involve multiple teams, in which case it is advisable to invite multiple teams. You can also conduct these workshops use-case-wise where you involve teams who are going to be affected by that particular use case.

You need to create the goals of the workshop. Refer to *Figure* 5.5 for some ideas.

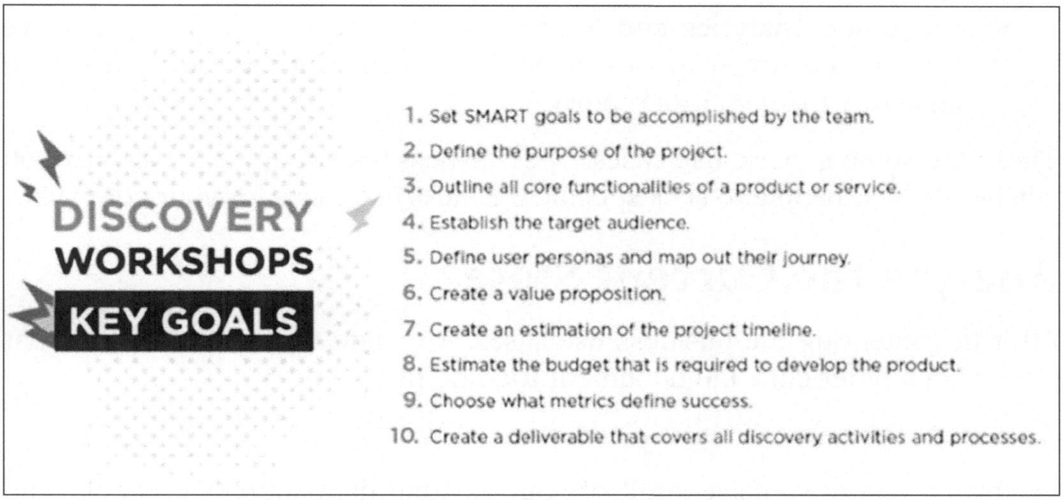

Figure 5.5: *Discover session goals*
(*Source*: **https://www.iteratorshq.com/blog/what-are-discovery-workshops-and-why-are-they-important/**)

Some examples of business use cases that are common for a CDP implementation are as follows:

- **Personalized Marketing**: CDPs enable businesses to deliver highly personalized marketing campaigns by utilizing comprehensive customer profiles.
- **Customer Segmentation**: CDPs allow businesses to segment their customer base based on various criteria such as demographics, purchase history, engagement levels, and more.
- **Customer Journey Optimization**: CDPs help businesses gain insights into the customer journey across different touchpoints and channels.
- **Cross-Selling and Upselling**: CDPs enable businesses to identify cross-selling and upselling opportunities by analyzing customer behavior, purchase history, and preferences.
- **Customer Retention and Churn Prevention**: CDPs provide valuable insights into customer behavior, allowing businesses to identify signals of potential churn.
- **Omnichannel Marketing**: CDPs help businesses deliver consistent and cohesive experiences across multiple channels, such as email, social media, mobile apps, and websites.

- **Customer Analytics and Reporting**: CDPs provide a comprehensive view of customer data, enabling businesses to perform in-depth analytics and generate reports.

These are some generic use cases. The business leaders in your organization will be the best people to seek specific business use cases for your company.

Analyze the Current State

After documenting the business use cases, it is time to evaluate the current state of customer data and document the findings.

Document the current state of customer data

Perform a comprehensive audit of your existing data sources, systems, and processes. Identify the types of data you collect, where it resides, and how it is currently managed. Assess the data's quality, completeness, and consistency to determine any data gaps or issues that need to be addressed during the implementation.

Follow these steps to analyze the current state of customer data:

- **Identify Data Sources**: Determine the various sources of customer data within your company. These may include transactional systems, CRM databases, marketing automation tools, website analytics, social media platforms, customer surveys, and more.
- **Assess Data Quality**: Evaluate the quality and accuracy of the customer data available. Look for issues such as duplicate records, incomplete data, inconsistencies, and data entry errors.
- **Data Integration**: Assess the level of data integration within your organization.
- **Compliance and Security**: Evaluate your company's compliance with relevant data privacy regulations, such as GDPR or CCPA. Assess the security measures in place to protect customer data from unauthorized access and breaches.
- **Analyze Data Analytics Capabilities**: Evaluate your company's data analytics capabilities. Assess whether you have the necessary tools, technologies, and skilled personnel to analyze customer data effectively.
- **Data Governance and Documentation**: Assess the governance and documentation practices surrounding customer data in your company.

Evaluate data readiness

In addition, assess the readiness of your data for integration into the CDP. Consider factors such as data quality, data formats, data governance, and data security. Identify any data cleansing or transformation requirements to ensure that the data integrated into the CDP is accurate, reliable, and compliant with data privacy regulations.

Assess system integration requirements

Determine the integration points between the CDP and your existing systems, such as CRM, marketing automation, e-commerce platforms, or analytics tools. Identify the data flows, APIs, and connectors needed to establish seamless data exchange between systems. Evaluate the compatibility and readiness of these systems for integration with the CDP.

Evaluate technical infrastructure

Assess your organization's technical infrastructure, including hardware, software, network capabilities, and scalability requirements. Determine if any upgrades or enhancements are needed to support the CDP implementation effectively.

Evaluate and Select the CDP Vendor

There are tons of CDP vendors available in the market (see *Figure* 5.6). Choosing the right one for your organization's needs is no easy task. We could write a book only on choosing the right CDP vendor!

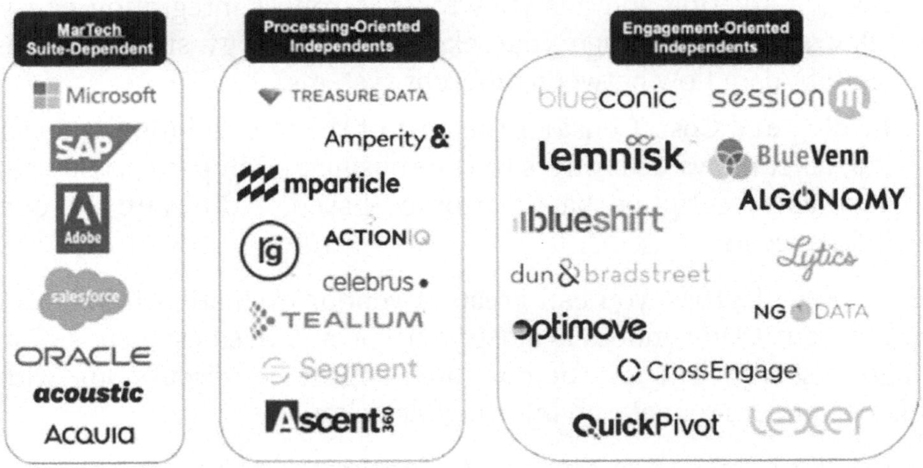

Figure 5.6: *Numerous CDP vendors in the market today and the list is growing every day*

However, let us share a few basics to get right while choosing a vendor. One of the common problems found in companies across the globe is that vendor selection is made by individuals or teams who have little idea of the real requirements. They choose a vendor based on either the cost of ownership or if that application is popular among the peer companies. However, every company's needs are different, even if they are in the same industry. So, companies need to carefully consider before choosing a vendor.

Here are a few points you should remember while choosing a CDP vendor:

- **Vendor Selection Team**: The vendor selection team should not only have the purchasing team members and the senior executives but also other business stakeholders who are going to be benefitted out of the system. If you involve your project team early, they will be invested in the decision. Business stakeholders will know which CDP can fulfill their needs and their inputs are invaluable in choosing the correct vendor.
- **Scalability and Performance**: Consider the scalability and performance of the vendor's CDP solution. Will it be able to handle your current data volume and future growth? Look for performance benchmarks and customer testimonials to gauge their capabilities.
- **Privacy and Security**: Data privacy and security are crucial considerations. Review the vendor's data governance policies, compliance with regulations (such as GDPR or CCPA), and security measures to protect customer data.
- **Integration Ecosystem**: Assess the vendor's integration capabilities with other marketing and analytics tools. A robust integration ecosystem allows you to leverage your existing technology stack and ensures smooth data flow between different systems.
- **Pricing and Cost**: Consider the cost of the CDP solution and evaluate it against the value it offers to your business. Compare pricing models, such as subscription-based or usage-based, and ensure there are no hidden costs

Based on these factors, you can create a vendor evaluation framework and assess different CDP vendors against your specific business needs. Conduct thorough research, request demos, and engage in discussions with the shortlisted vendors to make an informed decision.

Depending on your business needs, the technical talent available, and the degree of control you want to have on the CDP, you can choose between:

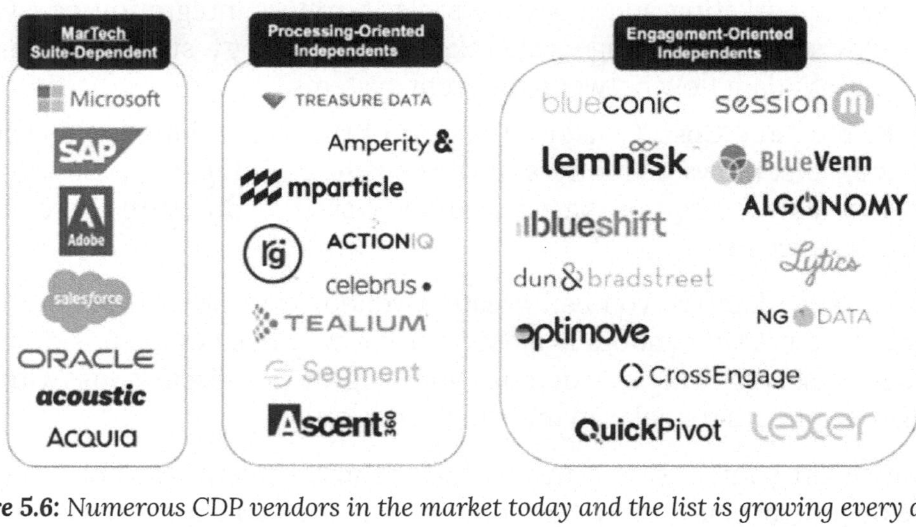

- Martech Suits
- Engagement-oriented CDP
- Data management-oriented CDP

Define and Design

After selecting the CDP vendor, we begin the define and design phase. In this phase, we prioritize business use cases (as we can't solve them all at once), create the implementation plan, and prepare for the implementation phase.

Certain activities needs to be completed for a successful **define and design** phase. Let us take a look at them one by one.

Prioritize Business Use Cases

In the discovery phase, we suggested noting all business use cases, irrespective of their priority or feasibility. Along with the use cases, it is a best practice to note down the various metrics that will help you track the impact of the implementation on each use case. Now, we need to delve deeper into the list of use cases and prioritize a few of them for the first build.

> **Note**: It is never a good idea to implement all your use cases at once, as it takes a lot of time to demonstrate value to the stakeholders. The ideal approach is to select one to three use cases that can be solved within a six-month timeframe. This way, you will be able to demonstrate the business benefits of the CDP in 6 months. For example, personalized offers for customers can be one such use case. Consider adopting an iterative approach to implementation. Start with a few high-priority use cases, implement them, and then assess the outcomes. Use the learnings from the initial implementation to refine and prioritize the next set of use cases. This allows for continuous improvement and adaptation based on real-world results.

Returning to prioritizing use cases, here are some methods you can use:

- **Eliminate the Use Cases Without Metrics**: If some of your use cases are in a raw shape, that is, the business does not have a solid idea to track the metrics and measure progress, then it is a better idea to drop those from the first build. Give the business some time to figure out how they want to measure the use cases and then we can accommodate those in the subsequent build phase.

- **Assess Data Availability and Quality**: Assess if the current data availability and quality are sufficient to solve the use case. If the use case involves significant changes to the way data is stored or requires re-modeling of data to fit the data quality needs, those use cases can be dropped from the first build attempt.
- **Consider Complexity and Feasibility**: Evaluate the complexity and feasibility of implementing each use case. Take into account factors like data accessibility, technical requirements, integration challenges, and resource availability. Prioritize use cases that are feasible to implement within a reasonable time frame and align with your organization's technical capabilities.
- **Evaluate Impact and Value**: Assess the potential impact and value of each use case. Consider the alignment with your business objectives and the expected outcomes. Prioritize use cases that have a higher potential for generating business value, such as increasing revenue, improving customer satisfaction, or driving operational efficiency.
- **Customer Journey and Touchpoints**: Analyze the customer journey and identify key touchpoints where implementing a CDP can have the most significant impact. Focus on use cases that can improve the customer experience at critical stages of the journey, such as acquisition, onboarding, engagement, retention, or upselling.

Creating a Customer Data Strategy

Customer data strategy is the process of collecting, organizing, and utilizing data about your customers to improve business outcomes.

To create an effective customer data strategy, perform the following:

- **Identify data sources**: Determine the various sources of customer data available to your organization. This may include transactional data, CRM systems, website analytics, social media platforms, customer surveys, and more. Understand the quality and accessibility of each data source.
- **Determine data requirements**: Identify the specific types of data you need to achieve your business goals. This could include demographic information, purchasing behavior, interaction history, customer preferences, and other relevant attributes. Prioritize the data elements based on their importance and relevance.

- **Establish data governance**: Develop a framework for data governance that defines the rules and processes for data collection, storage, privacy, security, and compliance. Ensure you comply with relevant regulations such as GDPR or CCPA to protect customer privacy.
- **Implement data collection mechanisms**: Determine the methods and tools to collect customer data efficiently and accurately. This might involve integrating data collection mechanisms across various touchpoints, such as websites, mobile apps, point-of-sale systems, or customer support interactions.
- **Establish guardrails to measure and evaluate the strategy**: Establish key performance indicators (KPIs) and metrics to measure the effectiveness of your customer data strategy. Continuously monitor and evaluate the outcomes to identify areas for improvement. Use these insights to refine your strategy and make data-driven decisions.

Your customer data strategy should be a living document and ideally will undergo changes as more information comes to light. Create an initial strategy but be flexible for change.

Define Implementation Roadmap and Timeline

After prioritizing the use cases (ideally one to three use cases for the first build), the next step is to define the implementation roadmap and timeline.

Based on the insights gained during the discovery phase, create a roadmap that outlines the implementation steps, milestones, and timelines for the prioritized use cases considering dependencies and resource availability. Define the scope of the initial implementation and any subsequent phases.

Here are some key points to remember:

- **Create a RACI (Responsible, Accountable, Consulted, or Informed) matrix**: A RACI matrix (see *Figure* 5.7) highlights the roles and responsibilities of the stakeholders in the implementation. It sets the right expectations from different stakeholders and makes sure that the implementation does not lose steam in due course of time.

Project tasks	Senior Analyst	Project Manager	Head of Design	SVP Finance	SEO Lead	Sales Director	Senior Management
Phase 1: Research							
Econometric model	R	I	I	A	C	I	I
Strategic framework	A	I	I	R	I	I	C
Risk factors	R	I	I	A	I	I	I
Phase 2: Structure							
Product specs	I	A	R	I	C	C	C
Design wireframe	I	C	R	I	C	I	C
User journey	I	C	R	I	C	C	C
User experience testing	I	C	R	I	C	C	C
Evaluation framework	I	R	C	I	C	I	C
Development backlog	I	R	C	I	C	I	C
Delivery roadmap	C	R	A	C	C	C	I

***Figure* 5.7:** *A sample RACI matrix*

- **Identify Key Tasks and Activities**: Break down the implementation process into key tasks and activities. Start by identifying the major steps or milestones that need to be accomplished. Then, further, break down each milestone into smaller tasks that are required to achieve it.
- **Sequence the Tasks**: Determine the logical order and dependencies of the tasks. Identify any tasks that need to be completed before others can start. This will help you establish the proper sequence of activities and ensure a smooth flow of work
- **Set Milestones**: Determine key milestones or checkpoints that mark significant stages or achievements in the implementation process. These milestones can serve as progress indicators and help you track the overall project timeline.
- **Communicate and Align**: Clearly, communicate the implementation roadmap and timeline to all stakeholders involved. Ensure that everyone understands the sequence of tasks, key milestones, and their respective responsibilities. Align expectations and gain buy-in from stakeholders.

Remember that implementation roadmaps and timelines may need to be adjusted as the project progresses and new information becomes available. Maintain open lines of communication, regularly review and update the roadmap, and ensure that the timeline remains realistic and achievable.

Risk Assessment and Mitigation Strategy

Identify potential risks and challenges associated with the CDP implementation. These may include data security risks, integration complexities, resource constraints, or change management issues. Develop a plan to mitigate these risks and ensure a smooth implementation process.

Follow these guidelines for risk assessment and mitigation:

- **Identify Risks**: Begin by brainstorming and identifying potential risks that could affect your project or organization. These risks can be internal (for example, organizational structure, resource constraints) or external (for example, market conditions, regulatory changes). Involve key stakeholders and subject-matter experts to ensure a comprehensive list.
- **Assess Probability and Impact:** Evaluate each identified risk in terms of its likelihood of occurring and the potential impact it could have. Assign a probability rating (for example, low, medium, high) and an impact rating (for example, minor, moderate, severe) to each risk.
- **Prioritize Risks**: Determine the priority of each risk by considering its probability and impact ratings. Focus on high-probability risks with severe potential impact, as well as risks that are likely to occur early in the project or have significant implications.
- **Develop Mitigation Strategies:** Once risks are prioritized, develop specific strategies to mitigate or minimize their impact. These strategies should be tailored to each risk and can include preventive measures, contingency plans, risk transfer (for example, insurance), risk avoidance (for example, changing project scope), or risk acceptance (for example, when the cost of mitigation outweighs the potential impact).

Create a Business Requirement Document

After prioritizing and finalizing the use cases that will be built in the first build phase, it is time to create a business requirement document. This is usually done by a business analyst working on the project or the data product manager.

A Business Requirement Document (BRD) is a comprehensive document that outlines the objectives, scope, functional requirements, and constraints of a proposed business solution. Here's an outline of the sections typically included in a BRD:

1. **Introduction:**
    - Purpose of the document
    - Overview of the project
    - Background information
2. **Business Objectives**:
    - Clearly state the business objectives and goals that the proposed solution aims to achieve
    - Align the objectives with the organization's overall strategy
3. **Scope**:
    - Define the boundaries and extent of the project
    - Identify what is included and excluded from the proposed solution
4. **Stakeholders**:
    - List and describe the stakeholders involved in the project
    - Identify their roles and responsibilities
5. **Functional Requirements**:
    - Provide a detailed description of the required system functionality
    - Break down the requirements into specific features and capabilities
    - Use a structured approach, such as user stories or use cases, to capture functional requirements
6. **Non-Functional Requirements**:
    - Outline the non-functional requirements, which describe system characteristics such as performance, security, reliability, scalability, usability, and more.
    - Specify any constraints or limitations that need to be considered
7. **Data Requirements**:
    - Identify the data requirements for the proposed solution
    - Describe the types of data needed, data sources, data storage, and data integration considerations
8. **Assumptions and Dependencies**:
    - Document any assumptions made during the requirements-gathering process
    - Identify any external dependencies that may impact the project

9. **Risks and Mitigation Strategies**:
   - Identify potential risks and uncertainties associated with the project
   - Describe mitigation strategies and contingency plans to address these risks
10. **Project Timeline and Deliverables**:
    - Provide an estimated timeline for the project, including key milestones
    - Specify the expected deliverables at each stage of the project
11. **Approval and Sign-off**:
    - Include a section for stakeholders to review, approve, and sign-off on the document
    - Document the date of approval and the names of approving stakeholders

The preceding is just a template, and the actual BRD structure will vary from one CDP project to another.

Create a Tracking Plan

To understand how users interact with your product, it's important to track their behavior, ensuring compliance with all privacy and data governance laws. Tracking user behavior helps you make your product better.

Before setting up tracking, develop a tracking plan. A data tracking plan is a document that outlines the events the business needs to track and the tracking methods it will use. It will cover details like where events need to go in the code base and why they are necessary from a business perspective.

Tracking plans serve multiple purposes. First, they promote alignment and ensure that all stakeholders are on the same page regarding data collection and implementation. Additionally, these plans facilitate seamless utilization and comprehension of the collected data by engineering, product, marketing, and analytics teams. Ideally, your tracking plan should be in a format like Google Sheets or Wiki, which is easily shared and updated by multiple stakeholders (see *Figure* 5.8).

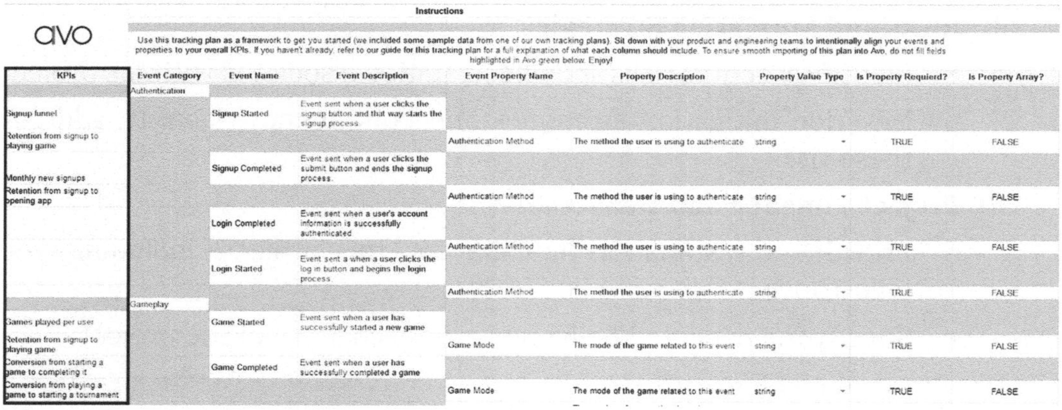

Instructions

Use this tracking plan as a framework to get you started (we included some sample data from one of our own tracking plans). Sit down with your product and engineering teams to intentionally align your events and properties to your overall KPIs. If you haven't already, refer to our guide for this tracking plan for a full explanation of what each column should include. To ensure smooth importing of this plan into Avo, do not fill fields highlighted in Avo green below. Enjoy!

KPIs	Event Category	Event Name	Event Description	Event Property Name	Property Description	Property Value Type	Is Property Requierd?	Is Property Array?
	Authentication							
Signup funnel		Signup Started	Event sent when a user clicks the signup button and that way starts the signup process					
Retention from signup to playing game				Authentication Method	The method the user is using to authenticate	string	TRUE	FALSE
Monthly new signups		Signup Completed	Event sent when a user clicks the submit button and ends the signup process.					
Retention from signup to opening app				Authentication Method	The method the user is using to authenticate	string	TRUE	FALSE
		Login Completed	Event sent when a user's account information is successfully authenticated					
				Authentication Method	The method the user is using to authenticate	string	TRUE	FALSE
		Login Started	Event sent a when a user clicks the log in button and begins the login process					
				Authentication Method	The method the user is using to authenticate	string	TRUE	FALSE
	Gameplay							
Games played per user		Game Started	Event sent when a user has successfully started a new game					
Retention from signup to playing game				Game Mode	The mode of the game related to this event	string	TRUE	FALSE
Conversion from starting a game to completing it		Game Completed	Event sent when a user has successfully completed a game					
Conversion from playing a game to starting a tournament				Game Mode	The mode of the game related to this event	string	TRUE	FALSE

***Figure 5.8:** Tracking Plan Template by Avo*
(Source: **https://www.avo.app/blog/avos-ultimate-tracking-plan-template-w-downloadable-worksheet***)*

A good tracking plan does the following:

- Summarizes which events and properties need to be added
- Justifies why they need to be tracked
- Details where in the code base they need to be added
- Informs stakeholders of progress/completion

Build Phase

With the define and design phase under your belt, you are now ready to start the build phase. Your team should be prepared with the prioritized use cases that will be built during the first build phase. Data assessment reports will provide insights into the current state and the required effort to reach the desired state.

If any of your use cases involved tracking user events, your team will need to implement the tracking plan that was created during the define phase. We have discussed user tracking, tracking plans, and event data in *Chapter* 2. Now, let's move on to the implementation of the tracking plan.

Implement the Tracking Plan

Implementing a tracking plan on the client side typically involves integrating an Software Development Kit (SDK) provided by your analytics or tracking platform. The exact steps may vary depending on the specific SDK and platform you're using, but we can provide you with a general overview of the process.

Here's a step-by-step guide to the process:

- **Choose an Analytics or Tracking Platform**: Select an analytics or tracking platform that supports SDK implementation on the client side.
- **Obtain the SDK**: Visit the website or documentation of your chosen platform and find the SDK for the programming language or framework you are using. Typically, the SDK will be available for popular languages such as JavaScript, Swift, or Java.
- **Include the SDK in Your Project**: Add the SDK to your project by following the installation instructions provided by the platform. This usually involves downloading the SDK file or adding a dependency to your project's configuration file (for example, **package.json** for Node.js projects or Podfile for iOS projects).
- **Initialize the SDK**: In your codebase, locate the appropriate place to initialize the SDK. It's often done in a central location, such as the entry point of your application or a configuration file. Initialize the SDK by providing any required configuration parameters, such as API keys or project identifiers.
- **Define Event Tracking**: Determine the events you want to track according to your tracking plan. These can include user actions, page views, or custom events specific to your application. Refer to the SDK documentation to learn how to define and send these events using the SDK's provided functions or methods.
- **Implement Event Tracking**: Place the relevant tracking code at the appropriate locations in your application's codebase to capture the desired events. For example, if you want to track when a user signs up, you might call a function like `trackEvent` ('`UserSignedUp`') in the relevant signup handler.
- **Test and Verify**: Run your application and perform actions that trigger the events you're tracking. Verify that the events are being sent successfully to the tracking platform. You may be able to view real-time event data in your analytics dashboard or use debugging tools provided by the platform.

Connect Data Sources to the CDP

To connect data sources to a CDP, you typically need to follow these general steps:

- **Identify Data Sources**: Determine the various data sources you want to connect to your CDP. These can include internal systems such as your customer relationship management (CRM) system, transactional databases, email marketing platforms, mobile apps, website analytics, and external sources like social media platforms or third-party data providers. Refer to *Table* 5.1 to find out where you can potentially find the different types of data.

Type of Data	Where It Can be Found
Contact data	CRM systems
Engagement data	Email Service provider, e-commerce systems, or marketing cloud
Purchase data	Point-of-sale system (POS)
Preferential data	Marketing or CRM systems
Service interaction data	Customer service management systems
Behavioral data	e-commerce, marketing, web and mobile apps, CRM systems

Table 5.1: *Different types of data and where they can be found*

- **Understand Data Structure and Format**: Gain a thorough understanding of the data structure and format of each data source. This includes identifying the types of data available, data fields, data formats (for example, CSV, JSON, database tables), and any unique identifiers that can be used to match or merge data across sources.
- **Assess Integration Options**: Research the integration options provided by your CDP. Many CDPs offer pre-built connectors or Application Programming Interfaces (APIs) that facilitate data ingestion from various sources. Explore the documentation or resources provided by your CDP to understand the available integration methods.
- **Preprocess and Transform Data**: Depending on the format and structure of your data sources, you may need to preprocess and transform the data to ensure compatibility with your CDP. This can involve cleaning data, restructuring or mapping fields, and standardizing data formats.

- **Set Up Data Integrations**: Use the integration options provided by your CDP to establish connections with each data source. This typically involves configuring the integration settings, specifying the data source credentials or access tokens, and defining the frequency or schedule for data synchronization.
- **Data Ingestion**: Initiate the data ingestion process by starting the integration or synchronization between the CDP and the data sources. The CDP will begin pulling or receiving data from the connected sources based on the configured settings.
- **Data Mapping and Unification**: As data flows into the CDP, you may need to map or unify fields across different data sources. This step ensures that data is correctly associated and consolidated within the CDP, allowing a unified view of customer profiles and behavior.
- **Data Quality Assurance**: Implement data quality checks and validation processes to ensure the accuracy, consistency, and integrity of the ingested data. This can involve data cleansing, deduplication, and error handling to maintain data quality standards.
- **Test and Monitor**: Validate the data integration by testing and verifying that the desired data is successfully flowing into the CDP. Monitor the data integration process to detect any issues or discrepancies and promptly address them.

Store the Customer Data

Once the connections are established, your applications will start sending data. The customer data has to be stored where it is easy to retain it and use it for downstream applications. Some CDPs come with database storage wherein they store customer data within the same application. Other CDP vendors give you the flexibility to store the data in a data warehouse of your choice. Hence, you can store data in AWS Redshift, AWS S3, Azure Data Lake, and more (see *Figure* 5.8).

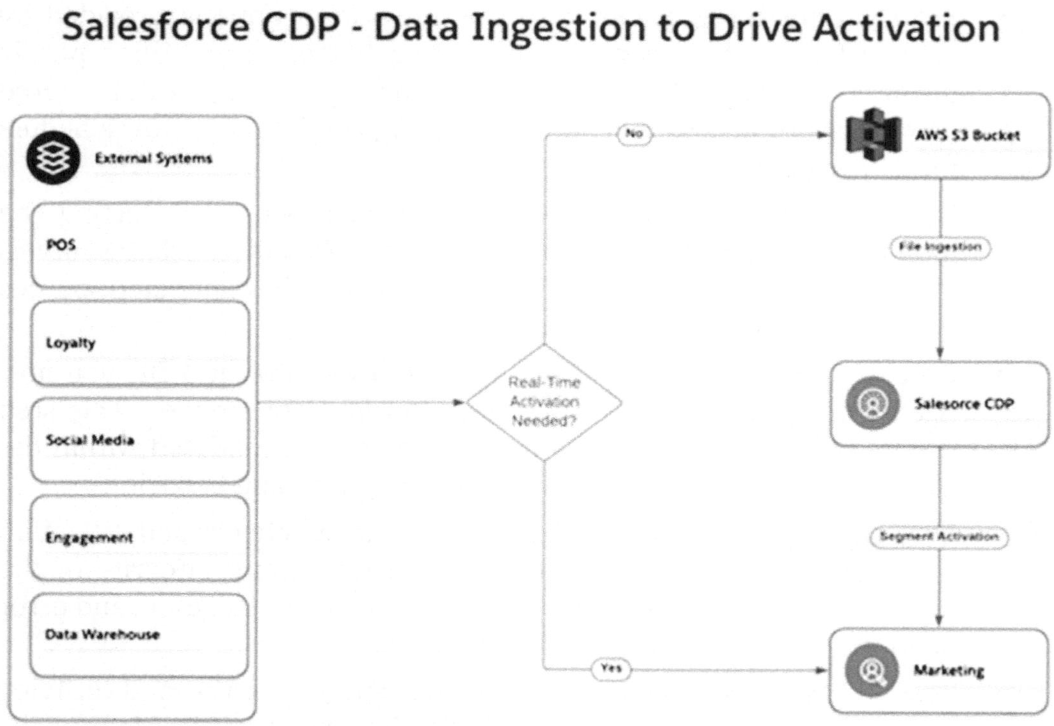

Figure 5.9: *Store data in the warehouse or in the CDP platform itself*

The decision to store the data should be taken during the data assessment stage in the define and design phase. Storing data in your own data warehouse has its advantages, as your developers are already familiar with the database. However, some CDPs have made data transformation easy for business users with just a few clicks. For more real-time purposes, storing in a CDP is a better option. If not, then using your database is a viable solution.

Identity Resolution

We have discussed identity resolution in *Chapter 2: Introduction to Customer Data Platform*. Performing identity resolution is important to uniquely identifying customer profiles. Most CDPs help in performing identity resolution based on certain criteria. Alternatively, you can create your own models to perform identity resolution with the data stored in your data warehouse.

Consent Management

Consent management is a critical aspect of developing a Customer Data Platform (CDP) that complies with privacy regulations and respects user preferences. Building a consent management platform involves understanding privacy regulations, identifying legal requirements, building preference management, and more. However, fortunately, many CDPs offer these services, and you can utilize them to stay ahead of the compliance requirements. If you are building it yourself, then it requires separate brainstorming sessions. We will not be covering consent management in detail in this book. However, we will touch upon this topic again in a later chapter.

Deployment

Now, we come to the final phase of the CDP implementation process: Deployment. With the data flowing through the applications to our CDP, it is time to use the data to meet the business objectives.

Customer Data Segmentation

Segmentation involves identifying particular characteristics or actions that are common among a subset of profiles in your customer database to create distinct groups for targeted marketing purposes. For instance, in an email campaign titled "Did you forget to buy your t-shirt?", you might want to target individuals who have recently searched for t-shirts but haven't made a purchase in the last 30 days. By employing various segments, you can tailor your marketing efforts to different audiences, resulting in a more personalized and effective marketing experience.

With your customer data, you would want to create segments for different use cases. Since you have accumulated the data from different sources, and stitched the customer profiles into unique profiles, now, you will be able to segment the customer based on business needs.

CDPs offer segmentation tools that allow marketers to define and create customer segments based on specific criteria and attributes. These tools typically provide a user-friendly interface to set segmentation rules and apply filters to segment the customer base effectively. CDPs enable the creation of dynamic segments that automatically update as customer data changes or new data is added. This ensures that segments remain current and aligned with customer behaviors and preferences.

Creating a segment will differ from one CDP platform to another. The best way to learn it is to check the documentation for that particular vendor.

We will take a look at a hypothetical example and use Salesforce CDP as the CDP vendor. Let us now see how a Salesforce admin will create segments in Salesforce CDP.

Bianca, an NTO marketer, accesses Salesforce and begins working with the Salesforce CDP app. In the `Segment` tab (see *Figure* 5.9), she examines the existing segments within her organization.

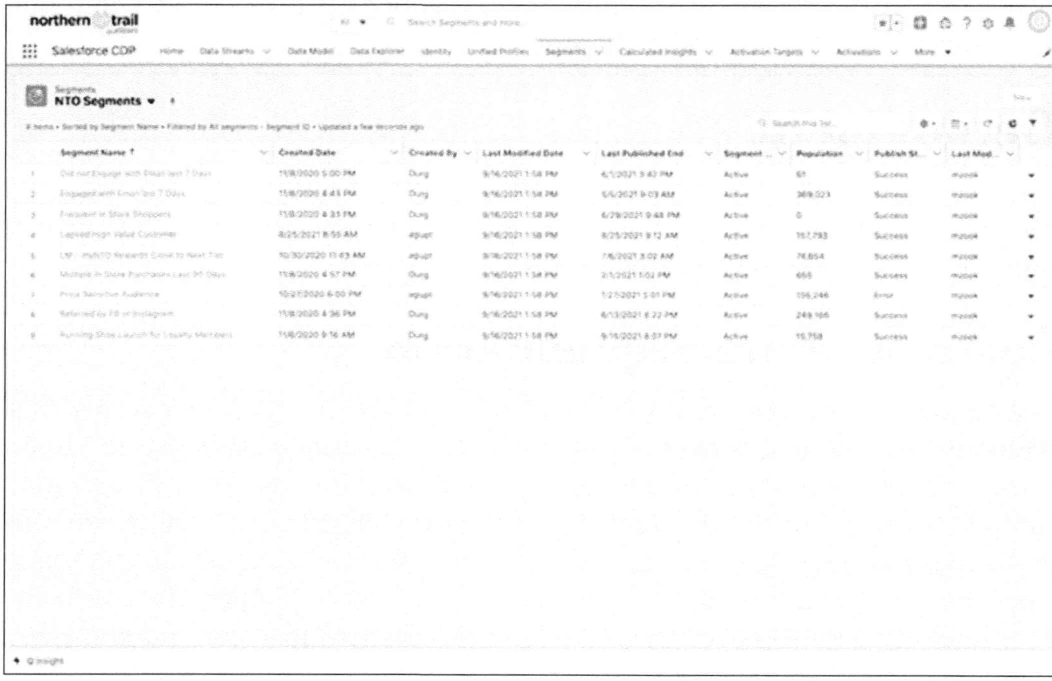

Figure 5.10: *Segments tab in Salesforce CDP*
(*Source:* **https://admin.salesforce.com/blog/2022/segment-your-audiences-with-salesforce-cdp**)

She creates a new segment by selecting the `New` option and assigning a name to it (see *Figure* 5.10). Bianca ensures that her unified customer data serves as the data source for this segment. She then sets the frequency at which the segment should be published or updated and saves her settings.

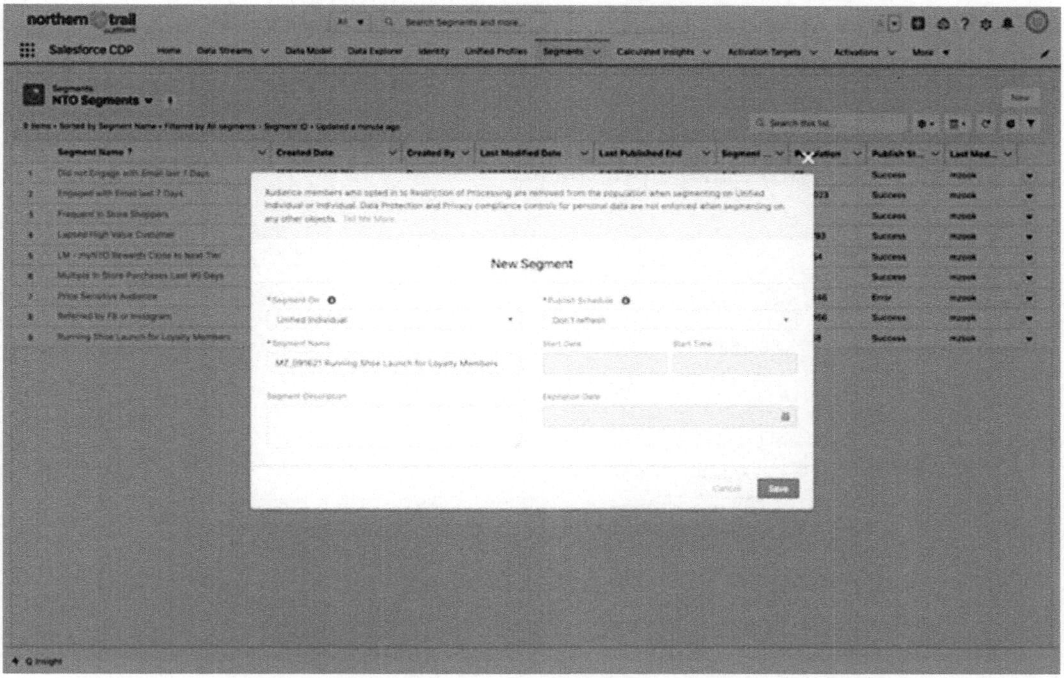

Figure 5.11: *Create a new segment in Salesforce CDP*
(*Source:* **https://admin.salesforce.com/blog/2022/segment-your-audiences-with-salesforce-cdp**)

Bianca can now apply filters using any attribute from her unified data. For the shoe launch, she establishes specific criteria for targeting customers. She wants to focus on NTO loyalty program members with a lifetime value exceeding $100, who have also browsed shoes on the NTO website at least once.

There are certain customers that Bianca wants to exclude from the segment. She specifies that customers who made a purchase within the last 30 days or have an open case should not be included. Additionally, any customers who received an email engagement in the past 7 days should be excluded, considering that the segment will be used for an email campaign by NTO marketers.

She drags the desired attribute onto the canvas, defines the criteria, and proceeds to the next filter. With just a few clicks, she sets up all the necessary filters.

Bianca can observe the impact on the audience size in real-time. Initially, the segment consisted of over 21 million customers, but now it has been refined to just over 85,000 customers (see *Figure* 5.11). This significant reduction indicates that these customers are highly relevant to the NTO sneaker launch and are more likely to make a purchase.

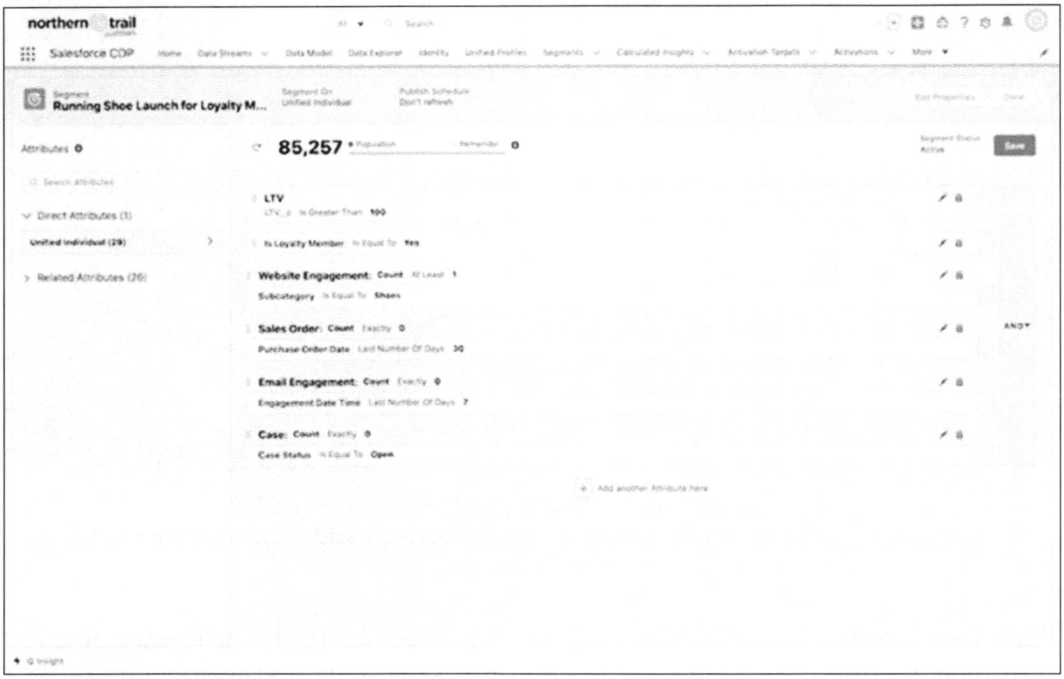

***Figure* 5.12:** *A created segment shows the target customer count* (*source-* **https://admin.salesforce.com/blog/2022/segment-your-audiences-with-salesforce-cdp**)

Different CDP tools offer different ways for segmentation. The point here is that you have to create the customer segments before proceeding toward activating the data.

Customer Data Activation

Once customer segments are created, the next step is to use the segments for customer activation.

Data activation is the process of using data to inform business decisions and activities. You put data into action by making it accessible on business applications. One example is having real-time e-commerce data accessible in email marketing software (to send personalized messages based on customers' latest purchases).

While activation in a Customer Data Platform (CDP) used to refer to the process of leveraging customer data and insights to activate targeted marketing campaigns or initiatives, it now extends beyond marketing use cases. It is used to deliver personalized and relevant experiences to specific customer segments.

Activation means using the segmented data and making it available for business tools such as:

- Customer service chats
- Analytics software
- SMS marketing tools
- Advertising platforms
- Accounting SaaS

To transfer the data you gather to the downstream tools, you have the option to utilize reverse ETL tools or develop custom integrations tailored to your specific requirements. Most CDP tools make it very easy to connect with downstream applications, offering connectors similar to those used for bringing data into the CDP from connecting data sources. These connectors help to connect with different downstream applications, such as advertising platforms, CRM platforms, BI tools, and other third-party applications. There are applications like Mulesoft, which can help in integrating your CDP with the downstream applications.

Once you start using the segmented data in your downstream applications, you can create personalized experiences for your customers.

Segmented data is used for various purposes, as follows:

- Personalized marketing
- Retargeting and look-alike modeling
- Social media advertising
- Personalized app experience
- Personalized recommendations
- Product analytics and usage metrics tracking, among other use cases

Let us take a look at one particular use case using segmented data from a Customer Data Platform (CDP) to enhance the personalization and user experience of a mobile app (android or iOS). By leveraging the insights and information gathered through your CDP, you can tailor the app experience to meet the specific needs and preferences of individual users by:

- **Personalized Content**: Use the segmented data from your CDP to deliver personalized content within the mobile app. For example, customize product recommendations, offers, or promotions based on each user's preferences and past behavior. Show relevant content or messages that resonate with each user segment.
- **Dynamic App Experience**: Customize the app's interface, layout, or features based on the specific needs of each user segment. For instance, show different menu options, display personalized greetings, or highlight relevant sections of the app based on the user's segment.
- **Push Notifications**: Craft personalized messages that align with each user segment's preferences and behaviors. Send notifications about relevant updates, new features, promotions, or personalized recommendations to increase user engagement. Companies like Zomato and Swiggy do it at scale with millions of users.
- **User Journey Optimization**: Analyze user behavior and interactions within the app using the data from your CDP. Identify common user paths, pain points, or areas of improvement for each segment. Optimize the app's user journey based on these insights, making it more intuitive and personalized for each segment.

After successfully activating the customer data for one or two business use cases, it's celebration time for your team - your first MVP is successful! Now, the goal is to monitor the performance of the activation and accordingly make changes. Document the learnings from this exercise and repeat it for other use cases. Hopefully, with each build, your team will get better at implementing the CDP for different use cases.

Conclusion

The implementation process of a Customer Data Platform (CDP) is a complex yet essential endeavor for businesses aiming to leverage their customer data effectively. Throughout the implementation journey, several key factors contribute to a successful outcome.

First and foremost, careful planning and thorough assessment of the organization's needs are critical. This involves defining clear objectives, understanding the existing data infrastructure, and identifying the desired outcomes from implementing a CDP. By conducting a comprehensive analysis, businesses can align their CDP implementation strategy with their specific requirements, ensuring a smoother transition and maximizing the platform's benefits.

Next, selecting the right CDP solution is vital. With numerous options available in the market, it is crucial to evaluate various vendors based on factors such as scalability, flexibility, data security, integration capabilities, and ease of use. Collaborating closely with the IT team and relevant stakeholders can help in choosing a CDP that aligns with the organization's technical landscape and long-term goals.

Once a CDP is chosen, the implementation process begins with data preparation and integration. This stage involves gathering data from various sources, cleaning and standardizing it, and establishing connections between different systems. Ensuring data accuracy and consistency is paramount to deriving meaningful insights and enabling effective personalization efforts.

Additionally, implementing proper data governance measures is essential. Defining data access controls, privacy policies, and compliance guidelines helps safeguard sensitive customer information and ensures adherence to regulatory requirements. It also builds trust with customers, demonstrating a commitment to data protection and ethical data practices.

During the implementation process, collaboration between cross-functional teams is crucial. Marketing, IT, and data analytics teams should work together closely to align their objectives, establish data flows, and create a unified customer view within the CDP. Effective communication and ongoing training sessions can foster a culture of data-driven decision-making and enhance the understanding of the CDP's capabilities throughout the organization.

Finally, continuous monitoring and optimization are essential post-implementation. Regularly reviewing the CDP's performance, data quality, and the achieved outcomes can uncover areas for improvement and provide insights into customer behavior. This iterative process allows organizations to refine their segmentation, personalization, and targeting strategies, thereby enhancing customer experiences and driving business growth.

In the upcoming chapter, we will understand the steps for implementing Salesforce Data Cloud. If this chapter was more theoretical for your taste, the next one will provide a practical guide for the implementation of Salesforce Data Cloud.

Points to Remember

- Careful planning and thorough needs assessment are crucial for successful CDP implementation.
- Selecting the right CDP solution is vital, considering factors like scalability, security, and integration capabilities.
- Data preparation and integration involve gathering, cleaning, and standardizing data from various sources.
- Implementing proper data governance ensures data security, compliance, and customer trust.
- Collaboration between cross-functional teams, including marketing, IT, and data analytics, is essential for alignment and a unified customer view.
- Ongoing monitoring and optimization of the CDP's performance and data quality are necessary.
- The regular review helps uncover areas for improvement and provides insights into customer behavior.
- Meticulous planning, robust data integration, strong data governance, and collaboration contribute to successful implementation.
- A customer-centric approach and effective utilization of a CDP lead to deeper customer insights and personalized experiences.
- CDP implementation fosters long-term customer loyalty and satisfaction while driving business growth.

Questions

1. Why is careful planning and thorough assessment of an organization's needs critical in the implementation process of a Customer Data Platform (CDP)?
2. What are the key factors to consider when selecting the right CDP solution for a business?
3. How do data preparation and integration contribute to the successful implementation of a CDP?
4. Why is implementing proper data governance measures essential during the implementation of a CDP?
5. What are the benefits of collaboration between cross-functional teams during the implementation of a CDP?

6. Why is continuous monitoring and optimization important after implementing a CDP?
7. Can you explain the importance of defining clear objectives and identifying desired outcomes before implementing a CDP?
8. What are the main considerations for evaluating CDP vendors in terms of scalability, flexibility, data security, integration capabilities, and ease of use?
9. How does effective data governance build trust with customers and ensure adherence to regulatory requirements?
10. How can ongoing training sessions and communication enhance the understanding of a CDP's capabilities within an organization?

CHAPTER 6

Implementing Salesforce Customer Data Cloud

Introduction

This chapter will walk you through the implementation steps for Salesforce Data Cloud. In the previous chapter, we discussed the implementation of a generic CDP. We know there are four phases in the implementation process: discovery, design, build, and deployment. These phases are generic and relevant to any implementation project. Salesforce Data Cloud implementation will also go through the same process. However, we will introduce the Salesforce recommended way of implementing Data Cloud. The concepts are similar with different packaging.

We will not reiterate the planning and preparation process here. Instead, we will jump directly into the steps an admin or a Salesforce Data Cloud engineer needs to take to implement Data Cloud. We will go through the steps in sequence in this chapter. By the end of the chapter, the reader will become familiar with the Data Cloud UI and will be able to undertake Data Cloud Admin tasks. Let us begin.

Structure

In this chapter, we will cover the following topics:

- Solution Overview
- Setup and Administration
- Connecting Data Sources
- Data Modeling
- Identity Resolution
- Calculated Insights
- Segmentation
- Activation

Solution Overview

Before you begin the implementation, it is important to perform the preparation, discovery, and design phases highlighted in the previous chapter. We can start the build or configuration phase after concluding these phases.

> **Note:** Salesforce Data Cloud is now known as Salesforce Customer Data Cloud or Data Cloud.

You can refer to the timeline in *Figure* 6.1, recommended by Salesforce to implement the Data Cloud.

Figure 6.1: *Timeline for Data Cloud implementation*

If we map the Salesforce recommended phases to the phases we proposed, it will look like this:

- Plan = Discovery phase
- Architect = Define and design phase
- Construct = Build phase
- Validate = Build phase
- Deploy = Deployment phase

In *Figure* 6.2, you can view the different roles and their requirement in the various phases of the project.

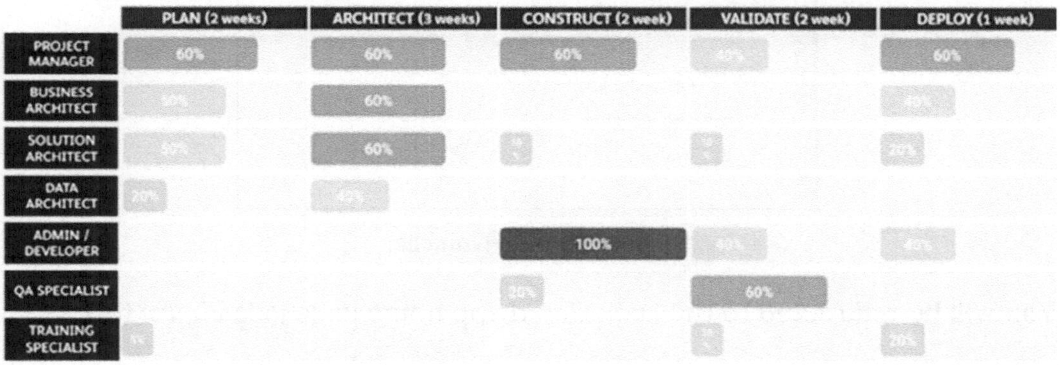

Figure 6.2: *Resources and their requirement in the different phases of the implementation*

Setup and Administration

Before we get started with the implementation, here is a recap of the necessary steps to take before getting started:

- Identify project stakeholders
- Identify data sources and integrations
- Understand system requirements
- Identify Data Cloud users
- Document all business requirements

With these in place, we can start the implementation of Salesforce Data Cloud, starting with the build phase or the construct phase in the project timeline.

Assuming that you have a Salesforce Data Cloud org provisioned, and you are a system admin in that org, let us get started with the pre-implementation steps.

On the Salesforce Data Cloud org, open the Customer Data Cloud app. On the home page, click the **App launcher** (the button with nine dots) and search for **Customer Data Cloud** (see *Figure 6.3*).

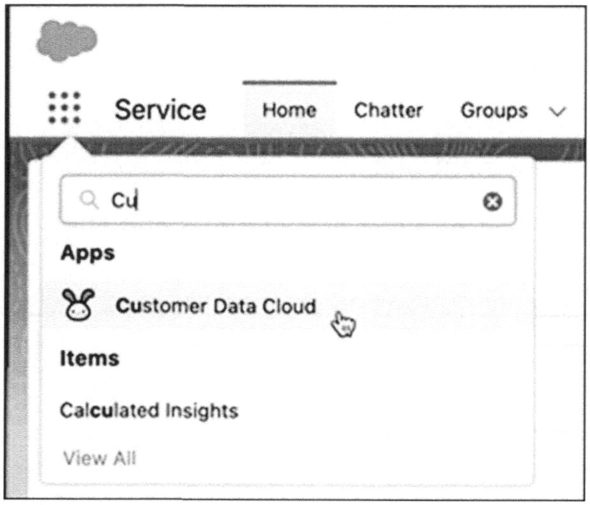

Figure 6.3: *App Launcher*

You will be redirected to the Data Cloud app home page (see *Figure 6.4*).

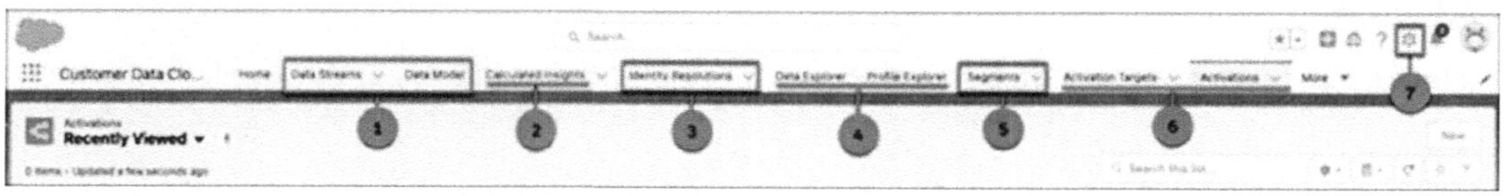

Figure 6.4: *Data Cloud app home page*

The different tabs are as follows:

1. **Data Streams and Model**: Data streams are the connected data sources added to your Data Cloud instance. The data model is focused on data.
2. **Calculated Insights**: Predefined and calculated metrics that can help marketers build segments.
3. **Identity Resolutions**: To resolve identities and create unique customer profiles.
4. **Data Explorer and Profile Explorer**: Data-viewing tools, allow a view into ingested data and unified profiles.
5. **Segments**: Create audience segments.
6. **Activation Targets and Activations**: Manage where the segments are exported, such as Marketing Cloud.

7. **`Setup Gear`**: Used for doing all the admin work.

We assume that the user performing the systems has all the admin permissions.

In the first chapter, we discussed permission sets. The Data Cloud has two permission sets, as shown in *Tables 6.1 and 6.2*:

Permission Set	Description
Customer Data Cloud Admin	Users with this permission set can access all functionality within Data Cloud, including mapping data to the data model and creating data streams, identity resolution rulesets, and calculated insights
Customer Data Cloud User	Users with this permission set can view Data Cloud features

***Table 6.1**: Customer Data Cloud Permission Set*

Data Cloud for Marketing has the following permission sets:

Permission Set	Description
Customer Data Cloud for Marketing Admin	Users with this permission set can manage day-to-day configuration needs, support, maintenance, and improvement and perform regular internal system audits
Customer Data Cloud for Marketing Manager	Users with this permission set can manage an overall segmentation strategy, including creating activation targets and activations
Customer Data Cloud for Marketing Specialist	Users with this permission set can create segments
Customer Data Cloud for Marketing Data Aware Specialist	Users with this permission set can map data to the data model and create data streams, identity resolution rulesets, and calculated insights

***Table 6.2**: Data Cloud for Marketing Permission Set*

To assign the Customer Data Cloud Admin permission set to your user, follow these steps:

1. Log in to the Salesforce org.
2. Click the gear icon on the homepage and select **`Setup`**.
3. In the quick find box, type **`user`**.
4. Click **`users`** and then select your **`username`**.
5. On your **`User`** page, under **`Permission Set Assignments`**, click **`Edit Assignments`** (see *Figure* 6.5).

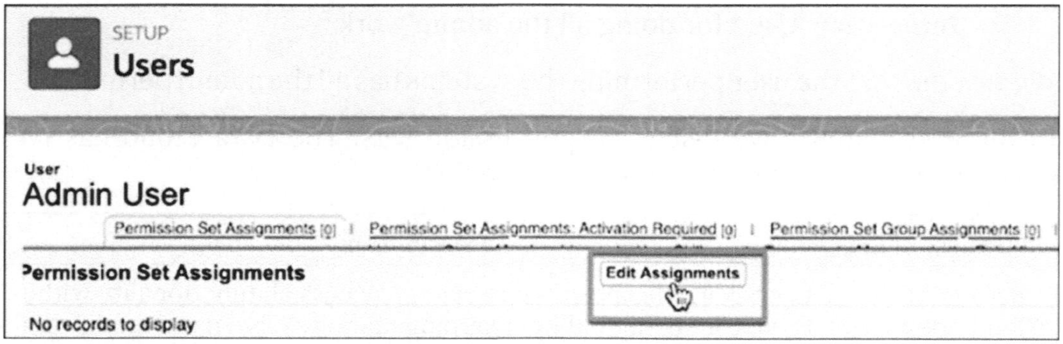

Figure 6.5: *Assign permission sets*

6. Select the **`Customer Data Cloud Admin permission set`** and click the **`Add arrow`** icon.
7. Click **`Save`**.

To complete Customer Data Cloud Setup, follow these steps:

1. Click the gear icon and select **`Customer Data Cloud Setup`** (see *Figure 6.6*).

Figure 6.6: *Customer Data Cloud Setup*

2. Click the **`Get Started`** button.
3. The setup will take a few minutes to complete. You will receive a green success message when it is done.

The pre-implementation steps are now complete, and we can begin with the implementation.

Connecting Data Sources

The next step is to connect the data sources with Data Cloud. Data Cloud provides out-of-the-box connections to most data storage solutions as well as other applications where customer data resides. This includes offerings from the Salesforce ecosystem as well as other vendors. Using MuleSoft Anypoint platform APIs, you can connect any source with the Salesforce Data Cloud. MuleSoft supports almost 300 connectors to databases, SaaS platforms, storage resources, and network services. With just a few steps, we can connect these sources of data with Data Cloud. Let's start by connecting Salesforce Marketing Cloud to get marketing data into Data Cloud.

Connecting Marketing Cloud

Perform the following steps to connect to Marketing Cloud:

1. Navigate to the **`Setup`** gear and click **`Customer Data Cloud Setup`**.
2. Under **`Configuration`**, select **`Marketing Cloud`** (see *Figure* 6.7).

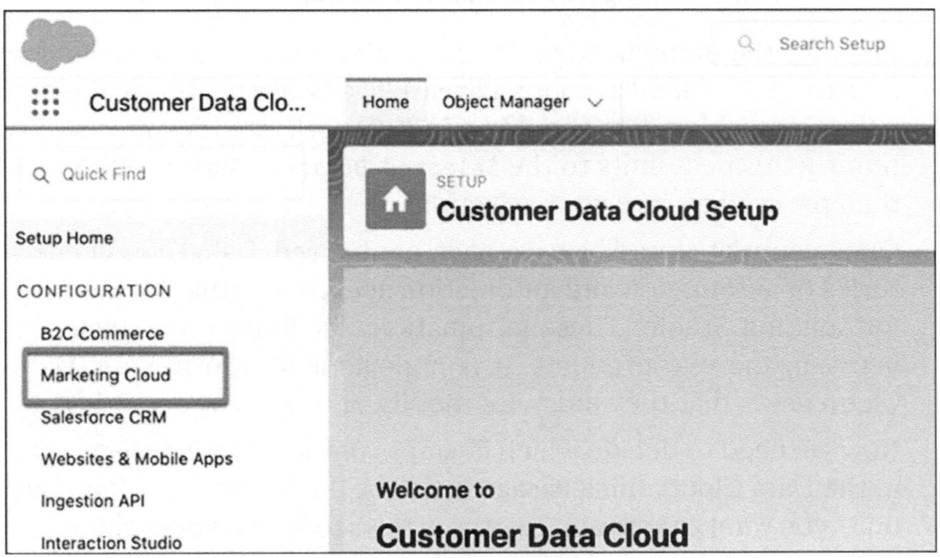

Figure 6.7: *Select Marketing Cloud*

3. Enter the credentials for your Marketing Cloud by clicking **`Manage`**. Enter your Marketing Cloud admin username and password.
4. Moving forward, we proceed with the Data Source Setup step. Click **`Manage`** to choose the data bundles you wish to import into the Data Cloud (see *Figure* 6.8). There are three bundles available: Email, MobileConnect, and MobilePush. While these sources are automatically

selected for import, please only choose the data bundles corresponding to the channels you currently utilize. Once you've made your selections, click the **Start** button to confirm.

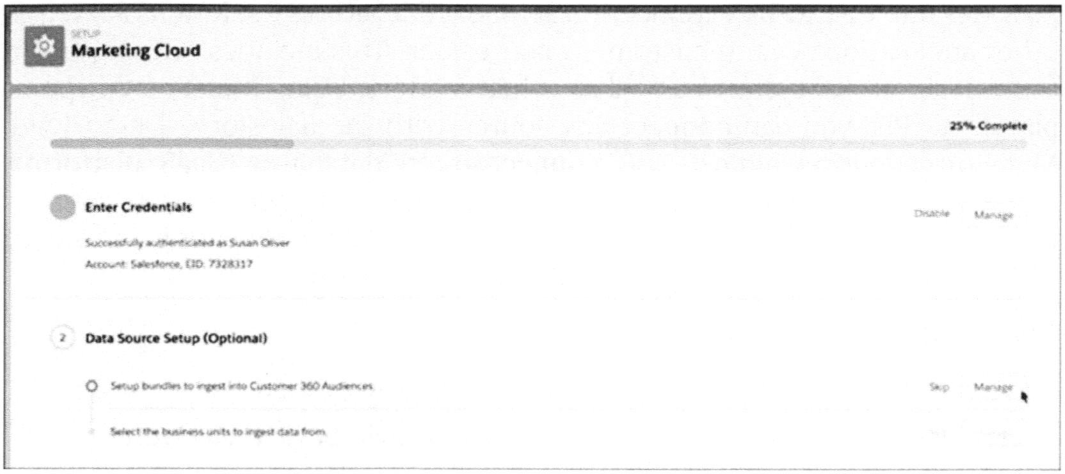

Figure 6.8: *Data Source Setup*

5. It is now the moment to verify the business units capable of supplying data to a Data Cloud account. Please click **Manage** to choose the business units from which data should be ingested. Utilize the arrows to add or remove business units to the **Selected Business Units (BUs)** field, and then proceed to save your selections.

   Once your data bundles have been configured, Data Cloud generates a series of automation and automation activities within Marketing Cloud Automation Studio. These automations facilitate the transfer of data between the two products. It is important to inform your Marketing Cloud users that they must not modify or edit these activities.
6. Now we need to decide which business units to activate segments from in the Data Cloud. Click **Manage** to select the Marketing Cloud business units you want to activate. Use the arrows to include or exclude business units in the **Selected business units** field, and then save your choices.
7. Once the progress bar is set to 100%, then you are done with the setup.

Connecting Sales and Service Cloud

Perform the following steps to connect to Sales and Service Cloud:

1. Under the **Setup** gear, select **Customer Data Cloud Setup**.
2. Under **Configuration**, select **Salesforce CRM**.
3. Click **Connect**.

4. You have the option to click Connect for the Salesforce org where Data Cloud is provisioned. You can also click Connect next to Connect Another Org (see *Figure* 6.9). Enter your user credentials to establish the connection with Data Cloud.

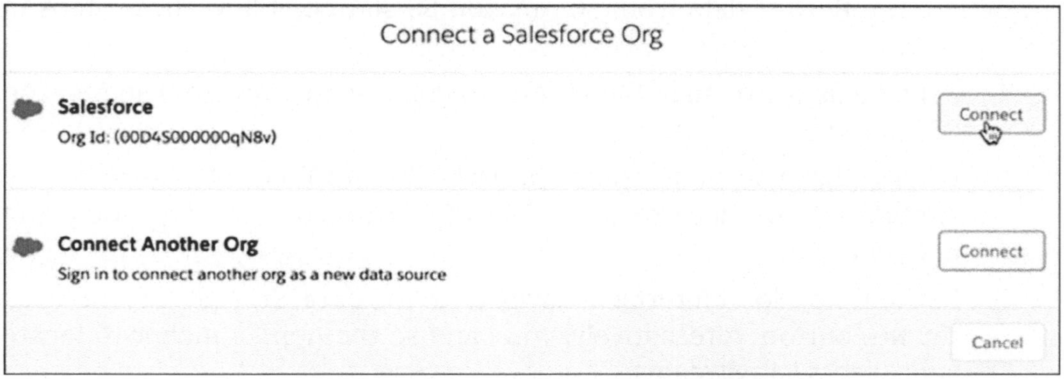

***Figure 6.9**: Connect Salesforce Orgs*

5. Once you have your Salesforce org(s) connected, you can view the connection details from the **`Setup`** screen. Come back at any time to add additional orgs or to delete an existing connection (see *Figure* 6.10).

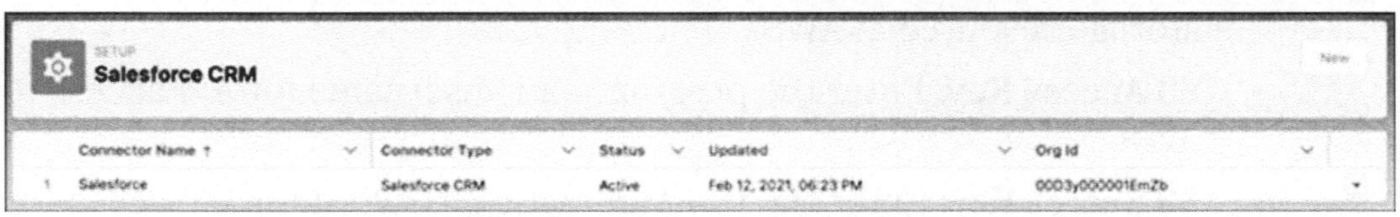

***Figure 6.10**: View connected CRM orgs*

6. In the same way, you can also connect your B2C Commerce Cloud or B2B Commerce Cloud. The B2C Commerce Cloud connector enables access to the customer profile and transactional (purchase and product) data from the B2C Commerce Cloud. This data enables enhanced insights and analytics use cases, and when combined with other data points, improves personalization opportunities. The B2C Commerce Cloud connector can connect one or more B2C Commerce production instances to a single CDP instance.

The prerequisites for this connection are as follows:

- The B2C Commerce instance should be implemented and owned by a customer.
- Commerce Einstein must be activated for data to flow from B2C Commerce to CDP.

- The user configuring the connection needs to have access to B2C Commerce Business Manager.

Connecting Amazon S3 Data Stream

To initiate the flow of data from an Amazon S3 source, follow these steps in Data Cloud:

1. Set up a data stream in Data Cloud to enable data flow from an Amazon S3 source.
2. Ensure that you understand the Data Stream Edit Settings and have configured the necessary S3 Bucket Permissions for Ingestion and Activation.
3. In the Data Cloud interface, navigate to the `Data Streams` tab and click the `New` button. Alternatively, you can use the App Launcher to locate and select Data Streams.
4. Choose `Amazon S3` as the data source.
5. Provide the credentials for accessing the S3 bucket and configure the source details as follows:
    - **S3 Bucket Name**: Specify the name of the specific public cloud storage resource in AWS.
    - **S3 Access Key**: Enter the programmatic username for API access to AWS.
    - **S3 Secret Key**: Enter the programmatic password for API access to AWS.
    - **Directory**: Specify the path name or folder hierarchy that leads to the physical location of the file.
    - **File Name**: Provide the name of the file that needs to be retrieved from the specified directory. You can use wildcards like `abc.csv` to match files containing `abc` in their name. Each time the data stream runs, it imports all files that satisfy the wildcard pattern.
    - **Source**: Indicate the external system from where the data is sourced. You can use the same source for multiple data streams.
6. Fill in the complete object details. You have two options:
    - Create a data lake object (DLO) according to the specified naming standards.

- Use an existing DLO. In this case, make sure to familiarize yourself with the guardrails associated with using an existing DLO to create a data stream.

7. Review the table fields and make any necessary edits.
8. Add new formula fields if required. You can map these fields to an existing DLO field or create a new DLO field. For more information, refer to the Formula Expression Library and Formula Expression Use Cases.
9. Provide the deployment details and click the `Deploy` button.
10. Click `Start Data Mapping`.
11. Map your DLO to the semantic data model to utilize the data in segments, calculated insights, and other use cases.

There are many other data sources that can be connected to the Data Cloud, such as Azure storage, Google Cloud, web and mobile applications, and more. We will not be able to cover all of them in this book. You can refer to Salesforce Data Cloud documentation for more details on connecting different data sources with Data Cloud.

Data Ingestion and Modeling

After connecting the data sources, next we ingest the data into Data Cloud. Before we can move to data modeling, it is important to understand how the data is ingested in the Data Cloud. Creating your data model can be a challenging task. It requires a thorough understanding of the data collection methods, the current data structure, and the relationships between different data sources. Additionally, it entails consolidating all this data into a comprehensive and useful customer view. Salesforce Data Cloud provides you with the necessary tools to accomplish this goal by enabling the creation of a unified customer view, empowering you to effectively engage with your customers.

There is a two-phased approach to bringing the data, as follows:

- **Data ingestion**: Ensure that all fields from a data set are brought in without any alterations. This way, you will always have the option to revert to the original data format if needed, especially in case of errors or changes in business requirements during the setup process. Additionally, you can expand the data set by creating extra formula fields to tidy up nomenclature or perform calculations on a row-by-row basis. Each data set will be represented by a data stream in Data

Cloud.

- **Data modeling**: Map the data streams to the data model to create a harmonized view across sources.

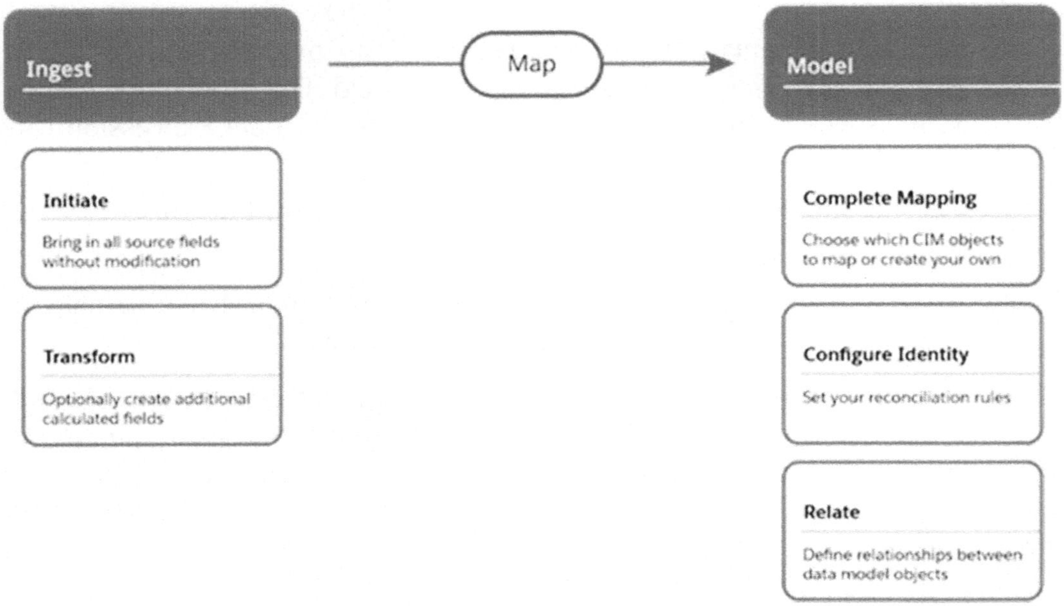

Figure 6.11: *Steps to bring in data in Data Cloud (Source:* **https://trailhead.salesforce.com/content/learn/modules/customer-360-audiences-data-ingestion-and-modeling/prepare-to-build-your-data-model?trail_id=explore-customer-360-audiences**)

Let us understand how the Data Cloud data model works before we proceed with the steps for data modeling.

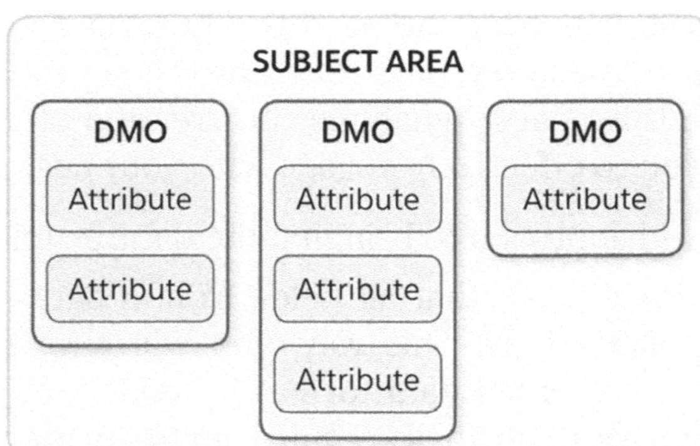

Figure 6.12: *Salesforce Data Cloud Data Model (Source:* **https://trailhead.salesforce.com/content/learn/modules/customer-360-audiences-basics/get-to-know-the-cloud-information-model#:~:text=For%20marketers%2C%20the%20Customer%20360%20Data%20Model%20is,or%20tracking%20customer%20loyalty%20are%20called%20**

data%20bundles)

Subject Area

A subject area is a business concept or term used to group similar data objects to aid in data modeling, for example, sales orders, loyalty, or engagement data. Each subject area contains one or more data model objects.

Data Stream

A data source brought into Data Cloud, for example, a Marketing Cloud customer data extension. These data streams can be based on batched data or real-time data streams.

Data Model Object (DMO)

A data model object (DMO) is a collection of data, consisting of attributes, which is formed from data streams, insights, and other data sources. These DMOs can be categorized as standard or custom, depending on the specific requirements of the business. Standard DMOs typically include common entities such as sales orders, party identification, email engagement, and more. Custom DMOs, on the other hand, are tailored to address the unique needs of the organization.

Attribute

An attribute, sometimes referred to as a field, is a particular piece of information present in a DMO, such as a customer's first name. This is comparable to a Marketing Cloud data extension field.

Foreign Key

A foreign key is a common link found between data sources that build data relationships, for example, a customer ID number.

Data Bundles

Data bundles serve the purpose of linking data source objects (data from various origins) to DMOs and establishing DMO relationships, which ultimately facilitates segmentation. Salesforce offers predefined standard data bundles by default (see *Figure* 6.13). These standard data bundles simplify the process of mapping incoming data to the Data Cloud data model. However, you have the flexibility to opt out of using the standard data bundles and instead, create your custom mappings as per your requirements.

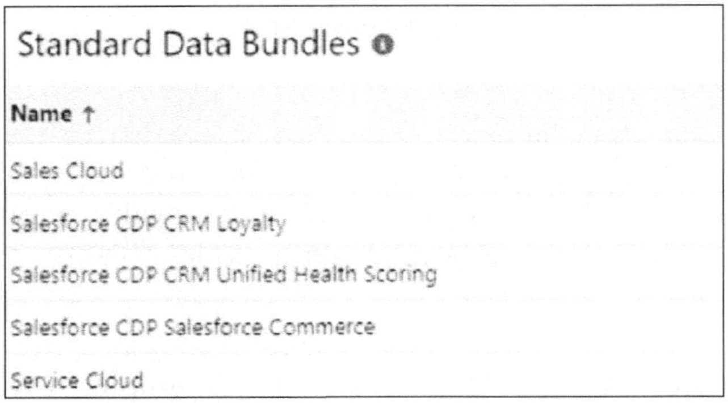

Figure 6.13: *Some standard data bundles for connecting to Salesforce* CRM

Data Ingestion

Returning to the steps for ingesting data, we will now demonstrate the steps for ingesting and modeling data from Salesforce Sales Cloud. For ingesting and modeling data from other sources, please refer to the Data Cloud documentation for detailed steps (the reference to the documentation is provided at the end of this chapter):

1. Click the **App Manager** and select **Data Cloud**.
2. Navigate to the **Data Stream tab**.
3. Select the **All Data Streams** list view, and then click the **New** button on the right.

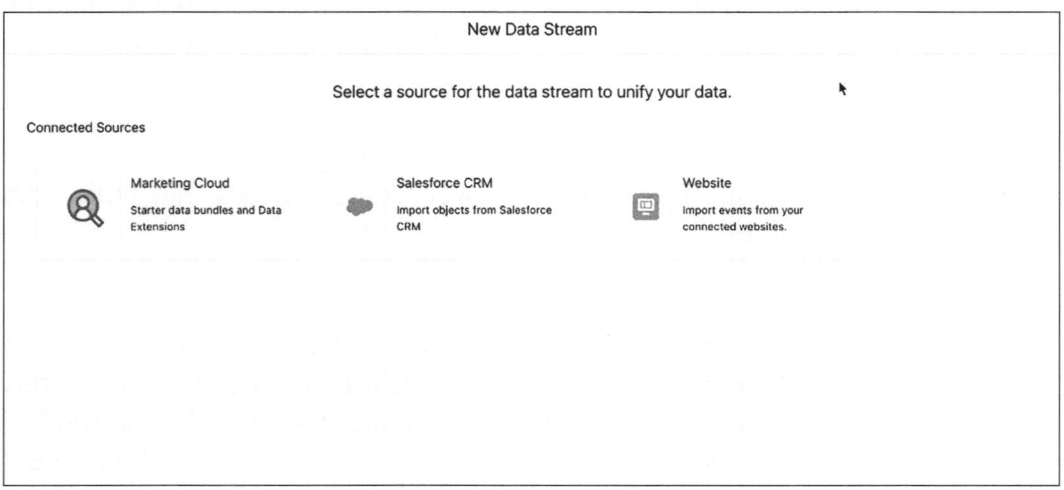

Figure 6.14: *New Data Stream View*

4. Click the **Salesforce CRM** in the connected source section (see *Figure* 6.14).

5. Select the Salesforce Org, and then either choose **`Data Bundles`** or **`All Objects`** and select the objects from which you want to ingest data (see *Figure 6.15*). Click **`Next`**.

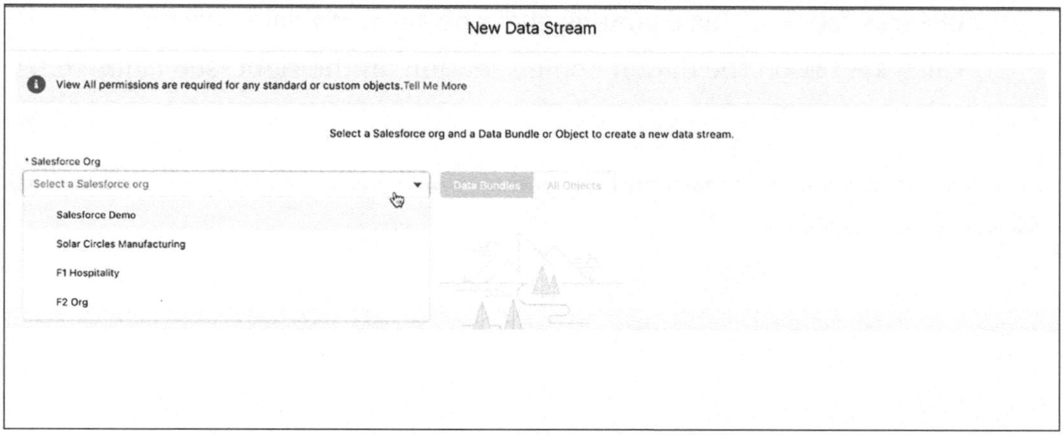

Figure 6.15: *Select the data bundles from which to ingest data*

6. Select the desired fields. If you want to do certain transformations, then use the **`New Formula Field`** option. Click **`Next`**.
7. **`Review`** and **`Deploy`** (see *Figure 6.16*).

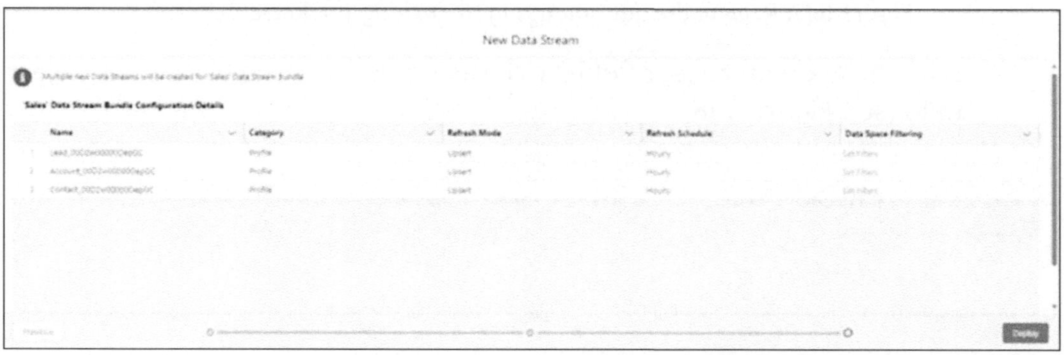

Figure 6.16: *Review the data stream bundle selection and deploy*

Data Modeling

After ingesting data from different sources, we need to map the incoming data to data objects in Data Cloud.

We will now go through an example of mapping the data we ingested from Salesforce CRM. For more details on mapping data coming from other sources, please refer to the Salesforce Data Cloud documentation.

To map the data, follow these steps:

1. Ingest data from three objects: Accounts, Lead, and Contact. You can go to these data streams from the **`Data Streams`** tab or the **`Data Lake Objects`** tab. For this example, click the **`Accounts`** data stream.
2. Click **`Review`** on the data mapping section on the right (see *Figure 6.17*).

Figure 6.17: *Review the data mapping by clicking the Review button*

3. Map the **`Account object`** fields with the corresponding **`Data Lake Object`** field (see *Figure 6.18*).

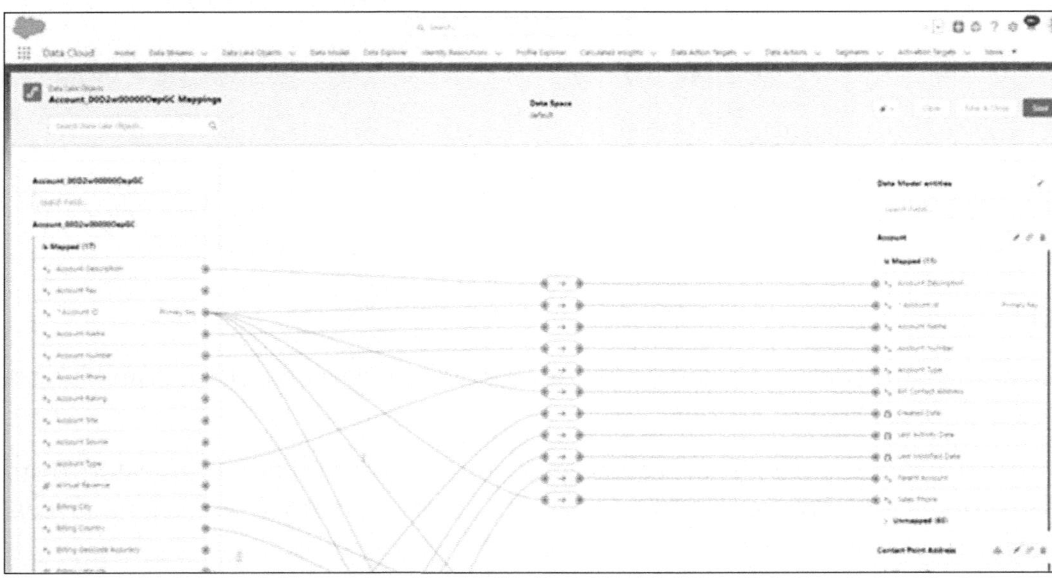

Figure 6.18: Data Mapping screen

4. Click any of the joins in the middle to delete the mapping. Search for the field to be mapped and click the field. Then, drag the mouse to a field on the right side and click that field to map it to the concerned Data Lake Object field (see *Figure* 6.19). Save the mapping.

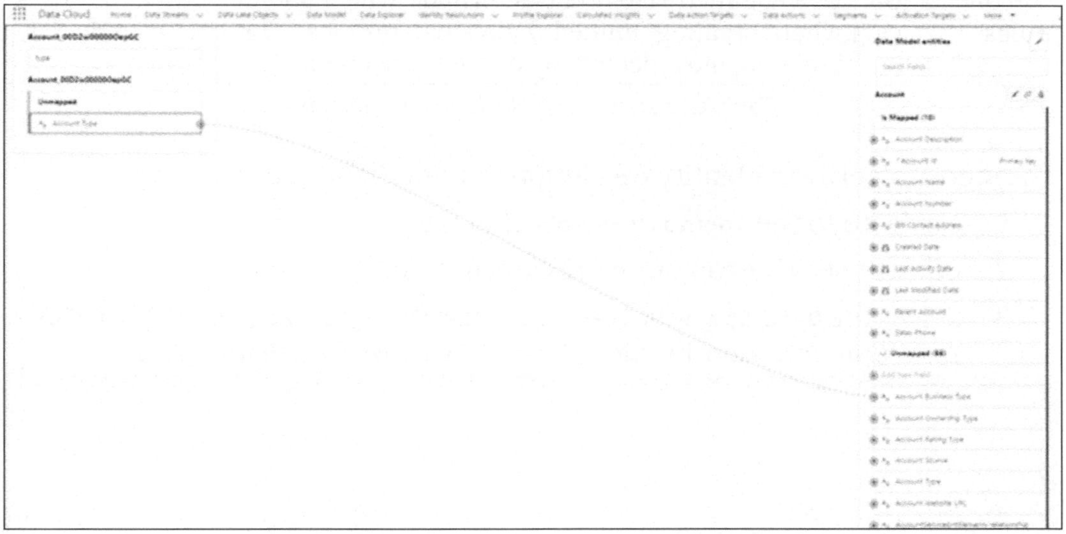

Figure 6.19: *Map a field to the corresponding field in the Data Lake Object model*

5. Repeat the process for all other sources of data. Once done, you will have completed the data modeling stage.

Identity Resolution

Before we view the steps, we need to perform for identity resolution in Data Cloud, let us understand the terminologies in identity resolution:

Terminology	Meaning
Ruleset	A user-selected combination of match and reconciliation rules is used to combine source records to resolve identity and create unified profiles (see identity resolution rulesets)
Ruleset Job	The ruleset job processes source profiles according to the map, match, and reconciliation rules you configure to create and update your unified profiles
Identity Resolution Rulesets	Rulesets are a combination of match and reconciliation rules used to combine source records to resolve identity and create unified profiles

Terminology	Meaning
Match Rules	A set of rules used to link multiple records into a unified individual within identity resolution rulesets
Reconciliation rules	User-defined rules that determine which source the system uses when creating unified individual profiles. Options include last updated, most occurring, or source sequence

Table 6.3: *Identity resolution terminologies*

The steps to perform identity resolution in Data Cloud are as follows:

1. Navigate to the **`Identity Resolution`** tab.
2. Click the **`New`** button on the right-hand side.
3. Select the **`Data Space`**, **`Primary Data Model Object`**, and provide a **`Ruleset ID`** to uniquely identify the ruleset. Click **`Next`** (see *Figure* 6.20).

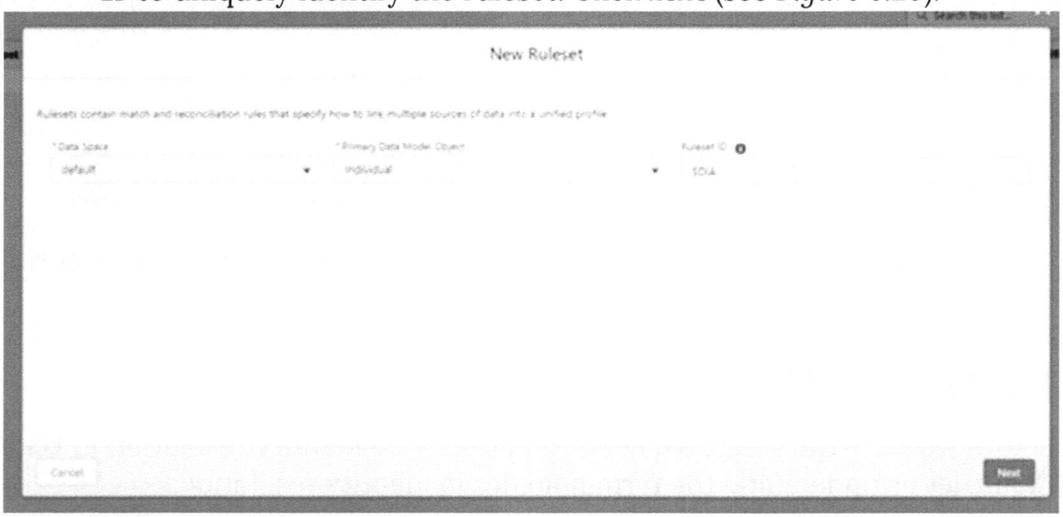

Figure 6.20: *Create New Ruleset*

4. Enter a Ruleset name and Ruleset description and click **`Save`**.
5. Click the **`Ruleset`** in the list view to open the ruleset.
6. Under **`Ruleset`** properties, click the **`Configure`** button under **`Match Rules`**.
7. Select one of the active match rules and click **`Next`**.
8. Add the match rule criteria as per the requirement. Click **`Next`** (see *Figure* 6.21). Finally, click **`Save`**.

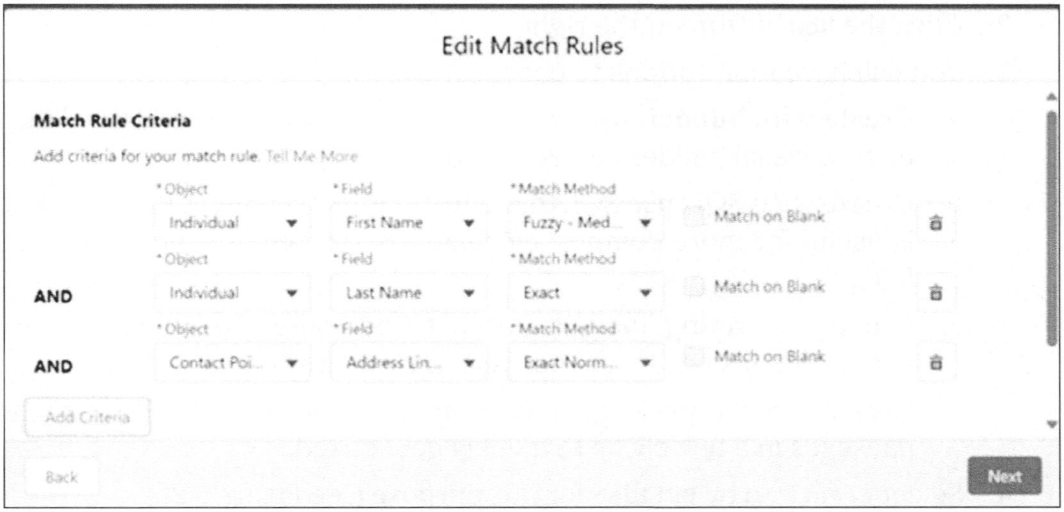

Figure 6.21: *Edit Match Rules*

9. You can change the reconciliation rules; the default is selected as **`Most Frequent`**.
10. Run the ruleset by clicking the **`Run Ruleset`** button. It can take up to 1 day to run the rulesets and unify the profiles. After unification, Salesforce will show the consolidation rate and the total unified profiles vs. the total profiles received. You can tweak your rulesets to fine-tune the identity resolution model.

Calculated Insights

The Calculated Insights feature empowers you to establish and compute multidimensional metrics based on the entirety of your digital data stored in Data Cloud. Using this feature, you can create various metrics, including Recency, Frequency, Monetary Value (RFM) scores, engagement scores, churn rates, most viewed categories, product cluster analysis, customer satisfaction scores (CSAT), and any other specialized metrics. These metrics can be generated at different levels, such as profile, segment, and population, providing valuable insights and analysis for your business.

You do not need to write queries to generate insights. Once the calculated insights are set up, it will automatically calculate the metrics for you.

Let us see how to implement calculated insights in Data Cloud by following these steps:

1. Click the **`Calculated Insights`** tab on the home screen.

2. Click the **New** button on the right.
3. You will have four options to choose from:
    a. **Create with builder**: useful for business users. It can create insights using a visual builder and zero code.
    b. **Create with SQL**: use SQL to create your metrics and dimensions. It is useful for more complex calculations and requires knowledge of SQL.
    c. **Create streaming insights**: used to compute streaming metrics across dimensions from your real-time data sources.
    d. **Create from a package**: create insight from installed Salesforce packages in a few clicks to quickly get started.
4. Select **Create with Builder** for our purpose (see *Figure* 6.22).

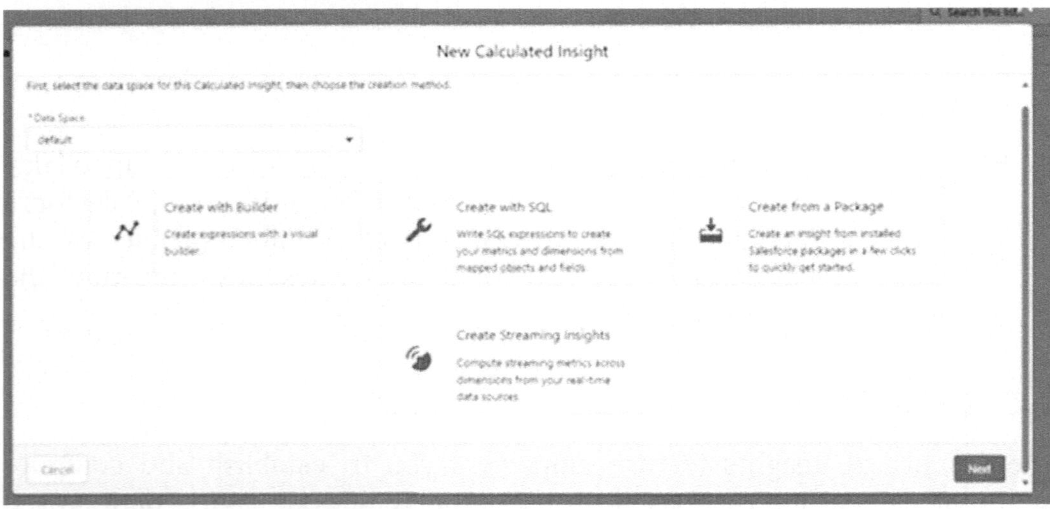

Figure 6.22: *Create Calculated Insights*

5. Out of the two options, select **Calculated Insights** and click **New**.
6. Click the **Select an Object** button.
7. Select the input data and click the **Next** button.
8. Create your logic using the options available to arrive at your metric. Alternatively, you can choose the **SQL** option in the earlier menu if you are more familiar with the SQL language. **Save** and **Run**.

Segmentation

Now, let's move to the segmentation stage, which is the most important stage for marketers. Marketers use segmented profiles to run their marketing campaigns. To perform segmentations in Salesforce Data Cloud, follow these steps:

1. Navigate to the **`Segmentation`** tab on the Data Cloud home page.
2. Click the **`New`** button. Select the data based on which segmentation will be done and provide a name for the segment (see *Figure 6.23*).

Figure 6.23: *Create New Segment*

3. If you want to build your segment on the last two years of engagement data, choose **`Standard Publish`**. The publish schedule can then be either 12 hours or 24 hours. If you want to build your segment using the last seven days' data, choose the **`Rapid Publish`** option. You can then select the **`Publish Schedule`** as 1 hour or 4 hours (see *Figure 6.24*).

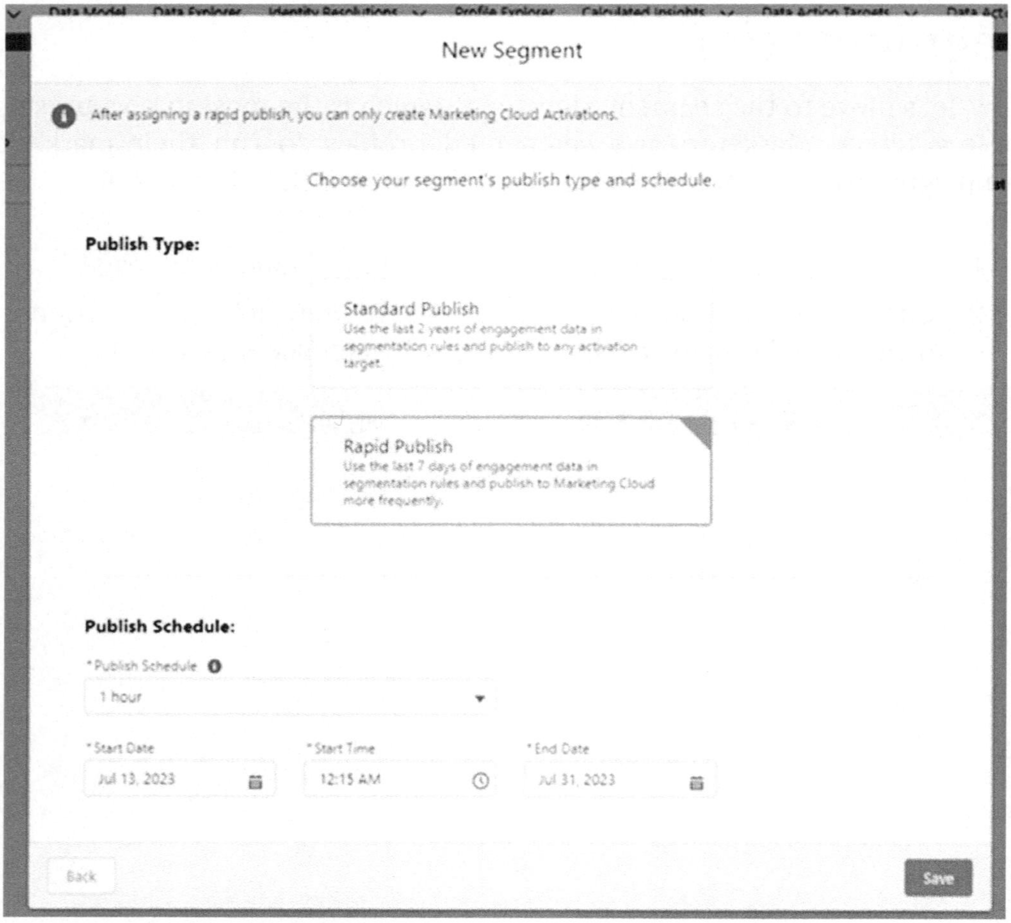

Figure 6.24: *Select Publish type and Publish Schedule*

4. Click **Save**.
5. On the screen that comes up, select the **Edit Rules** button to configure the segmentation rules.
6. Include or exclude certain attributes to arrive at the desired segment (see *Figure 6.25*).

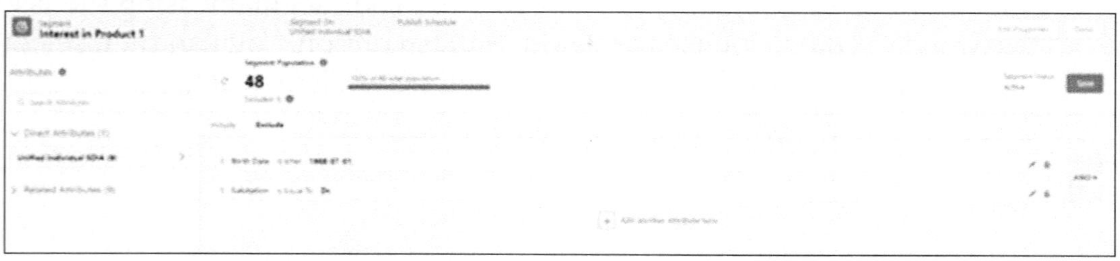

Figure 6.25: *Include or exclude attributes while creating a segment*

7. Once your segment is created, click the **`Publish Now`** option to publish the segment (see *Figure* 6.26). Once published, you can use the segment for Activations.

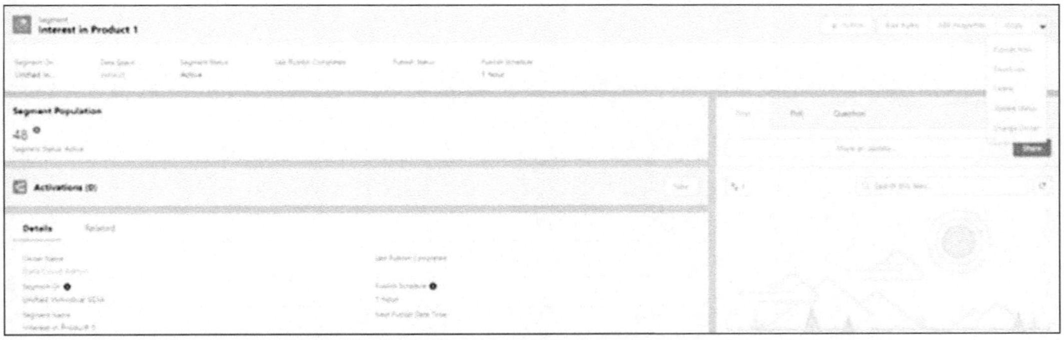

Figure 6.26: *Click Publish Now to publish the segment before activation*

Activation

The final stage is activation. We will use the segments created to send the data for our business use cases like marketing, analytics, and more. Before we can activate our segment, we need to create Activation targets.

To create an activation target, follow these steps:

1. Navigate to the **`Activation Target`** tab. If not visible on the home page, click the **`More`** dropdown and select the **`Activation Targets`** option.
2. Click the **`New`** button.
3. As of the day of the publication of this book, Data Cloud supports four activation targets: Data Cloud, Meta Ads, Google Ads, and Amazon S3 (see *Figure* 6.27). Salesforce keeps adding new activation targets, so you may see more options when you are reading this book.

Figure 6.27: *Data Cloud Activation Target*

4. Provide an activation target name and click **`Save`**. You will be redirected to the login page for your Google Ads account. Login with the correct credential and the activation target will be set.

Once the Activation Target is created, we can proceed with Activations by following these steps:

1. Navigate to the **`Activation`** tab. Click the **`New`** button.
2. Enter the segment and the Activation Target and Activation Membership and click the **`Continue`** button.
3. Select your contact points.
4. Selecting contact points is optional for S3 activations. In S3, the order of attributes in the activation doesn't match the order in the CSV file output.
    a. When contact points are mapped, select an existing path or click **`Edit`** to add, reorder, or delete sources and change source types and priority for each contact point.
    b. Click **`Next`**.
5. To activate additional attributes, click **`Add Attributes`**.
    a. Drag up to 100 additional attributes to the canvas and click **`Save`**. When activating additional attributes, primary or foreign key fields aren't available as an option as they aren't exposed for activation. To

see primary or foreign key fields during activation, create a formula field that copies those fields. This formula field is included as an additional attribute for activation.

   b. To add a unique preferred attribute name for any attributes, click the **`pencil icon`**.

   c. Click **`Next`**.

6. Enter a name and description for your activation, and click **`Save`**.

Your segment publishes on the next publish scheduled for the selected activation target.

Once the segments are activated, it completes the flow in Data Cloud. Now you have to use the activation platforms to run campaigns, perform analytics, and more on the data. Your workflow in Data Cloud is complete.

Although there are more details to the workflow than what we covered in this book, we have not gone into the specific technical details. The objective of this book is to give you an overview of the steps you need to perform in Salesforce Data Cloud to successfully go-live. There are other technical details in each step, which were beyond the scope of this book. For detailed instructions on the technical details, please refer to the Salesforce Data Cloud technical documentation. The reference to the documentation is provided at the end of this chapter.

For each of the steps we covered in this chapter, there are many considerations to take care of. Each step has many other options that need exploring. We have covered the happy path from start to finish with enough detail to get you started on Salesforce Data Cloud. For more details, it is advisable to go through the technical documentation, watch the series of videos listed in the resources section, or consult with a Salesforce Data Cloud implementation partner.

Conclusion

Implementing Salesforce Data Cloud can be a transformative step in your organization's data-driven journey. By avoiding common pitfalls such as inadequate data governance, poor integration planning, and neglecting data privacy and security, you can leverage the full power of Salesforce CDP to gain a holistic view of your customers, enhance personalization efforts, and drive meaningful interactions. With clear objectives, thorough data preparation, and ongoing monitoring and measurement, you can harness the potential of Salesforce CDP to deliver superior customer experiences, make data-driven decisions, and achieve long-term success in today's highly competitive business landscape.

By following the flow mentioned in the chapter and referring to the Salesforce Data Cloud documentation, you can implement Data Cloud and harness the true potential of the customer engagement data.

In the next chapter, we will understand the concepts of data security and data privacy and explore these in the realm of customer data platforms. We will go through best practices to ensure data security and privacy and understand the different laws that ensure companies adhere to the best practices.

References

- Salesforce Data Cloud Documentation: **https://help.salesforce.com/s/articleView?id=sf.customer360_a.htm&type=5**
- Salesforce Data Cloud Implementation playlist: **https://www.youtube.com/watch?v=sn3qimlECic&list=PLOWi4YJyd0lS6pgKP0IxqlCe-H7zZ0rJiJ**

CHAPTER 7
Data Security and Privacy

Introduction

In today's digital age, where vast amounts of data are generated and shared every second, the protection of personal information has become a paramount concern. Data security and privacy are critical elements for individuals, businesses, and organizations across various sectors. The importance of safeguarding sensitive data, preventing unauthorized access, and respecting individuals' privacy rights cannot be overstated.

This chapter explores the multifaceted world of data security and privacy, shedding light on the fundamental concepts, challenges, and solutions for protecting data in an increasingly interconnected and data-driven world. We delve into the principles, best practices, and technologies employed to ensure the confidentiality, integrity, and availability of data, as well as the legal and ethical considerations surrounding data privacy.

The chapter begins by establishing a foundation for understanding and defining key terms and concepts related to data security and privacy.

We examine the significance of data security, considering the potential consequences of data breaches, unauthorized access, and cyberattacks. We delve into the evolving threat landscape, exploring common attack vectors and techniques employed by malicious actors. Understanding the risks is crucial for comprehending the importance of implementing robust data security measures.

The chapter then delves into the principles and practices of data security. We introduce the concepts of encryption techniques, access controls, authentication mechanisms, and network security measures. We discuss the importance of security policies, incident response plans, and security audits in mitigating risks and ensuring the resilience of data systems.

Moving beyond data security, we shift our focus to data privacy. We explore the legal and regulatory landscape governing data privacy, discussing prominent frameworks, such as the General Data Protection Regulation (GDPR) and the California Consumer Privacy Act (CCPA).

Within data privacy, we investigate the concepts of consent, data minimization, purpose limitation, and individual rights. We explore the challenges associated with obtaining informed consent. Additionally, we consider the impact of emerging technologies, such as artificial intelligence, big data analytics, and the Internet of Things on data privacy, raising important ethical considerations.

We explore the distinction between data security and data privacy, highlighting the interconnected nature of these domains and their shared goal of protecting sensitive information.

We understand the role Customer Data Platform (CDP) plays in adhering to data security and data privacy compliances and security best practices for CDP. We will then understand the cookie-less tracking mechanism, which is where user tracking mechanisms are heading. In a largely cookies-less world, we will try to know how to track users without compromising their security and privacy.

Finally, we conclude the chapter by considering the future of data security and privacy. We discuss emerging trends, technological advancements, and evolving regulatory landscapes, as well as the ongoing challenges and opportunities that lie ahead.

By the end of this chapter, readers will gain a deep understanding of the complex and interconnected nature of data security and privacy.

Structure

In this chapter, we will cover the following topics:

- Data security
- Data privacy
- Data security and privacy features in a CDP
- Cookie-less tracking and its impact
- Future of data security and privacy

Data Security

Let us understand what data security is. Data security refers to the protection of data from unauthorized access, use, disclosure, alteration, or destruction. It involves implementing measures and safeguards to ensure the confidentiality, integrity, and availability of data. Data security aims to prevent unauthorized individuals or entities from gaining access to sensitive information and to mitigate the risks associated with data breaches, cyberattacks, or accidental data loss.

It's a concept that encompasses every aspect of information security, from the physical security of hardware and storage devices to administrative and access controls, as well as the logical security of software applications.

Why is data security so crucial?

To understand the cost implication of data security, here is a finding: "*According to IBM's Cost of a Data Breach Report, the average data breach costs rose from $3.86 million to $4.24 million in 2021–the highest average total cost in the 17-year history of their report.*"

The cost of a data breach per country is shown in *Figure 7.1*:

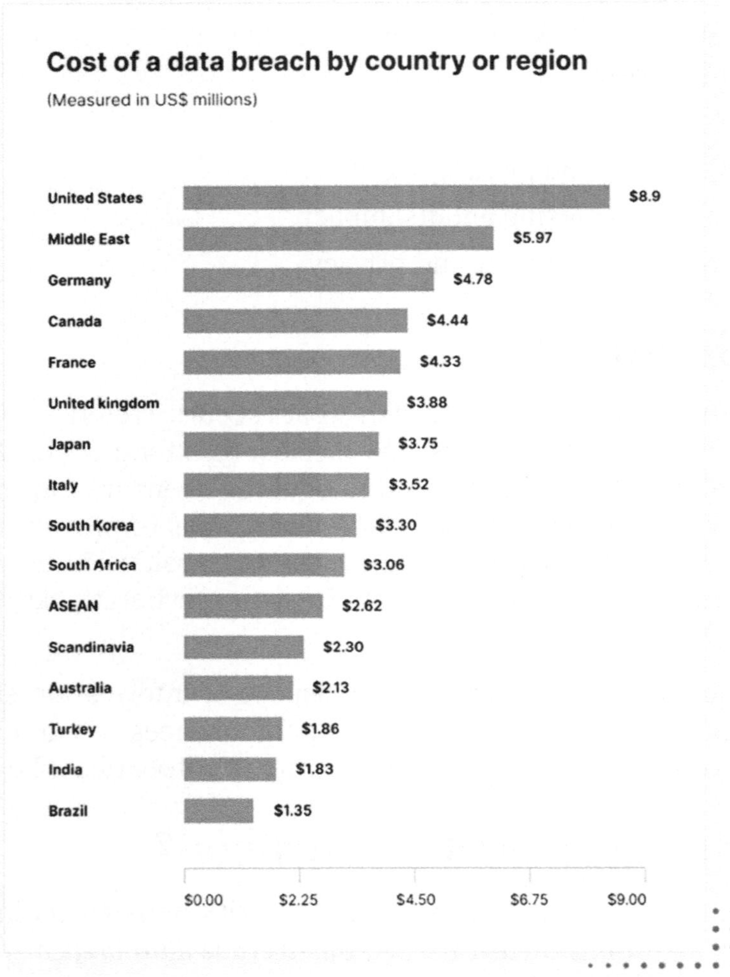

Figure 7.1: *Cost of data breach in different countries*
(*source*-**https://www.imperva.com/learn/data-security/data-security/**)

A data breach is not only bad financially as it can lead to fines and penalties, but it also damages the years of reputation a company has gathered. A company data breach will destroy the trust and confidence of its customers and clients.

Data security is crucial due to the following factors:

- **Protecting Confidentiality**: Data security ensures the confidentiality of sensitive information.

- **Safeguarding Integrity**: Data integrity refers to the accuracy, consistency, and reliability of data.
- **Ensuring Availability**: Data security measures also ensure the availability of data when needed.
- **Regulatory Compliance**: Many industries and jurisdictions have specific data protection regulations and standards that organizations must comply with. Non-compliance can result in severe penalties and legal consequences.
- **Maintaining Customer Trust**: In an era where data breaches and privacy incidents are increasingly common, maintaining customer trust is paramount.

Risks to data security

There are various risks to data security that organizations and individuals should be aware of. Understanding these risks is essential for implementing effective security measures and mitigating potential vulnerabilities. Here are some common risks to data security:

- **Unauthorized Access**: Unauthorized individuals or entities gaining access to sensitive data is a significant risk. This can occur through various means, including hacking, social engineering, insider threats, weak access controls, or stolen credentials. Unauthorized access can lead to data breaches, data loss, identity theft, financial fraud, and other malicious activities.
- **Malware and Cyberattacks**: Malicious software, commonly known as malware, poses a significant risk to data security. This includes viruses, ransomware, spyware, worms, and trojans. Cyberattacks can exploit vulnerabilities in systems and networks, leading to unauthorized access, data theft, system disruption, or damage. These attacks can occur through phishing emails, malicious downloads, compromised websites, or network intrusions.
- **Data Breaches**: A data breach occurs when unauthorized individuals gain access to sensitive data. This can happen due to cyberattacks, insider threats, weak security controls, or human error. Data breaches can result in the exposure of personal information, financial loss, reputational damage, regulatory penalties, and legal consequences. The impact of a data breach can be severe, affecting individuals, organizations, and even the broader ecosystem.

- **Lack of Encryption**: Failing to encrypt sensitive data puts it at risk if it is intercepted or accessed by unauthorized individuals. Encryption is essential for protecting data confidentiality, especially when data is stored or transmitted across networks. Without encryption, data can be easily accessed and read by attackers if systems are compromised.
- **Physical Threats**: Physical threats to data security involve the risk of physical access to data centers, servers, or storage devices. Unauthorized individuals gaining physical access can steal or compromise hardware, extract data, or disrupt systems. Physical security measures, such as access controls, video surveillance, and secure storage facilities, are essential for mitigating physical threats.

Mitigating data security risks

To mitigate data security risks, companies take different steps. The method will vary based on the type of threat. There are the following popular methods to maintain the security of data:

- **Encryption**: Encrypting data involves converting it into a code that can only be accessed with a decryption key. This ensures that, even if data is intercepted, it remains unreadable and secure.
- **Access Control**: Implement strict access controls to limit data access to authorized individuals or roles. Use techniques like role-based access control (RBAC) and permissions management to ensure data is only accessible to those who need it.
- **Regular Data Backups**: Performing regular backups of data helps in the event of data loss due to accidents, cyberattacks, or hardware failures. Backups ensure that data can be restored to a previous state if needed.
- **Strong Authentication**: Require strong authentication methods, such as multi-factor authentication (MFA) to verify the identity of users before granting access to sensitive data.
- **Data Masking/Anonymization**: Masking or anonymizing sensitive data in non-production environments ensures that even if unauthorized access occurs, the data remains protected.
- **Firewalls and Intrusion Detection/Prevention Systems (IDS/IPS)**: Employ firewalls and IDS/IPS solutions to monitor and block suspicious network traffic and potential cyber threats.

In addition to these, there are three critical components of ensuring data security. Let's explore each of these elements:

- **Security Policies**: Security policies are a set of guidelines, rules, and procedures that outline how an organization handles its data and information assets. These policies establish a framework for data security practices, access controls, user responsibilities, and acceptable use of resources. By defining clear and comprehensive security policies, organizations can create a strong security culture and ensure that employees, contractors, and stakeholders understand their roles in safeguarding sensitive data.
- **Incident Response Plans**: An incident response plan is a documented strategy that outlines the steps to be taken when a cybersecurity incident or data breach occurs. It provides a structured approach to detect, respond to, and recover from security incidents effectively and efficiently. An incident response plan includes procedures for reporting incidents, containing the damage, investigating the root cause, and implementing corrective actions to prevent similar incidents in the future. Having a well-prepared incident response plan is essential in reducing the impact of security breaches and restoring the integrity of data systems promptly.
- **Security Audits**: Security audits involve systematic assessments of an organization's data systems, infrastructure, and security practices to identify vulnerabilities, weaknesses, and compliance gaps. Security audits can be conducted internally or by third-party professionals. Regular security audits help organizations proactively identify potential security risks and ensure that security measures are being implemented correctly. The findings from security audit guide the organization in strengthening its security posture and making informed decisions about security improvements and investments.

Implementing and enforcing security policies, developing effective incident response plans, and conducting regular security audits are integral to safeguarding data systems, mitigating risks, and ensuring the overall resilience of an organization's data infrastructure.

Data privacy

Data privacy refers to the protection and control of personal information or data belonging to individuals or entities (*Figure* 7.2). It involves the right of individuals to have control over their personal data and to decide how and to what extent that data is collected, used, processed, shared, and stored by organizations or other entities.

Figure 7.2: *Data Privacy (source-***https://www.cyberark.com/resources/blog/data-privacy-day-data-protection-lessons-from-the-2010s***)*

Key aspects of data privacy include:

- **Consent**: Data privacy emphasizes obtaining informed and explicit consent from individuals before collecting, processing, or using their personal data.
- **Purpose Limitation**: Organizations should only collect and use personal data for specified, legitimate purposes, and not retain it longer than necessary.
- **Data Minimization**: Data privacy promotes the collection and processing of only the minimum amount of personal data required for the intended purpose.
- **Security**: Ensuring the confidentiality, integrity, and availability of personal data through appropriate security measures is a critical aspect of data privacy.
- **User Rights**: Data privacy grants individuals certain rights over their personal data, such as the right to access, correct, delete, or export their data.
- **Transparency**: Organizations are encouraged to be transparent about their data collection and processing practices, providing clear and easily accessible privacy notices.
- **Data Breach Notification**: In the case of a data breach that could affect the privacy of individuals, organizations are typically required to notify the affected parties promptly.

- **Cross-Border Data Transfers**: When personal data is transferred across borders, data privacy regulations often require that adequate safeguards be in place to protect the data.

To delve into more details, within the realm of data privacy, several fundamental concepts play a crucial role in protecting individuals' data. Let's delve into each of these concepts:

- **Consent**: Consent is a fundamental aspect of data privacy. It refers to obtaining explicit permission from individuals before collecting, processing, or using their personal data. Consent should be informed, specific, and freely given. Organizations must clearly explain the purpose of data processing and any potential third-party sharing. Individuals have the right to withdraw their consent at any time.
- **Data Minimization**: Data minimization is the principle of collecting and processing only the minimum amount of personal data necessary for a specific purpose. This means limiting data collection to what is directly relevant and essential to achieving the intended objective. By adopting data minimization practices, organizations can reduce the risk of privacy breaches and ensure they are not holding unnecessary personal information.
- **Purpose Limitation**: Purpose limitation is closely related to data minimization. It entails using personal data solely for the purposes explicitly stated and agreed upon at the time of data collection. Organizations should not process data for purposes that are incompatible with the original reason for collection without obtaining additional consent.

These concepts form the foundation of data privacy protection, ensuring that individuals have control over their personal data and that organizations handle data responsibly, ethically, and in compliance with relevant privacy laws and regulations. Implementing these principles helps build trust between organizations and individuals, fostering a respectful and secure data environment.

Data privacy is a fundamental right and is safeguarded by various privacy laws and regulations in different countries and regions. For example, the European Union's General Data Protection Regulation (GDPR) and the California Consumer Privacy Act (CCPA) in the United States are prominent data privacy laws that provide strong protections for personal data. We will study about them in detail later in the chapter.

Why data privacy is so crucial now?

Data privacy has become increasingly crucial in recent times due to several significant factors and developments:

- **The proliferation of Data**: With the exponential growth in digital technologies and the widespread adoption of the internet and connected devices, vast amounts of personal data are being generated, collected, and processed every day. This data includes sensitive information, such as financial details, health records, and personal preferences, making it essential to protect individuals' privacy.
- **High-Profile Data Breaches**: Several high-profile data breaches have occurred in recent years, exposing millions of personal data to malicious actors. These breaches have raised public awareness about the importance of data privacy and the need for robust security measures to safeguard personal information.
- **Increased Cybersecurity Threats**: Cyberattacks, such as ransomware, phishing, and social engineering, are on the rise. These threats pose significant risks to individuals' personal data, leading to identity theft, financial fraud, and other forms of cybercrime.
- **Stricter Regulations**: Governments worldwide are enacting more stringent data protection laws to protect individuals' privacy rights. Laws like the GDPR in the European Union and the CCPA in the United States impose significant penalties for non-compliance, prompting organizations to prioritize data privacy.
- **Concerns about Data Misuse**: The improper use of personal data, such as unauthorized data sharing or profiling, has raised concerns about the potential misuse of information for targeted advertising, manipulation, or discrimination.
- **Digital Transformation and Remote Work**: The ongoing digital transformation and the rise of remote work have resulted in increased data sharing and data access points, making data privacy more challenging to maintain and control.
- **Building Trust with Customers**: Data privacy is a critical aspect of maintaining customer trust. Customers are more likely to engage with organizations that prioritize and protect their privacy rights, leading to stronger customer relationships and loyalty.
- **Global Data Transfers**: Data is often transferred across borders for various business purposes. This poses challenges in maintaining data

privacy and complying with different privacy regulations in different jurisdictions.

- **Ethical Considerations**: Data privacy is not just a legal or regulatory issue but also an ethical one. Respecting individuals' privacy rights demonstrates an organization's commitment to ethical data handling and responsible corporate behavior.
- **Protection of Sensitive Information**: Personal data often includes sensitive information, such as medical records, financial details, and biometric data. Ensuring data privacy is crucial to prevent unauthorized access to such sensitive information.

Important Privacy Frameworks

We will study in detail about the two important data privacy frameworks, the General Data Protection Regulation (GDPR) and the California Consumer Privacy Act (CCPA). The two frameworks are for the protection of privacy for the citizens of Europe and the residents of California in the USA, respectively. They will help us appreciate the role the Government and the regulating bodies should play in protecting the privacy rights of citizens.

General Data Protection Regulation (GDPR)

The General Data Protection Regulation (GDPR) is a comprehensive data protection and privacy regulation enacted by the European Union (EU) to enhance and harmonize data privacy laws across its member states. It came into effect on May 25, 2018, replacing the previous Data Protection Directive of 1995. The GDPR is considered one of the most stringent and influential data privacy regulations globally.

Key Principles of GDPR:

- **Lawfulness, Fairness, and Transparency**: Data processing must have a lawful basis, be conducted fairly, and individuals must be informed about how their data will be used.
- **Purpose Limitation**: Personal data should be collected and processed for specific, explicit, and legitimate purposes, and not further processed in a manner incompatible with those purposes.
- **Data Minimization**: Organizations should only collect and retain the minimum amount of personal data necessary for the specified purposes.

- **Accuracy**: Data must be accurate, and organizations are required to take reasonable steps to keep it up to date.
- **Storage Limitation**: Personal data should be stored for no longer than necessary for the purposes for which it is processed.
- **Integrity and Confidentiality**: Organizations must implement appropriate security measures to protect personal data from unauthorized access, loss, or damage.
- **Accountability**: Organizations are responsible for demonstrating compliance with GDPR principles and must be able to show how they comply with the regulation.

Key Rights of Data Subjects under GDPR:

- **Right to Access**: Individuals have the right to request access to their personal data held by organizations.
- **Right to Rectification**: Data subjects can request the correction of inaccurate or incomplete personal data.
- **Right to Erasure (Right to be Forgotten)**: Individuals have the right to request the deletion of their personal data under certain circumstances.
- **Right to Restriction of Processing**: Data subjects can request the limitation of processing their data in specific situations.
- **Right to Data Portability**: Individuals have the right to receive their personal data in a structured, commonly used, and machine-readable format and transfer it to another organization.
- **Right to Object**: Data subjects can object to the processing of their personal data in certain cases.
- **Rights Related to Automated Decision-Making**: Individuals have the right to contest and seek human intervention when decisions are made solely based on automated processing, including profiling.

GDPR and Extraterritorial Scope:

The GDPR has extraterritorial reach, meaning it applies to organizations outside the EU that process the personal data of EU residents if the processing activities are related to the offering of goods or services to, or monitoring the behavior of, EU data subjects.

Non-Compliance and Penalties:

Organizations found to be in breach of the GDPR can face significant fines, which can be up to 4% of their global annual revenue or €20 million, whichever is higher, depending on the severity of the violation (*Figure* 7.3).

***Figure* 7.3**: *GDPR implications* (**source-https://www.emotiv.com/glossary/gdpr/**)

The GDPR aims to empower individuals with more control over their personal data and encourage organizations to handle data responsibly, securely, and transparently. Its impact has been significant, driving data privacy discussions worldwide and influencing the enactment of similar privacy regulations in other regions.

California Consumer Privacy Act (CCPA)

The California Consumer Privacy Act (CCPA) is a comprehensive data privacy law that was enacted in the state of California, United States. It went into effect on January 1, 2020, and provides California residents with enhanced privacy rights and control over their personal information. The CCPA is one of the most influential data privacy laws in the United States and has served as a model for other state-level privacy legislation (*Figure* 7.4).

***Figure 7.4**: California Consumer Privacy Act*

Key Provisions of the CCPA:

- **Consumer Rights**: The CCPA grants California consumers several rights concerning their personal information, including the right to know what personal data is collected, sold, or disclosed about them, the right to request deletion of their personal information and the right to opt-out of the sale of their data.
- **Notice and Transparency**: Businesses subject to the CCPA are required to inform consumers about their data collection and sharing practices by providing a clear and easily accessible privacy notice.
- **Right to Opt-Out of Data Sale**: Businesses that sell consumers' personal information must provide a clear and conspicuous "*Do Not Sell My Personal Information*" link or button on their websites, allowing consumers to opt out of the sale of their data.
- **Non-Discrimination**: Businesses are prohibited from discriminating against consumers who exercise their CCPA rights, meaning they cannot deny goods or services, charge different prices, or provide different quality levels based on a consumer's exercise of their privacy rights.
- **Data Security Obligations**: Businesses are required to implement reasonable security measures to protect consumer's personal information from unauthorized access, disclosure, and other potential breaches.
- **Applicability and Thresholds**: The CCPA applies to businesses that meet specific thresholds, such as having annual gross revenues over a certain amount, handling personal information of a certain number of

California residents, or deriving a significant portion of their revenue from selling personal information.

- **Children's Privacy:** The CCPA includes provisions related to collecting and selling personal information from minors, requiring affirmative opt-in consent for minors under the age of 16 and parental consent for those under 13.
- **Data Processing Agreements**: Businesses that share personal information with service providers are required to have written contracts that govern how the service providers handle that data.

Enforcement and Penalties:

The California Attorney General enforces the CCPA. In case of violations, businesses can face penalties of up to $2500 per violation or up to $7500 for intentional violations.

Impact and Influence:

The CCPA has had a significant impact on privacy discussions in the United States and has prompted other states to consider similar privacy legislation. It paved the way for the enactment of the California Privacy Rights Act (CPRA), a ballot initiative that further enhances data privacy rights in California and creates a dedicated privacy enforcement agency.

Overall, the CCPA empowers consumers in California with greater control over their personal information and encourages businesses to be more transparent and accountable in their data-handling practices.

Challenges of obtaining consent

Obtaining informed consent and practicing transparency in data handling are crucial aspects of data privacy, but they come with certain challenges that organizations must address to build trust with their customers and comply with data protection regulations:

- **Complexity and Length of Privacy Notices**: Privacy notices that explain data processing practices and obtain consent can be lengthy, technical, and complex. Many users may find it challenging to understand the implications of providing consent, leading to a lack of genuine informed consent.
- **Consent Fatigue**: Users are often bombarded with numerous consent requests across different platforms and services. This can lead to

consent fatigue, where users may accept without fully understanding what they consent to or simply ignore the requests altogether.

- **Ambiguity and Lack of Clarity**: Privacy notices may lack clarity or use ambiguous language, making it difficult for users to grasp the full scope of data collection, use, and sharing activities.
- **Opt-Out vs. Opt-In**: Some organizations may use the default "opt-out" settings, pre-selecting options that favor data collection or sharing. This approach shifts the burden to users to actively.
- **Lack of Awareness and Education**: Some users may not fully comprehend the implications of data sharing and may not be aware of their privacy rights. A lack of awareness and education can hinder informed consent.

The distinction between data security and data privacy

Data security and data privacy are two related but distinct concepts that play vital roles in protecting sensitive information. Understanding the difference between the two is essential for organizations to implement effective measures for safeguarding data. Data security is about protecting data from unauthorized access and cyber threats, while data privacy is about respecting individuals' rights and ensuring proper handling of their personal information (*Figure 7.5*).

Figure 7.5: *Data security vs data privacy (source-* **https://www.stealthlabs.com/blog/data-security-vs-data-privacy-an-imperative-distinction-to-protect-data/**)

Data security and privacy features in a CDP

Data security and privacy are critical considerations when it comes to a Customer Data Platform (CDP). CDPs provide features to streamline and implement data security and privacy measures across the entire data stack.

- **Centralized storage of customer data**

  A few years ago, Mary Meeker's Industry Trends report revealed that the average enterprise utilizes up to 91 cloud marketing tools. However, using so many tools often leads to customer attributes and events being scattered across different systems, causing duplicate data points or complete separation. For instance, a customer's mobile conversion history might be in the attribution provider, while their audience memberships are tracked in the marketing automation tool, and location history is stored in the location context provider, all with varying tracking methods. This fragmentation makes it challenging to unify engagements and fully comprehend the customer journey. Not only do isolated customer data sets hinder delivering connected experiences, but they also pose significant security risks. When customers inquire about their stored data, it's difficult to retrieve it promptly from diverse systems, and complying with data-sharing preferences becomes complex. This lack of transparency may lead to a breach of customer trust. To address these issues, Customer Data Platforms centralize and streamline customer data infrastructure, enabling efficient querying of customer data records. Responding to individual data requests is easier with a CDP.

- **Process Data Subject Requests (DSR)**

  Processing DSR in a CDP involves a systematic approach to ensure compliance with data protection regulations and respect for individuals' data rights. When a DSR is received, the first step is to verify the identity of the data subject to prevent unauthorized access. The CDP then locates and compiles all relevant personal data associated with the individual from various connected data sources. Depending on the nature of the request, the CDP may proceed with rectifying inaccurate data or permanently erasing specific information. Throughout the process, data security and privacy measures are strictly adhered to, safeguarding the confidentiality and integrity of the data. Processing DSRs in a CDP allows organizations to efficiently and transparently manage individuals' data, fostering trust and demonstrating a commitment to data privacy.

- **Consent management using CDP**

  Consent management in a CDP is a crucial component of ensuring data privacy and compliance with data protection regulations. CDPs typically offer robust consent management features that allow organizations to obtain, record, and manage user consent for data collection and processing activities. Through consent management, users are presented with clear and transparent information about how their data will be used, giving them the opportunity to provide or withdraw consent for specific purposes. The CDP maintains a detailed record of each user's consent status, ensuring that data processing aligns with the individual's preferences. Additionally, consent management in a CDP enables organizations to handle various data subject requests, such as accessing, rectifying, or deleting personal data, following users' privacy rights. By implementing comprehensive consent management, organizations can build trust with their customers, demonstrate a commitment to data privacy, and enhance their ability to deliver personalized experiences while respecting individuals' rights to control their data. CDPs take off the headache of managing consent for users.

Cookie-less tracking and its impact

Let us understand what is a cookie and why it is used. A cookie is a small text file that a website places on a user's device when they visit the site. Cookies play a crucial role in enhancing the user experience and improving website functionality. They enable websites to remember user preferences, login information, and past interactions, allowing for a personalized and seamless browsing experience. Cookies also assist website owners in understanding user behavior, such as the pages visited, time spent, and interactions made, enabling them to analyze website performance and make informed optimizations. Moreover, cookies facilitate targeted advertising and retargeting efforts, ensuring that users receive relevant content and advertisements based on their interests and browsing history. Overall, cookies are essential tools that contribute to smoother navigation, personalization, and overall efficiency for both website visitors and owners.

A cookie is very useful for providing a personalized web experience for millions of users. However, there are certain reservations about the use of cookies. There are valid reservations about the use of cookies in tracking user behavior online. While cookies serve legitimate purposes, such as enhancing user experience and website functionality, concerns arise primarily around data privacy and user consent. As cookies collect information about users' browsing activities, there is apprehension about the potential misuse of this data by third parties for targeted advertising or unauthorized tracking. Moreover, some users might not be fully aware of the extent of data collection and tracking through cookies, raising issues of transparency and informed consent. The widespread use of cookies also leads to the creation of extensive user profiles, which raises questions about the level of data control users have over their personal information. As a result, there is a growing demand for stricter data protection regulations and the adoption of more transparent and user-centric cookie practices to address these reservations and protect user privacy in the digital landscape.

Due to privacy concerns, companies are shifting away from cookies, thus creating a cookie-less world. Companies like Apple have already banned third-party cookies in the Safari browser, which means marketers will no longer be able to track user sessions in Safari. This solved privacy concerns but raised challenges for marketers to personalize the user experience. Till now, we had a choice whether to let third-party cookies track our sessions and to what extent. But now more and more companies to looking to ban the use of third-party cookies due to the privacy concerns it poses.

The future then becomes a cookie-less one. Marketers need to work past this challenge in order to stay relevant to their customers. Some of the challenges faced by marketers in a cookie-less world are:

- **Challenges in Personalization**: Without cookies, it becomes harder for marketers to track user behavior, user sessions across browsers and devices, and preferences accurately. This can hinder personalized marketing efforts, as understanding individual user journeys and tailoring content becomes more challenging.
- **Cross-Device Tracking**: Traditional cookies have limitations in tracking users across different devices. With cookie-less tracking, there may be difficulties in maintaining a unified view of a user's interactions on various devices, leading to fragmented data and less effective targeting.
- **Advertising and Retargeting**: Cookie-less tracking can impact ad targeting and retargeting efforts, making it more challenging for advertisers to deliver relevant ads to specific audiences.
- **Data Accuracy and Attribution**: The accuracy of tracking user interactions may be reduced without cookies, leading to potential

challenges in attributing conversions to specific marketing efforts accurately.

Fall of cookies and the rise of first-party data

The fall of cookies and the rise of first-party data mark a significant shift in the digital marketing landscape. With increasing privacy concerns, technological limitations, and the adoption of ad-blockers, third-party cookies have become less reliable for tracking user behavior. As a result, businesses are turning to first-party data, which they directly collect from their customers or website visitors. First-party data includes information such as customer preferences, purchase history, and interactions with the brand, providing a more accurate and reliable source of insights. By leveraging first-party data, organizations can build deeper customer relationships, deliver personalized experiences, and ensure compliance with data protection regulations. This shift also emphasizes the importance of fostering trust with customers through transparent data collection practices and offering value in exchange for their data. As the reliance on first-party data grows, businesses are reevaluating their marketing strategies to embrace data ownership and enhance customer-centric approaches in the ever-evolving digital era.

Future of data security and privacy

The emergence of technologies like artificial intelligence (AI), big data analytics, and the Internet of Things (IoT) has revolutionized the way data is collected, processed, and utilized, but it also raises significant concerns about data privacy and ethical considerations. AI algorithms and machine learning models can extract valuable insights from massive amounts of data, but this poses challenges in ensuring data anonymity and preventing potential biases. Big data analytics allows organizations to analyze vast datasets to understand consumer behavior and trends, but it also raises questions about data ownership and the potential for unauthorized data access. The IoT enables interconnected devices to collect and exchange data, enhancing convenience, but it also brings forth concerns about data security and unauthorized data sharing, particularly when sensitive personal information is involved. The use of these technologies demands a careful balance between innovation and data privacy protection, emphasizing the need for transparent data practices, user consent, and strict adherence to ethical guidelines to safeguard individual rights and prevent potential data misuse.

As these emerging technologies continue to advance, ethical considerations become more crucial in safeguarding data privacy. Organizations must adopt privacy by design principles, ensuring that privacy and security measures are integrated into the development of new technologies and systems from the outset. Transparency and clear communication with users are vital to obtaining informed consent and informing them about data collection, processing, and sharing practices. Robust data protection mechanisms, such as encryption and access controls, are essential to mitigate the risk of data breaches and unauthorized access to sensitive information. Moreover, governments and regulatory bodies play a pivotal role in establishing comprehensive data protection regulations and enforcing ethical standards in the use of emerging technologies. By fostering a culture of data privacy and ethical responsibility, businesses can harness the power of AI, big data analytics, and IoT while preserving individual privacy rights and building trust with their customers and users.

Future trends in data security and privacy are shaped by technological advancements, evolving regulations, and changing consumer attitudes. Some key trends to watch out for in data security and privacy are:

- **Zero-Trust Architecture**: The concept of zero-trust security is gaining traction, emphasizing the need to verify and validate every access request, regardless of the user's location or device. This approach ensures that no user or system is inherently trusted, reducing the risk of unauthorized access and data breaches.
- **Privacy-Preserving Technologies**: With increasing concerns about data privacy, there is a growing focus on privacy-preserving technologies. Techniques like differential privacy, federated learning, and homomorphic encryption enable data analysis and sharing while preserving individual privacy and confidentiality.
- **Biometric Authentication**: Biometric authentication methods, such as fingerprint and facial recognition, are becoming more prevalent as a secure alternative to traditional passwords. These methods enhance user authentication and reduce the risk of identity theft.
- **Decentralized Identity and Blockchain**: Blockchain technology is being explored for decentralized identity management, providing users with greater control over their personal data and enabling secure, verifiable, and tamper-resistant identity verification.
- **Ethical AI and Algorithmic Transparency**: As AI and machine learning applications proliferate, there is a growing demand for ethical AI

practices and algorithmic transparency to address concerns about biased decision-making and potential discrimination.

- **Quantum-Safe Encryption**: With the advent of quantum computing, quantum-safe encryption methods are being developed to protect data from potential quantum-based attacks in the future.

These trends reflect the ongoing efforts to strike a balance between leveraging data for innovation and safeguarding individual privacy rights. The future of data security and privacy will continue to be shaped by advancements in technology, evolving regulatory landscapes, and the growing importance of building trust with users and consumers.

Conclusion

Data security and privacy have emerged as critical and pressing concerns in our increasingly data-driven world. As technology advances and the volume of data generated continues to surge, safeguarding sensitive information and ensuring the confidentiality of personal data have become paramount. The potential risks of data breaches, cyberattacks, and unauthorized access highlight the need for robust security measures and comprehensive privacy frameworks. Organizations and individuals must remain vigilant and proactive in implementing stringent security protocols, employing encryption techniques, and adhering to relevant data protection regulations. Balancing the benefits of data-driven innovations with the protection of individual rights is a delicate task that requires continuous collaboration between governments, businesses, and individuals. By fostering a culture of responsible data handling and emphasizing the value of transparency, trust, and accountability, we can collectively create a safer digital environment that respects and upholds the rights of all users. Through ongoing efforts, education, and technological advancements, we can strive to achieve a future where data security and privacy are not just aspirations but tangible realities.

In the next chapter, we will study a few companies or brands that have successfully implemented a CDP solution or a Salesforce Data Cloud solution. We will understand their goals, the impact and the outcome of implementing the Salesforce Data Cloud. See you in the next one.

Chapter 8
Success Stories with Salesforce Data Cloud

Introduction

We have come a long way in the book and understood concepts related to CDP and Salesforce Data Cloud or Data Cloud. We have also understood how to implement Data Cloud solutions. In this chapter, we will study a few organizations that have successfully implemented a CDP solution or a Salesforce Data Cloud solution. We will understand their motivations for implementing Data Cloud, how they went about implementing it, and understand the outcome it had on their business.

Understanding the success stories of companies that have been there and done that will help us orient ourselves for a successful implementation.

Note: Salesforce Data Cloud is now known as Salesforce Customer Data Cloud or Salesforce Data Cloud.

Structure

In this chapter, we will cover the following topics:

- Importance of success stories

- Success Story 1: Ford
- Success Story 2: Formula 1
- Success Story 3: Casey's
- Success Story 4: Banco Inter
- Success Story 5: School Specialty

Importance of success stories

Learning about success stories has a lot of benefits. It creates a positive frame of mind for the implementation team as they get to know other companies have benefited from the solution and they can too. It gives validation to the management team that the product vendor they have chosen has demonstrated success in the past and can help their team be successful.

Here are some other benefits of understanding and analyzing success stories:

- **Best practices**: Successful Data Cloud implementation projects showcase best practices, strategies, and methodologies that have been proven to work effectively. Understanding these approaches can help organizations avoid common pitfalls and make informed decisions during their implementation process.
- **Efficiency and cost-effectiveness**: By studying successful projects, organizations can identify efficient and cost-effective ways to implement Data Cloud. Learning from others' experiences can save time and resources, ensuring a smoother implementation journey.
- **Real-world examples:** Successful case studies offer real-world examples of how Data Clouds have been used to drive business outcomes. This helps stakeholders envision how it can be tailored to their specific needs and industry.
- **Measurement of success**: Examining the success metrics and key performance indicators (KPIs) from successful projects helps organizations set realistic goals for their implementation. It also enables them to measure their success against industry benchmarks.
- **Innovation and adaptation**: Analyzing successful projects provides insights into how Data Cloud implementations evolve. It helps organizations stay innovative and adapt their strategies to changing market conditions and customer demands.
- **Risk mitigation**: Learning from others' experiences allows organizations to anticipate potential challenges and risks in their implementation.

This knowledge helps them put in place risk mitigation strategies and contingency plans.

To appeal to a broad audience, we have selected companies from different industries who have been trailblazers and have adopted Salesforce Data Cloud to harness the true potential of their customer data. We have selected different industries to highlight that success is not industry specific. With the right approach and use cases, you can tailor Data Cloud to solve the challenges in your industry.

We have one success story from each industry covering automobile manufacturing to sports entertainment. This should give a broad idea that Salesforce Data Cloud can be implemented across different industries.

Let us start with the first success story.

Success story 1: Ford

Industry: Automobile

About the company

Ford is a universal brand name (*Figure* 8.1). In case you have not heard about this iconic brand, let us first introduce the company.

Figure 8.1: *Ford Company Logo*
(**https://corporate.ford.com/home.html**, *copyright © 2020 Ford Motor Company*)

Ford Motor Company, commonly referred to as Ford, is one of the most iconic and influential automakers in the world. Founded by Henry Ford in 1903, the company has played a pivotal role in revolutionizing the automotive industry. Ford is credited with introducing the assembly line production method, which significantly increased efficiency and lowered production costs, making automobiles more accessible to the general public. This innovation culminated in the mass production of the Model T, an affordable and reliable car that became a symbol of the American automotive revolution. Over the years, Ford has continued to innovate and produce a diverse range of vehicles, including trucks, SUVs, and electric vehicles, maintaining its status as a global leader in the automotive market.

Ford, although known for its big SUVs and powerful engines, has recently started making electric vehicles. Ford Mustang Mach-E, an all-electric SUV, blends the iconic Mustang name with the innovation of electric mobility, offering impressive performance and long-range driving capability. Another recent introduction is the Ford F-150 Lightning, an all-electric version of the popular F-150 pickup truck, which was unveiled in 2021.

Customer experience is important for Ford to maintain the status of the brand. Every touchpoint with the customer is crucial. From the inquiry stage to the final delivery of the vehicle, Ford wants to provide an exceptional customer experience. Recent changes in the automobile industry dynamics have further fueled the need for a superior customer experience.

To provide that, Ford decided to invest in the Salesforce Data Cloud to meet the growing customer expectations.

Goals

Let us understand the goals that motivated Ford to implement Data Cloud:

- **Creation of a single source of truth for customer data**: Ford lacked a single source of truth for customer data and had customer data in disparate systems. Different dealers using different systems were a challenge. They wanted to create a single source of truth for customer data.
- **Unique customer profiles**: Ford lacked unique customer profiles as customers used different channels to interact with the brand. Inability to uniquely identify customers led to unwanted marketing communications or wrong messaging.
- **Simplify the customer journey**: Ford wanted to streamline the customer journey to increase retention and loyalty.
- **Measure customer satisfaction, customer engagement, and campaign effectiveness**: Ford wanted dashboards that can help the management team understand customer satisfaction, customer engagement, and campaign effectiveness.
- **Faster time to market**: They wanted a solution that could be deployed in months rather than years. They wanted to go to market quickly with the new solution.

Impact of implementing Salesforce Data Cloud

The adoption of Salesforce Data Cloud resolved many of the challenges faced by Ford. With Data Cloud, Ford created trusted relationships with personalized customer experiences. It achieved the following as a result of adopting Salesforce solutions:

- Unified customer data, activated it across channels, and matched customers to engagement behaviors.
- Proactively updated customers about their vehicle delivery status with personalized emails and SMS messaging.
- Provided dealers with leads and intelligent insights into customer behavior that helped drive brand loyalty.
- Measured customer service quality, customer engagement, and campaign effectiveness with intuitive dashboards.
- Accelerated time to value with strategic guidance and personalized technical expertise.

Outcomes

The following business outcomes were observed as a result of Data Cloud implementation:

- 99% reduction in email templates.
- 55% simplification of the customer journey.
- The initial rollout took 4 months. So for the implementation to add value to the business, it took just 4 months–a significant achievement for the implementation team.

What we can learn from Ford's experience

After understanding Ford's experience with Data Cloud implementation, we can learn the following:

- It is possible to show value to the business within 6 months. Ford did it in 4 months.
- We can simplify the customer journey significantly, thereby reducing friction in the process and increasing customer satisfaction levels.
- Having unique customer profiles helps us engage customers on a personal level, which is not possible without the use of Data Cloud.

Success story 2: Formula 1

Industry: Sports and entertainment

About the company

Formula 1 (as shown in *Figure* 8.2) is the commercial entity responsible for organizing and managing the Formula 1 World Championship. Established in 1950, Formula 1 has since evolved into a multi-billion-dollar business, captivating a vast global audience and substantial commercial interest. The company's primary objective is to oversee a series of high-profile racing events held across various countries, showcasing the world's most skilled drivers and technologically advanced racing cars. Serving as a mediator between teams, sponsors, broadcasters, and other stakeholders, Formula 1 ensures the seamless operation of the championship and the preservation of the sport's prestige and marketability.

***Figure* 8.2**: *Formula 1 Logo* (**https://www.formula1.com/en.html**)

As a company, Formula 1 derives a significant portion of its revenue through a combination of broadcasting rights, sponsorships, ticket sales, and licensing deals. Broadcasting rights are particularly lucrative, as the sport enjoys a massive TV and online viewership worldwide. Major brands and corporations are attracted to Formula 1 as a powerful platform to advertise their products and services to a global audience, leading to substantial sponsorship deals. The company also invests heavily in research and development to continuously improve safety measures and the overall racing experience. Formula 1 continues to evolve, embracing sustainability initiatives and technological advancements to remain at the forefront of global motorsport and thrill generations to come.

At the center of the Formula 1 business are the fans. Formula 1 fans are global, generally higher income groups, and technologically savvy. The fan experience is of paramount importance for Formula 1, as it plays a crucial role in shaping the sport's success and sustainability. Fans are the lifeblood of any sporting event, and in the case of Formula 1, they create an electric atmosphere that amplifies the excitement and drama of each race. Engaging and satisfying the diverse global fan base is essential for maintaining and growing Formula 1's viewership, attendance, and commercial appeal. Providing fans with an unforgettable experience at the racetrack, as well as through digital platforms and media, fosters a deep emotional connection to the sport and its stars. Their passion and loyalty drive the demand for merchandise, ticket sales, and sponsor engagement, which, in turn, contribute to the financial health and longevity of the championship. By prioritizing the fan experience, Formula 1 can continue to captivate and inspire generations of motorsport enthusiasts, ensuring its position as a premier sporting spectacle for years to come. Creating and providing an immersive and engaging fan experience is crucial for the motorsports business. Major chunks of F1's revenue come from broadcast rights, merchandise sales, and ticket sales.

To be at the forefront of the ever-changing digital experience for its fans, F1 partnered with Salesforce to provide its fans with the best experience: both offline and online.

Goals

The goals set by F1 can be summarized as follows:

- **F1 had to attract and retain fans across the globe**: With cash-rich sponsors comes the demand for increasing viewership. F1 had to increase its fan base and attract new fans across the globe. These fans have different aspirations, speak different languages, and engage with the sports in their unique way. A one-size fits all approach would fail to attract fans globally.
- **Increase fan engagement**: With the fan base it had, F1 wanted to increase fan engagement and retain them.
- **Increase brand value and revenue**: F1 wanted to convert fan engagement into brand value and revenue. They wanted fans to come and visit the race tracks on race day and buy licensed merchandise.

Impact of implementing Salesforce Data Cloud

- They created a single database for all fan data. This helped them understand their customers within the same platform.
- Created an end-to-end fan experience strategy with sales, service, and marketing.
- They have taken a step towards the ambitious strategy of becoming Net Zero Carbon by 2030.

What we can learn from Formula 1's experience

Fans are at the center of the F1 experience. Attracting new fans and retaining the existing ones at a global level is no easy task. Using a single database for customer data, understanding fans has become easier. We can learn the following from F1's experience:

- Salesforce Data Cloud can unify billions of user data records to create unique customer profiles.
- It is possible to create an end-to-end experience strategy using the Salesforce platform.
- Using Salesforce Data Cloud, we can engage users using personalized content, messages, and offers.

Success story 3: Casey's

Industry: Retail

About the company

Casey's is a well-established and prominent convenience store chain operating primarily in the Midwestern United States (*Figure* 8.3). Founded in 1959, the company has grown into one of the largest retailers in the region, with thousands of stores across multiple states. Casey's offers a diverse range of products, catering to the daily needs of its customers, including gasoline, groceries, snacks, beverages, and freshly prepared food items. The company is renowned for its friendly service and convenient locations, making it a go-to destination for travelers, commuters, and residents alike. With a strong focus on community engagement, Casey's actively supports various charitable initiatives, reflecting its commitment to making a positive impact on the neighborhoods it serves.

Casey's

***Figure* 8.3**: *Casey's Logo* (**https://www.caseys.com/**, *copyright ©2023 Casey's Retail Company)*

Known for its iconic pizza, Casey's has earned a reputation for providing quality food options alongside traditional convenience store offerings. The company's pizza is made with fresh ingredients, hand-tossed dough, and a variety of mouthwatering toppings, making it a popular choice for quick and delicious meals. Beyond its in-store services, Casey's has embraced digital innovation, offering online ordering and delivery options to meet the evolving preferences of its customers. As the company continues to expand its footprint and enhance its product offerings, Casey's remains dedicated to its founding principles of providing excellent service, value, and a sense of community, solidifying its position as a cherished and trusted brand in the Midwest.

Providing a great customer experience is crucial for Casey's for several reasons. Firstly, in the highly competitive convenience store industry, exceptional customer service sets Casey's apart from its rivals and helps build customer loyalty. When customers have positive interactions with friendly and attentive staff, and their needs are met promptly and efficiently, they are more likely to return to Casey's for their convenience store needs. Satisfied customers also tend to share their positive experiences with friends and family, leading to positive word-of-mouth referrals that can drive new business.

Secondly, a great customer experience enhances Casey's reputation and brand image. As customers consistently have positive interactions with the company, they develop a favorable perception of the brand.

Casey's has moved to digital interaction along with offline. Tracking customer behavior across the different channels is important to provide a consistent user experience. Its quality food options with its convenience store offerings are no longer enough to stay relevant to the customers. It has to provide them with a more personalized experience.

Challenges

Some of the challenges faced by Casey's are:

- Casey's wanted to shift from mass marketing to personalization at scale. It had a lot of customer data both online and offline but it had to unify and generate insights from that data. For that, a single source of truth for customer data was needed.
- The systems they used were not able to scale with the high volume of customer transaction records. They needed a solution that could scale with their business.
- They wanted to use AI to create and activate guest segments and unlock insights to drive an increase in visit frequency and transaction size.

Impact of implementing Salesforce Data Cloud

Casey's adopted Salesforce Data Cloud to accelerate focus on personalization and drive guest loyalty and business impact. It had the following impact:

- Shifted from mass marketing to personalization at scale y incorporating multiple data sets into a single source of truth
- Focused on personalization to create relevant and familiar experiences for guests, anticipate their needs, and add value to every interaction.
- Created and activated guest audience segments with AI, unlocking insights to drive an increase in visit frequency and transaction size.
- Focused on new ways of working, increasing agility and experimentation leading to scale and impact.

Outcome

- 10 million customer records were ingested.
- The speed of segment creation increased by 30x.
- 1.3 billion customer transaction records were processed.

What we can learn from Casey's experience

We can learn the following from Casey's experience:

- Casey's is a B2C brand and therefore deals with a huge volume of customer data. Salesforce Data Cloud's scalable solution enables them to ingest millions of customer records
- Personalized marketing was essential for their business. Using the AI features of Salesforce, they could offer their customers personalized offers to increase visit frequency to their stores both online and offline.
- Using Salesforce Data Cloud helped them to make a transition from just another convenience store to a brand that offered great customer experience thereby improving brand loyalty.

Success story 4: Banco Inter

Industry: Banking

About the company

Banco Inter (*Figure* 8.4), officially known as Banco Inter S.A., is a prominent Brazilian digital bank that has gained significant attention and popularity for its innovative approach to banking services. Founded in 1994 and headquartered in Belo Horizonte, Brazil, Banco Inter has evolved into one of the leading digital banking institutions in the country. It stands out for its emphasis on providing a range of financial services through digital channels, catering to the evolving preferences of tech-savvy customers. Banco Inter offers a variety of banking products, including savings accounts, checking accounts, loans, credit cards, and investment opportunities, all accessible through its user-friendly mobile app and online platform. Banco Inter is the first 100% digital bank in Brazil and the only one to provide a digital checking account free of charge.

Figure 8.4: *Casey's Logo (***https://inter.co/en/the-bank/***, copyright © 2023 Banco Inter S.A.)*

What distinguishes Banco Inter is its commitment to simplifying banking processes and improving customer convenience. By eliminating many of the traditional brick-and-mortar elements, the bank reduces operational costs and passes on these benefits to customers in the form of competitive interest rates and minimal fees. Its vibrant orange logo and branding have become recognizable symbols of the bank's modern and customer-centric approach. Banco Inter has not only gained traction among individuals seeking a seamless digital banking experience, but has also garnered attention from investors and industry peers for its growth potential and disruptive impact on the traditional banking landscape in Brazil.

Being a digital-first bank, Banco Inter has had to overcome the hesitations of customers who preferred offline banking. Although Inter's customers are mostly tech-savvy, building trust with their customers is not easy. They had to make the customer journey frictionless, right from account opening to transactions with the bank and support from the customer support team. They had to be proactive in understanding their customers' needs and offer personalization at scale. Offers need to be personalized for different segments of customers and it needs to be in real-time.

Challenges

- Data was stored in different sources. Inter had to unify the customer data and create customer profiles.
- They wanted to reach out to customers with the right offers at the right time.

- Inter wanted to improve the customer experience by sending relevant messages through targeted campaigns.
- They wanted to increase the productivity of the team.

Impact of implementing Salesforce Data Cloud

- Connected data from 6 sources to create a single, unified, customer profile and over 1706 segments to activate.
- Able to reach the right customer with automated personalized product offers at the right time.
- Created engagement score strategy based on email, push, web, and app performance data per business line in addition to sales propensity models.
- Improved the customer experience by only sending relevant, targeted campaigns, reducing the number of overall sends.

Outcome

- The ROI on the Salesforce Data Clouds was a multiple of 20.
- They could achieve 35x conversion.
- 33 million plus records were uploaded.
- 6 data sources were consolidated to create unified customer profiles.
- An average of 1 hour 30 mins of weekly bandwidth was returned for each member of the team, which led to improved productivity and reduced workload, thus improving employee satisfaction.

What we can learn from Banco Inter experience

Learnings from Banco Inter are as follows:

- To run a completely digital bank, one needs to evolve with the evolving trends of customer expectations. We can't evolve unless we understand what those expectations are. For that, we need to understand the customer pulse. The insights are hidden inside the vast amount of customer data the company has.
- The insights can only be unlocked with a CDP solution such as Salesforce Data Cloud. Without Data Cloud, Banco Inter will not be able to proactively work on customer expectations.
- After implementing Data Cloud along with other Salesforce ecosystem products, they were able to ingest millions of records, unify data from multiple data sources and supercharge their conversion rate.

Success story 5: School Specialty

Industry: Education

About the company

School Specialty Inc. (*Figure* 8.5) is a leading provider of educational products, services, and solutions that cater to the needs of educators, students, and schools across the United States. With a rich history dating back to its founding in 1959, School Specialty has evolved into a comprehensive resource for K-12 educational materials, classroom supplies, furniture, curriculum solutions, and more. The company's commitment to enhancing the learning environment and supporting educators has made it a trusted partner for schools seeking to create effective and engaging educational experiences.

Figure 8.5: *School Specialty Logo* (**https://www.schoolspecialty.com/**, *copyright ©2023 School Specialty, LLC*)

One of School Specialty's strengths lies in its diverse portfolio of offerings that encompass a wide range of subjects, teaching methodologies, and learning needs. From art and STEM (science, technology, engineering, and math) supplies to literacy resources and special education tools, the company provides educators with the tools they need to foster a dynamic and supportive learning environment. By collaborating closely with educators, administrators, and curriculum specialists, School Specialty develops tailored solutions that align with evolving educational trends and standards. Through its vast product range and dedication to innovation, School Specialty plays a pivotal role in shaping the educational landscape and empowering both teachers and students to succeed.

School Specialty operates in a B2B2C space where the products and solutions are bought by schools and institutions, but the end users are the students. To get feedback and improve their products, they not only need to collaborate with educators and curriculum specialists but also the students. Since they are dealing with student data, privacy, and security concerns are paramount. School Specialty must adhere to the best practices when it comes to ensuring data privacy and security.

Challenges

School Specialty aims to transform the learning environment with a single source of truth. To fulfill their goals, they had to overcome the following challenges:

- Data was collected and stored across different systems. Part of the data was offline. The first challenge was to collect, consolidate and unify the data from more than 13 data sources to create customer profiles.
- They were not able to offer personalization at scale based on customers' interests and preferences.
- Customer data should be connected across the Salesforce ecosystem.

Impact of implementing Salesforce Data Cloud

- School Specialty collected and unified customer profile and engagement data to create a world-class customer experience.
- They were able to deliver personalized messages at scale by activating customers' interests and preferences.
- They empowered sales reps to have more strategic conversations with their accounts around their spending allocation to optimize budgets.
- They established a data-driven culture to ensure customer data is connected across the entire Salesforce ecosystem.

Outcomes

School Specialty had a favorable outcome from their Salesforce Data Cloud implementation:

- They had a 67% consolidation rate.
- More than 30 million records were uploaded.
- 13 different data sources were consolidated to unify and create customer profiles.

What we can learn from School Specialty experience

Learnings from School Specialty were as follows:

- School Specialty wanted to understand their customers better and provide a personalized experience for them. Salesforce Data Cloud enabled them to do just that.

- By consolidating different data sources, they were able to unify and create customer profiles based on engagement data and deliver personalized messages to different segments. This liberated them from the shackles of cookie-cutter messaging. Their customers felt more engaged and valued.
- Salesforce Data Cloud was able to handle 13 different data sources with more data sources to be connected later, and ingestion of more than 30 million records. We can therefore be sure that scalability is not a challenge for Data Cloud.

Conclusion

We hope to learn about the five stories of successful Salesforce Data Cloud implementation and their impacts on the companies that motivated and encouraged you. Our goal of including these success stories was to demonstrate that companies across different industries were able to successfully implement and derive value from Data Cloud. These companies are the perfect source of inspiration for others who want to go on this journey. A well-thought-out and successful implementation can transform businesses and supercharge the customer experience. Ultimately, it leads to an outcome that all businesses desire: better ROI, higher customer satisfaction, and retention.

In the next chapter, we are going to look at future trends and the way forward to creating great customer experiences. We will look at the future of Salesforce Data Cloud and what customers can expect from Salesforce. We will also discuss the future of customer data platforms and why it is an exciting time to be invested in them.

CHAPTER 9

The Way Forward for Creating Great Customer Experiences

Introduction

In today's dynamic and highly competitive business landscape, the creation of exceptional customer experiences has emerged as a pivotal driver of success. Companies no longer view customer interactions as mere transactions; instead, they recognize them as opportunities to establish lasting relationships and build brand loyalty. To remain relevant and thrive in this customer-centric era, organizations must chart a strategic path forward that prioritizes innovation, personalization, and seamless integration across all touchpoints. In this age of heightened customer expectations and digital transformation, the way forward for creating great customer experiences demands a holistic approach that harnesses cutting-edge technologies, deep customer insights, and a commitment to delivering value at every turn.

In this chapter, we will discuss the emerging trends in the world of customer experience management. We will start with the most hyped word in the tech industry: generative AI. We will understand what Generative AI or Gen AI as it is commonly called, how they can bring a revolution to the world of tech, and what risks we should be worried about. Then we will understand Einstein GPT and Einstein Studio, which are AI offerings from Salesforce. We will delve into a few AI use cases in Data Cloud and thereafter know what to expect from Data Cloud in future releases.

Note: Salesforce Data Cloud is now known as Salesforce Customer Data Cloud or Salesforce Data Cloud.

Structure

In this chapter, we will cover the following topics:

- Emerging trend: Generative AI
- Einstein GPT and Einstein Studio
- AI use cases in Data Cloud
- Data Cloud: What to expect in the future releases

Emerging trend: Generative AI

One of the most captivating and transformative emerging trends in the world of technology is the rise of Generative AI, short for Generative Artificial Intelligence. As we navigate the digital landscape of the 21st century, Generative AI is emerging as a powerful force that is reshaping how we create, communicate, and interact with information. At its core, Generative AI leverages advanced machine learning techniques, particularly deep learning, to generate content that can range from text and images to music and even entire virtual environments. This technology enables machines to not only understand and replicate existing data but also to create entirely new and innovative content autonomously. The implications of this trend are far-reaching, touching domains as diverse as content creation, healthcare, art, and beyond.

Generative AI models use neural network architectures with billions of parameters, which are designed to simulate the functioning of the human brain. Common architectures include Recurrent Neural Networks (RNNs), Convolutional Neural Networks (CNNs), and more recently, Transformers. Transformers, with their attention mechanisms, have gained popularity for generative models due to their ability to capture long-range dependencies in data. These models are also called foundation models.

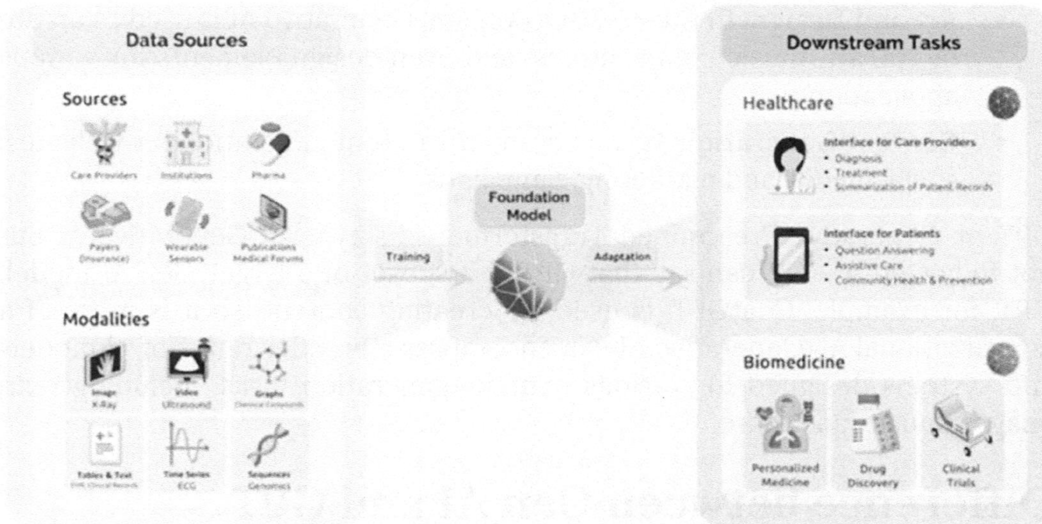

Figure 9.1: *Training a foundation model (source:* **https://blogs.nvidia.com/blog/2022/10/10/llms-ai-horizon/**)

Once trained, the generative AI model can produce new content. This is done by providing an initial input or "*seed*" to the model, which it then uses to generate a sequence of data. The generation process is often autoregressive, meaning the model predicts the next part of the sequence based on what it has already generated. This process continues iteratively until the desired length or complexity is achieved.

Generative models can exhibit creativity because they don't simply replicate data from their training set. Instead, they generate new content based on the patterns and knowledge they have acquired during training. The extent of creativity can be controlled by adjusting parameters such as temperature in text-based models. Higher values make the output more random and creative, while lower values make it more deterministic.

Some common applications of Generative AI include:

- **Text Generation**: Generative AI can be used to generate human-like text, including writing articles, poetry, or even writing code.
- **Image Generation**: It can create images that appear to be photographs of non-existent places, people, or objects.
- **Natural Language Processing (NLP)**: Generative AI is used in NLP tasks like chatbots, language translation, and even creating conversational agents that can hold coherent conversations.

- **Art and Design**: In the creative domain, Generative AI is used to create digital art, music compositions, and even design elements for various applications.
- **Content Generation**: It can automate content generation for websites, social media, and marketing campaigns.

GPT or Generative Pre-trained Transformer is a type of Generative AI but not fully Gen AI. You can say that GPT is a subset of a larger Gen AI model. GPT, for example, ChatGPT, is used for creating content, so it is more of a conversational AI. Generative AI can encompass a broader range of AI models and systems designed for various content-generation tasks, including text, images, music, and more.

Difference between Gen AI and GPT

GPT and Gen AI are related but not synonymous terms. Let's break down the key differences between them:

Definition

- **GPT**: GPT specifically refers to a series of natural language processing models developed by OpenAI. These models are primarily designed for text-related tasks, such as text generation, translation, summarization, and more.
- **Gen AI**: "Gen AI" is a broader term that encompasses a wide range of generative artificial intelligence technologies and models. It's not limited to language processing but includes various AI models capable of generating content in different forms, such as text, images, music, and more.

Scope

- **GPT**: GPT models are primarily focused on natural language understanding and generation. They excel at processing and generating text-based content and are often used in applications like chatbots, content generation, and language translation.
- **Gen AI**: "*Gen* AI" is a more encompassing concept that can include not only text generation but also other types of content generation, such as image generation, music composition, and creative content in various domains.

Examples

- **GPT**: Examples of GPT models include GPT-3 and GPT-4. These models are known for their text-generation capabilities and are widely used for natural language processing tasks.
- **Gen AI**: "*Gen AI*" can refer to a wide array of generative models and technologies, including non-text-based models like DALL-E for image generation and MuseNet for music composition.

Future Prospects of Gen AI

Gen AI is being seen as a new wave in the tech industry and may become even a bigger thing than the internet itself. The use of Gen AI currently is restrictive and usage is narrow but the future possibilities are immense. A few future potential use cases for Gen AI are as follows:

- **Content Generation and Automation**: Gen AI can play a significant role in automating content creation across different media, including text, images, videos, and music. This can benefit industries such as marketing, entertainment, and journalism by reducing the time and cost associated with content production. So far, we have seen the potential of ChatGPT and other AI tools, which can create human-like content. In the future, we might see more use cases.
- **Personalized Experiences**: Gen AI can enable highly personalized experiences for users. In marketing, it can generate tailored product recommendations and advertisements. In healthcare, it can help create personalized treatment plans based on individual patient data. CDP enthusiasts are most interested in this use case as it can revolutionize the industry and how companies interact with their customers.
- **Scientific Research and Discovery**: Gen AI can assist researchers in areas such as drug discovery, materials science, and data analysis by generating hypotheses, simulating experiments, and summarizing vast datasets. A lot of the time-consuming and labor-intensive work can be offloaded to Gen AI and the human mind can work on more complicated workloads.
- **Language Translation and Global Communication**: Gen AI models may offer near-real-time, highly accurate translation services that break down language barriers in communication, facilitating global collaboration and understanding.

Risks associated with Gen AI

Although Gen AI can be the biggest thing for the tech industry, it is also fraught with several key risks. If the government, companies, as well as those who will use AI, are not careful, the result could be catastrophic. As with nuclear energy, which can provide the cleanest fuel on the planet but also create the most dangerous weapon known to mankind, Gen AI can potentially ruin humankind if we are not judicious with its use.

Here are some key risks associated with Gen AI:

- **Bias and Fairness**: If not properly curated and supervised, Gen AI models can inherit and perpetuate biases present in their training data. This can result in discriminatory content and decision-making processes, impacting marginalized groups.
- **Misinformation and Deep Fakes**: Gen AI can be used to create highly convincing fake content, including deepfake videos and realistic but fabricated text. This can be exploited to spread false information, damage reputations, or manipulate public opinion. This can create riots, and even wars when politically sensitive content is used.
- **Disruption of Employment**: The automation of content creation and other tasks by Gen AI could lead to job displacement in industries that rely heavily on manual content generation, such as journalism, copywriting, and graphic design. Gen AI can potentially take away jobs that require repeated and simple manual labor, the work done by the most vulnerable section of society.
- **Lack of Control and Understanding**: As Gen AI models become more complex, understanding and controlling their decision-making processes can become increasingly challenging, potentially leading to unintended consequences.
- **Ethical Dilemmas**: The use of Gen AI raises ethical questions, particularly regarding issues like copyright infringement, plagiarism, and consent. Deciding who owns generated content and whether it can be used without attribution can be complex.

As Gen AI evolves, there will be a growing need for ethical guidelines, regulation, and oversight to ensure responsible and safe use. Efforts to prevent misuse, such as deep fakes and misinformation, will continue to be important.

Einstein GPT and Einstein Studio

This sections explains Einstein GPT and Einstein Studio.

Einstein GPT

Einstein GPT is a generative pre-trained transformer model created by Salesforce that can create personalized content across every Salesforce cloud with generative AI. For example, Einstein GPT can create personalized emails for sales representatives to send to their customers, generate tailor-made responses for customer service professionals to answer customer questions, generate targeted content for marketers to increase campaign response rates, and auto-generate code for developers more promptly.

Einstein GPT is a Gen AI tool that will train itself on the data from Salesforce Data Cloud and therefore will generate content unique to every organization. Customers who adopt Einstein GPT can choose to connect their data to Open AI's advanced AI models out of the box or use their own AI model or any other external AI model (see *Figure* 9.2). After training the model, customers can use natural language prompts similar to ChatGPT prompts within their Salesforce orgs to generate content that adapts to the changing customer information in their orgs in real-time.

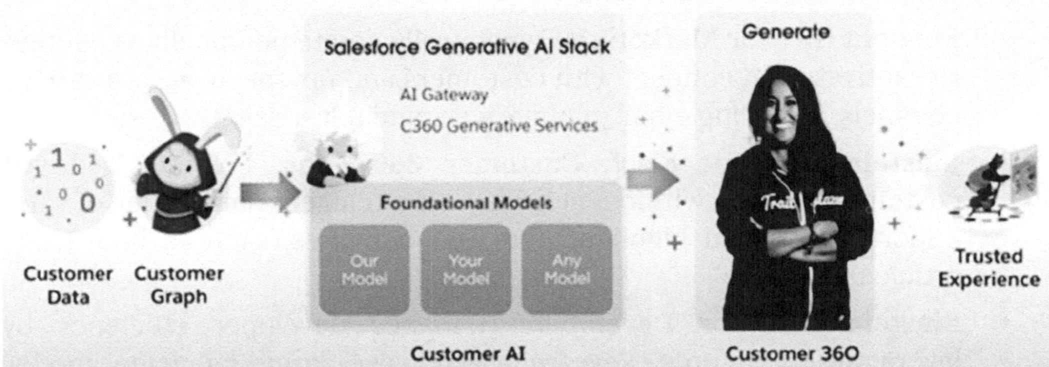

Figure 9.2: *Salesforce Generative AI stack*

Einstein GPT is in closed pilot till the publication of this book. When it becomes GA (generally available), Salesforce customers will be able to test it out.

For now, Salesforce has announced Einstein GPT for the following services:

- **Einstein GPT for Sales**: Automatically generate sales tasks, including crafting emails (see *Figure* 9.3), arranging meetings, and preparing for upcoming interactions.

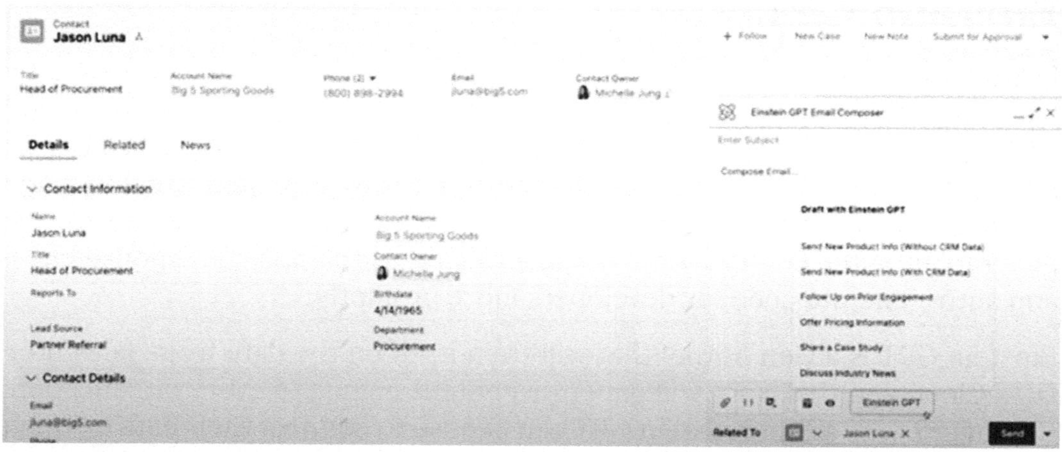

***Figure 9.3:** Einstein GPT Email Composer to help write personalized emails quickly*

- **Einstein GPT for Service**: Generate informative articles based on historical case notes. Automatically create customized agent chat responses to enhance customer satisfaction by providing tailored and efficient service interactions.
- **Einstein GPT for Marketing**: Dynamically create personalized content to captivate and connect with customers and prospects across various channels, including email, mobile, web, and advertising.
- **Einstein GPT for Slack Customer 360 apps**: Provide AI-driven customer insights within Slack, such as intelligent summaries of sales opportunities, and highlight end-user activities, such as knowledge article updates.
- **Einstein GPT for Developers**: Enhance developer efficiency by leveraging Salesforce Research's exclusive large language model. Employ an AI chat assistant to automatically generate code and inquire about queries in languages such as Apex, streamlining the development process.

Einstein Studio

Salesforce is making it easier for companies to use their own AI models for any sales, service, marketing, commerce, and IT application within Salesforce.

Einstein GPT can also be trained on your own AI model. To bring other AI models to Salesforce, it has launched Einstein Studio, which is now generally available.

Einstein Studio simplifies the process for data science and engineering teams to efficiently manage and deploy AI models, all while reducing costs. Businesses can seamlessly utilize their in-house data from Salesforce Data Cloud to train models, leveraging Salesforce's ecosystem of curated AI models, including Amazon SageMaker from Amazon Web Services (AWS), Google Cloud's Vertex AI, and other AI services (see *Figure* 9.4).

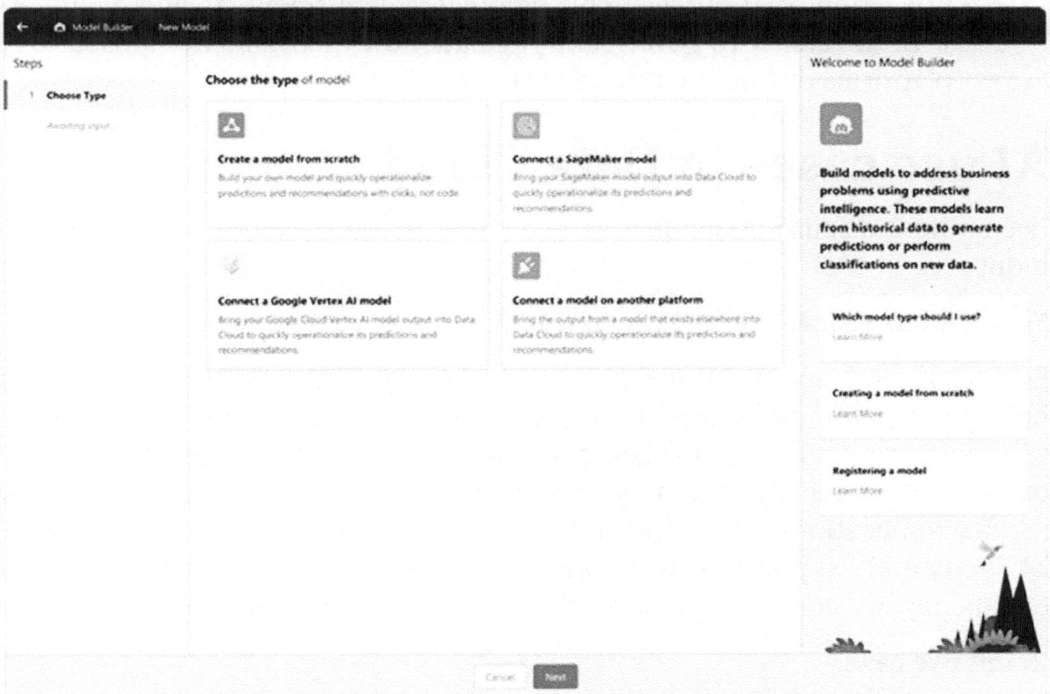

***Figure 9.4:** Einstein Studio helps you bring AI models to Salesforce*

With this Bring Your Own Model (BYOM) solution, customers gain the capability to integrate their custom AI models alongside the ready-made Large Language Models (LLMs) offered through Einstein GPT. This empowers them to deliver a holistic and rapid AI solution that combines both custom and pre-built AI capabilities.

The benefits of Einstein Studio are as follows:

- Einstein Studio accelerates the AI model training process by offering pre-built, zero-ETL integration. This simplifies and streamlines data movement between platforms, significantly reducing complexity and enhancing efficiency.

- Einstein Studio enables technical teams to effortlessly access their data in Data Cloud using a simple **point and click** approach. They can then proceed to construct and train their custom AI models for deployment across Salesforce applications. This streamlined process ensures that up-to-date and pertinent customer data informs AI predictions and facilitates the automatic generation of content.
- Einstein Studio offers a centralized control panel for overseeing the utilization of AI models. This empowers data scientists and engineers with the ability to govern and regulate how their data is exposed to AI platforms during the training process.

AI use cases in Data Cloud

Let us now discuss about few AI use cases in Data Cloud across different industries:

Financial use case

Financial service institutions can create custom cross-selling models that help recommend additional products or services to advisors based on real-time engagement data from clients. AI models can help in proactive fraudulent transaction detection and risk management. Using AI-powered customer service applications, chatbots, and virtual assistants powered by AI provide 24/7 customer support, answer queries, and assist with routine transactions, enhancing customer experiences while reducing operational costs.

Retail use case

A retailer can create a custom AI model to predict a customer's likelihood to buy specific outfits based on engagement data, such as their purchase history or online activity. They can then deploy the model and use Einstein Studio to deliver hyper-personalized product recommendations to customers via the most appropriate channel, including email, a mobile app, or social media.

Automotive use case

An automotive brand can use predictive AI to determine when a car is likely to need maintenance and detect fraudulent insurance claims. Generative AI can then be used to personalize customer marketing campaigns based on individual needs and preferences.

Travel use case

A travel agency can connect CRM data, such as customer booking history and travel preferences, with non-CRM data like destination reviews and weather forecasts. They can then deploy predictive and generative AI models to predict which destinations appeal to specific customers and generate personalized email recommendations for them.

Field Service use case

Proactive service with Data Cloud combines a unified view of customers and their assets – including customer purchase details, service history, and IoT signals on machine health – all in real-time and at scale. With this unified data, Einstein can automatically schedule service appointments and job duration, the necessary parts or tools needed, and the right technician for the job.

Data Cloud: What to expect in the future releases

Salesforce products are ever evolving. Salesforce continuously innovates its products and has three releases each year, summer, spring, and winter. In these releases, they fix bugs as well as introduce new features. With future releases, customers will find it easier to deal with certain tasks on the Data Cloud as well as try new features on the Data Cloud.

For Salesforce Data Cloud, Salesforce releases new features every month. For the month of August 2023, they have released:

Directly Ingest Parquet Files into Data Cloud: Data Cloud now has native support for the Parquet file format when ingesting data streams from Amazon S3, Google Cloud Storage (GCS), and Microsoft Azure Storage. Parquet, an open-source columnar storage format, is specifically engineered for optimal performance in large-scale data processing tasks, especially those involving substantial workloads. By adopting the Parquet format, you can seamlessly set up data streams for ingestion without the necessity of converting them to CSV, resulting in reduced intricacy and cost savings.

Future release

- **Use Your Own SFTP Server to Activate Segments**

  Bring in your own Secure File Transfer Protocol (SFTP) server to activate data to more external platforms.

This feature is in pilot and is yet to be made generally available. We can expect this in a future release.

- **Einstein GPT**

  Einstein GPT can be a game-changer for the Data Cloud. Currently, Einstein GPT is in closed pilot and will be released soon to the general public. We can expect many Data Cloud use cases from Einstein GPT, especially in the calculated insights, segmentation, and activation phase.

- **AI-Powered field service**

  AI-powered field service along with Data Cloud will greatly enhance the experience of frontline field workers. AI will power their skilling, service preparation, and service delivery experience.

Conclusion

It is an interesting time to be in the tech world. We are experiencing one-in-a-generation tech trends unfolding right before us. The AI revolution is upon us, and it might even be bigger than the internet revolution. AI will touch every aspect of human life.

Salesforce has been investing in AI for a while now. Salesforce has been experimenting with augmented AI and has already released many augmented AI applications and citizen data science tools. With the rise of Gen AI, Salesforce is now making investments in making Gen AI available on its platform and to its customers. Although it is too soon to test the usefulness of the products, it is surely a good time to get excited about the possibilities of Gen AI in the Salesforce ecosystem. Using a combination of Gen AI tools and Salesforce features, we can transform the customer experience landscape. Data Cloud can provide the much-needed data based on which Gen AI can be trained and therefore will provide relevant customer-specific solutions. We are excited and so should you.

In the next chapter, we will take a look at how to successfully pass the Data Cloud Accredited Professional Credential Exam. We will explain how to begin your preparation for the exam, go through the exam guide, and discuss in brief how to prepare for each section, preparation tips, and finally some mock questions with their solutions and explanations.

CHAPTER 10

Preparation for the Salesforce Data Cloud Consultant Exam

Introduction

We are finally on the last chapter of this book. If you have made it to the last chapter without skipping any of the chapters, congratulations. You are now ready to prepare for the Salesforce Data Cloud Consultant Exam. You are not yet ready to take the test. But you are ready to begin the preparation for it.

Throughout the entirety of the book, we discussed concepts related to the need for a customer data platform and went into the specifics. The book will help you manage and deliver on a Data Cloud implementation project. However, the exam needs more than that. You need to possess good product knowledge as well as technical knowledge of the Data Cloud product to successfully ace the exam.

In this chapter, we will explain how to begin your preparation for the exam, go through the exam guide, and discuss in brief how to prepare for each section, tips, and finally some mock questions with their solutions and explanations. By the end of the chapter, you should be prepared for the exam, provided you follow the steps mentioned in this chapter.

Note: Salesforce Data Cloud is now known as Salesforce Customer Data Cloud or Salesforce Data Cloud.

Structure

In this chapter, we will cover the following topics:

- How to start your preparation
- Understanding the exam guide
- How to prepare for each section of the exam
- Important information to remember for the exam
- Exam tips
- Mock questions with solutions and explanations

Starting your preparation

It is said that "*well begun is half done*". Starting your preparation for the exam in the correct way is key to staying on the path and passing the consultant exam.

Note: If your company is a Salesforce partner or you are a Salesforce employee then you will have access to the Salesforce Partner community, where you can access the Partner Learning Camp. In the partner learning camp, you need to complete the Get to Know Data Cloud Curriculum, which will prepare you for the exam along with the "*Prepare for Your Salesforce Data Cloud Consultant Credential*" trailmix.

To begin your preparation, you need to first check whether your company is a Salesforce partner. If you are working for a company that implements Salesforce for clients, then chances are your company is a Salesforce partner.

If your company uses Salesforce for its business, do check internally whether your company is a partner.

If your company is a partner, then reach out to your alliance partner or an executive who deals with Salesforce AE and ask for a partner credential for yourself. Once you have the partner credentials, you can start your preparations for the exam.

Here are the steps you need to perform to start preparing on the partner org portal.

1. Login to **https://partners.salesforce.com/** using your partner org credential (*Figure 10.1*)

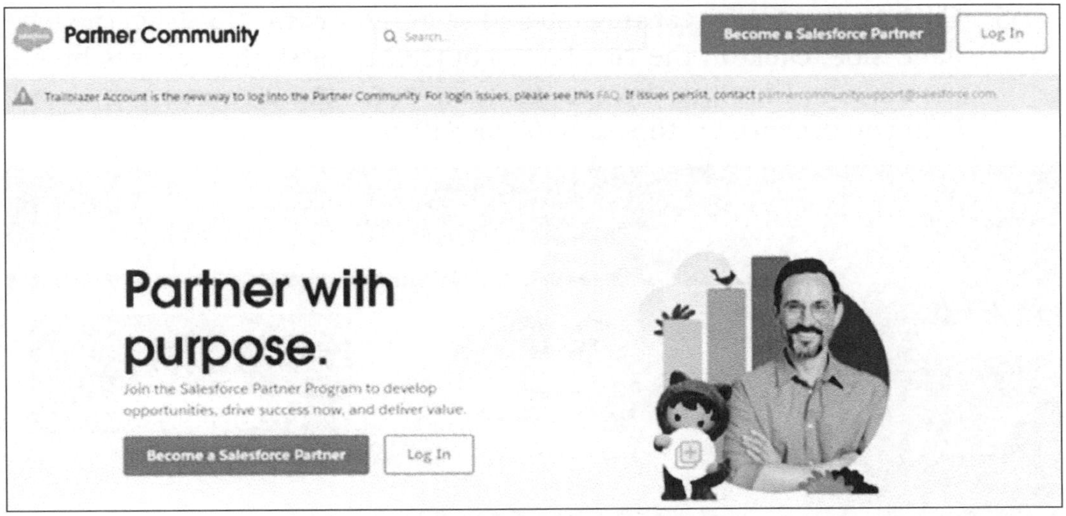

Figure 10.1: *Salesforce partner portal login page*

2. Click on the `Learn` tab.
3. Click on the `Start Learning` button inside the `Partner Learning Camp` (*Figure 10.2*)

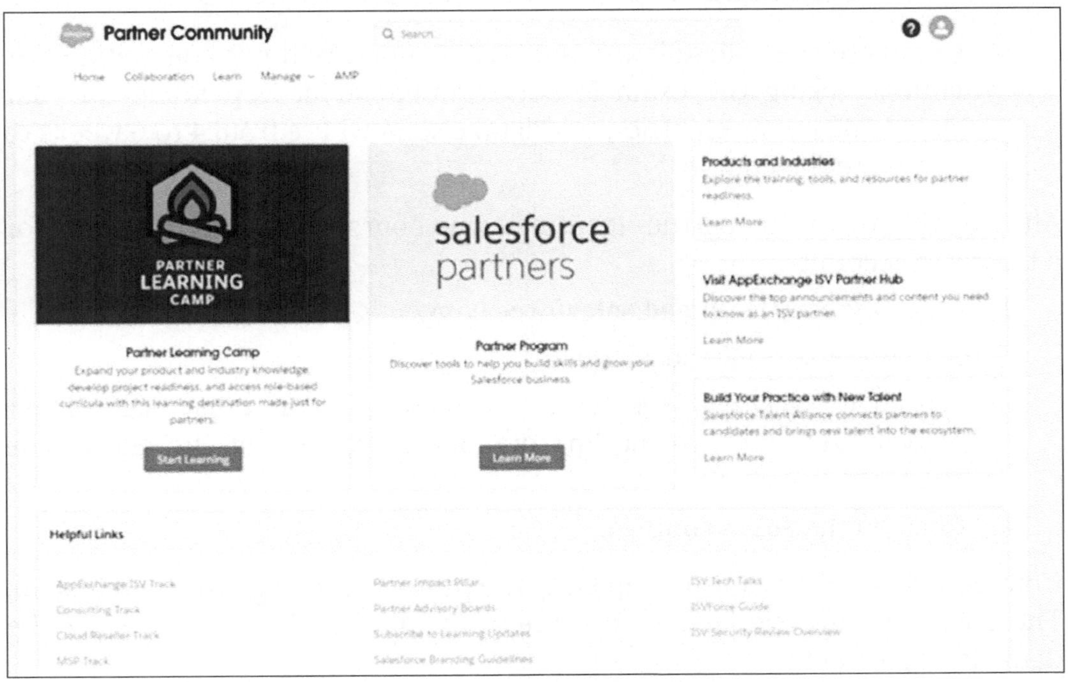

Figure 10.2: *Click on the Start Learning button*

4. You will be asked to log in using the trailblazer.me account. Click on the **`Log in`** button.
5. Click on the **`Browse Catalog`** tab and search for **`data Cloud`**. On the left-hand side, click on the **`Curriculum`** button to filter the courses by the curriculum. Enroll in the **`Get to Know Data Cloud`** course, which will help you prepare for the exam (*Figure* 10.3).

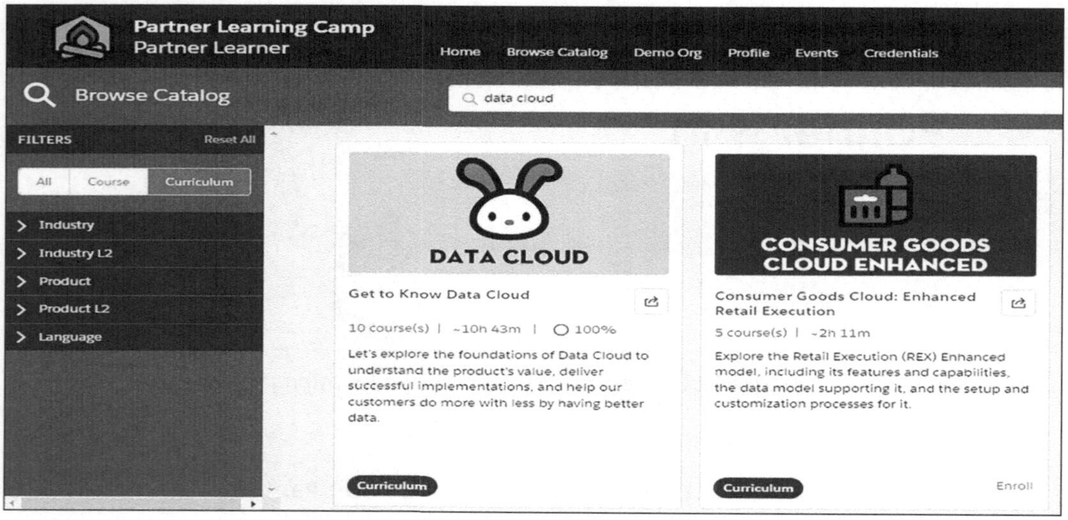

***Figure* 10.3:** *Enroll in the 'Get to Know Data Cloud' course*

6. Complete the course in a sequential manner. Without completing this course, taking the exam is not recommended. Depending on your speed and comprehension, it will take somewhere from 4 to 6 weeks to complete the course.

After signing up for the partner learning camp course, you need to sign up for a trailhead account.

1. Go to **https://trailhead.salesforce.com/**.
2. Sign up for a trailhead account.
3. Search for **`Prepare for your Salesforce Data Cloud Consultant Credential`**. Or go to the link number 2 provided at the end of the chapter.
4. Click on the **`Follow`** button.

Complete this trailmix after completing the partner learning camp curriculum. There will be some overlap between the two and it should help you revise the data cloud concepts.

Understanding the exam guide

After completing the `Get to Know Data Cloud` curriculum, it is time to understand the exam. Learning about a topic is one thing, but preparing for an exam is another. We need to understand the exam, the pattern, the type of questions asked, and why questions are framed as they are. Once we understand the exam, we have a better chance of clearing it on the first attempt.

About the Salesforce Data Cloud Consultant exam: Who is it for?

The Salesforce Data Cloud Consultant exam is ideal for consultants who have experience implementing and consulting on customer data platforms in a customer-facing role. The Salesforce Data Cloud Consultant is someone who demonstrates skills in designing, configuring, building, and implementing Data Cloud.

Salesforce highly recommends a combination of on-the-job experience, completion of relevant Partner Learning Camp (PLC) curriculum, trailmixes and self-study to maximize your chances of passing the exam.

About the Exam

Questions: 60 multiple-choice questions

Exam Duration: 105 mins

Passing Percentage: 62%

Fee: USD 200, plus applicable taxes as required per local law. Most partners receive certification vouchers which nullify the exam cost.

Delivery options: Proctored exam delivered onsite at a testing center or in an online proctored environment.

Recommended Courses to attend before the exam

The following courses should be completed:

- `Get to Know Data Cloud` along with the hands-on exercise in the course.
- Review Data Cloud Help Documentation. Link to be provided at the end of the chapter.
- Sign up for `Prepare for your Salesforce Data Cloud Consultant Credential` Trailmix. The link for both is shared at the end of the chapter.
- Salesforce Training or recordings if you can register for such courses during the preparation time.

- Videos on YouTube. Links to be provided at the end.

Table 10.1 displays the exam outline:

Topics	Weighting
Solution Overview	18%
Data Cloud Setup and Administration	12%
Data Ingestion and Modeling	20%
Identity Resolution	14%
Segmentation and Insights	18%
Act on Data	18%

***Table* 10.1:** *Exam Outline*

Exam Registration

To register for the exam, you need to go to **https://www.webassessor.com/** and sign up with your email ID. Later you have to connect your webassesor ID with your trailblazer id so that all the certification details are synced up.

To register for the exam, click on the `Register` for an Exam tab. Expand the Consultant Exams dropdown. You will see the Salesforce Certified Data Cloud Consultant (*Figure* 10.4).

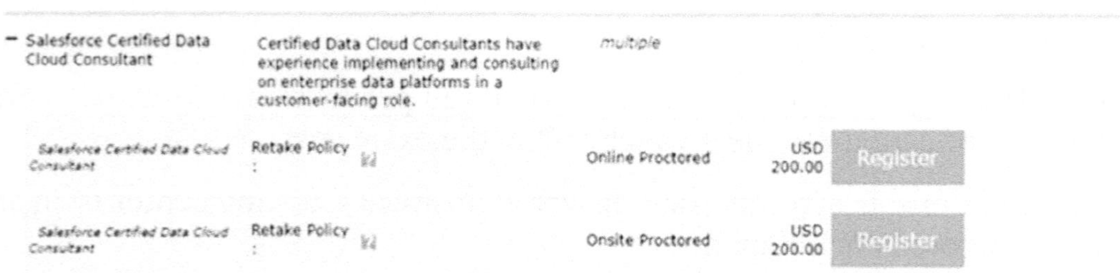

***Figure* 10.4:** *Either choose the online proctored or the onsite proctored*

Choose either the online proctored or the onsite proctored depending on how you want to take the exam. For the onsite proctored, you need to select a venue where you have to go and take the exam. There are exam centers in major cities around the world. For the onsite proctored, you can take the exam in the comfort of your house, provided you have a room that is free from distractions or noise.

Go ahead in the process and complete the payment and schedule your exam. We recommend booking a day at least 2-3 months after you have started your

preparation or once you feel that you are confident enough to take the exam on the chosen date.

Preparing for each section of the exam

To prepare for each section of the exam, it is essential to enroll and complete the Data Cloud curriculum. The course has the following sections, and each section covers certain topics from the exam outline:

1. **Data Cloud: Overview**

   This module explains what Data Cloud is, including its key features and common ways customers benefit from the platform. This covers the solution overview section of the exam.

2. **Data Cloud: Setup**

   The *Data Cloud: Setup* module explains how to navigate the Data Cloud interface, add user roles and permissions, and connect it to external data sources. It covers the setup part of the setup and administration section of the exam.

3. **Data Cloud: Data Ingestion**

   In this module, you will explore how to ingest data into Data Cloud from various sources. It will cover the data ingestion part of the exam.

4. **Data Cloud: Data Modeling**

   In this *Data Cloud: Data Modeling* module, you will discover how to map data to the Data Cloud data model designed from the Customer 360 Data Model. Covers the data modeling section.

5. **Data Cloud: Identity Resolution**

   In this *Data Cloud: Identity Resolution* course, you will explore how to unify customer data by using the identity resolution match and reconciliation rules. Covers the identity resolution section of the exam, which has the highest weightage.

6. **Data Cloud: Insights**

   Explore the insights capabilities of Data Cloud, including calculated insights, streaming insights, and visual insights builder. Covers the insights part of the segmentation and insights section.

7. **Data Cloud: Segmentation**

   In this *Data Cloud: Segmentation* course, you will be able to explore the segmentation capabilities of Data Cloud, including common segment examples and how to build segments in an account. Covers the segmentation part of the segmentation and insights section.

8. **Data Cloud: Activation**

   Explore how to configure the activation of segments in the Data Cloud and determine which activation targets are currently available in this module. Covers the activation section of the exam, which has the second highest weightage in the exam.

9. **Data Cloud: Administration**

   Investigate general Data Cloud administration tasks performed by an Admin, including maintenance, packaging, and troubleshooting in this module. It covers the administration part of the setup and administration section of the exam.

10. **Data Cloud: Implementation Basics**

    In this *Data Cloud: Implementation Basics course*, you will explore how to prepare for the implementation of the Data Cloud solution, identify applicable use cases, and deliver on projects. As such this module is not directly related to any of the exam modules, but gives a sense of the overall implementation basics. You can expect a few questions on the exam on this topic as well.

After going through these modules and completing the hands-on exercises that are a part of the curriculum, you will be around 60% prepared to take the test.

The remaining 40% of the preparation involves practicing sample questions and building proof of concepts (POC) or working on a Data Cloud implementation project. It is a chicken and an egg problem. For working on a Data Cloud implementation project, project managers will want a certification and at the same time, to get certified, having practical experience helps. Even to get a free Data Cloud org for your company to build POCs for your customers, you need to have at least two Salesforce Data Cloud Consultant certified. So it goes without saying, many would have to attempt the exam without actually working on a Data Cloud project.

You will get a chance to sign up for a free trial org while completing the curriculum. You can use that org to practice Data Cloud concepts. Create your own use case and build POCs on them for your own use only. Salesforce prohibits building POCs on those orgs for customer demos. Try using different approaches and tinkering with the features to get the best of the platform. Refer to the Data Cloud documentation for better understanding.

After that, it is time to practice sample questions for the data cloud exam. Make sure you are practicing questions before attempting the exam. Thoroughly understand the underlying concept for each question. It is not the answer that matters but the concept that the question is talking about. All concepts should be crystal clear. We will include a few sample questions for you to practice. You can get more such questions from different websites. Make sure you do not violate the code of conduct for the exam. Do not attempt or ask for actual exam questions as this violates the code of conduct. You are free to practice on sample questions but not on the actual exam questions or dumps as they are commonly known.

Important information to remember for the exam

Here is some important information that you should know about the exam. Make sure that you read through this section the night before you take the exam.

1. To connect a Salesforce org and ingest objects and fields, you need a `Data Cloud Admin permission` set OR `Data Cloud for Marketing Admin permission set` and `View All and Read permission` on the object being ingested.
2. There are no hard limits on the number of CRM org you can connect to Data Cloud. However, it will affect Data Cloud billing.
3. `Data Cloud and Loyalty management` must be installed within the same org for Activation to support loyalty management.
4. Data Cloud supports the Parquet file format for Amazon S3, Google Cloud Storage (GCS), and Microsoft Azure Storage data stream ingestion.
5. The total number of streaming data transforms is **25 per org**.
6. The Full Refresh extract method can only be used on data of **50 million records or smaller**. For larger data groups, use either Delta Extract by Date or by Number.
7. Provide the **Data Cloud Salesforce Connector permission set** access to the required objects and fields that are to be ingested in the org from which the CRM data is being ingested.

8. With Data Cloud, the system can only unify profiles if they are mapped correctly to the **individual object** and one other element: a contact point object or a party identifier object.
9. Within a Data Kit, we can bundle **data steam, data models, and calculated insights.**
10. Reconciliation rules operate across **Individual, Party Identification, and Contact Point Email** data model objects.
11. Deleting a ruleset permanently removes all **unified customer data, eliminates dependencies on data model objects, stops all processing of the ruleset**, and deletes the history of previous runs. In some cases, it's better to update the match or reconciliation rules instead of deleting the ruleset.
12. While mapping source data to the data model object, remember that fields related to **`address`, `phone number`, `email`,** or other contact points should not be mapped to the Individual object. We should map it to other objects, namely **`Contact Point Address`, `Contact Point Phone`,** and **`Contact Point Email`.**
13. While mapping a data model object (DMO) in the Profile or Other category, it is mandatory to map **`the primary key field`**. You can **`save the data mapping`** only after doing the same.
14. While mapping a DMO in the Engagement category, it is mandatory to map the **`primary key field and the Event dateTime field`**. You can save the data mapping only after doing the same.
15. To implement identity resolution, segmentation, and activation, it's essential to establish the necessary mappings for the party area data. You can use the Entity Relationships Diagram (ERD) for the Party area to plan the mapping. You must also map the Individual object and either a Contact Point or the Party Identification object must be mapped in data streams.

Exam tips

To ace the exam on the first go, follow the exam tips provided here:

- Read this book thoroughly, especially the chapters on Data Cloud, that is, *Chapter 3, Going beyond CDP: Salesforce Data Cloud; Chapter 4, Salesforce Data Cloud Architecture*; and *Chapter 6, Implementing Salesforce Customer Data Cloud*. Make sure you understand the basic concepts.

- Complete the curriculum in a sequential manner without skipping any of the topics or hands-on exercises.
- If you get a chance to work on a Data Cloud implementation project, then you are in luck. Else if you get a chance to build a proof of concept, volunteer for the same. If none of these options works out, then self-practice on the trial org.
- Practice enough sample questions to test your knowledge. While practicing questions or building or working on implementation, if you come across new information, make note of it.
- Read the Data Cloud documentation to clarify your doubts.
- Before the examination, read your notes and this book to revise the concepts.
- Go through the glossary section of the documentation to make sure you know all the terms.
- In the exam, instead of trying to select the correct answer, try to eliminate the wrong options first. In a typical question, there will be 4 options. Your chance of selecting the correct one is 25%. By reading the options, you will be able to eliminate one or two options that cannot be correct. These options will typically have incorrect information. If your concepts are clear, then you can eliminate these options. If you eliminate two options, your chance of selecting the correct option jumps to 50%.
- Use the elimination technique, especially for those questions where you are not sure of the answer.
- During the exam, in the first run, answer questions that you are 100% confident about. If you are not confident of a question's answer, mark it for review and move on. Go through the entire paper once in this manner. In the second run, answer questions from the reviewed questions. You may be able to answer some now by the process of elimination. For those questions, you can't, keep it in review and move on. Continue this process till all questions are answered.

Mock questions with solutions and explanations

Our objective here is to provide a few sample questions that will help you understand whether your preparation is up to the mark to appear for the exam.

These are not actual exam questions and should not be taken as an exhaustive list of questions. Actual exam questions may vary in terms of level of difficulty as well as the nature of the question itself.

We have provided explanations for each answer to help clarify the concept. Let us begin:

1. Select two use cases that can be addressed with Data Cloud.

   A. Harmonize data from multiple sources with a standardized and extendable data model

   B. Understand and act upon customer data to drive more relevant experiences

   C. Safeguard critical business data by serving as a centralized system for backup and disaster recovery

   D. Govern enterprise data lifecycle through a centralized set of policies and processes

   Answer: Options A and B.

   Explanation: Data Cloud is used to harmonize data from multiple sources with a standardized and extendable data model and to act on unified customer data to create more relevant and personalized experiences.

   C and D are not relevant as Data Cloud is not used as a centralized system for backup and disaster recovery and neither it is used to govern enterprise data lifecycle through a centralized set of policies and processes.

2. Which three dependencies can prevent a Data Stream from being deleted?

   A. A data stream attribute is mapped to a Data Model object

   B. A data stream attribute is used in Calculated Insight

   C. A data stream attribute is used in Segmentation

   D. A data stream is associated with a data kit

   Answer: Options A, B, and C.

   Explanation: According to Salesforce documentation, consider the following factors before deleting a data stream:

   - The underlying DLO can't be mapped to any data model objects.
   - The underlying DLO can't be referenced in Calculated Insights.
   - The data stream can't be associated with a data kit.

Hence A, B, and C are the correct options. Data Stream deletion is not dependent on segmentation.

3. Which three components of the Data Cloud can be bundled within a Data Kit?

    A. Activation

    B. Streaming Insight

    C. Segment

    D. Calculated Insights

    Answer: Option B.

    Explanation: The Steaming Insight method should be used when performing aggregations in windows of 15 minutes of data collected via the Interactions SDK and Mobile SDK. Streaming Insight allows you to query and aggregate data from real-time streams using the window function.

4. Which three components of the Data Cloud can be bundled within a Data Kit?

    A. Data stream

    B. Data Model

    C. Segments

    D. Identity resolution rulesets

    E. Calculated Insights

    Answer: Options A, B, and E.

    Explanation: Within a Data Kit, we can bundle data steam, data models, and calculated insights. Reference documentation: https://help.salesforce.com/s/articleView?id=sf.c360_a_packaging_in_customer_360_audiences.htm&type=5

    However, calculated insights should be packaged and used in an org that already has a corresponding data model established and mapped. Without the required data models, installed calculated insights cannot be deployed.

5. A customer intends to incorporate their transactional data from the data warehouse into the Data Cloud. Their data export options are limited to an SFTP site. What are two advisable methods for transferring this data into the Data Cloud?

    A. Initiate a manual file import using the Data Import Wizard.

B. Employ Salesforce's Dataloader application for a bulk upload from a desktop.

C. Transfer the file into Google Cloud Storage and then utilize the Cloud Storage Connector for ingestion.

D. Move the file into Amazon S3 and subsequently employ the Cloud Storage Connector for ingestion.

Answer: Options C and D.

Explanation: A and B can be eliminated as we cannot manually import the file using the Data import wizard nor can we use the Dataloader application to upload the file. We can ingest the data using Google Cloud and S3 cloud storage connectors if the files are present in the respective storage.

6. What sequence of DMO joins should be utilized within the Calculated Insight to facilitate the creation of a multi-dimensional metric aimed at determining a consolidated Customer Lifetime Value (CLV) for administrators?

   A. **`Unified Individual`** > **`Individual`** > **`Sales Order`**

   B. **`Unified Individual`** > **`Unified Link Individual`** > **`Sales Order`**

   C. **`Sales Order`** > **`Unified Individual`**

   D. **`Sales Order`** > **`Individual`** > **`Unified Individual`**

   Answer: Option B.

   Explanation: We need to join the Unified Individual DMO with the Unified Link Individual DMO to identify the customers uniquely. Along with that, we need to join the Sales Order DMO, which contains the total sales-related data to calculate CLV.

7. An administrator has configured the Salesforce CRM connector and set up a data stream for the Case object. A new custom field called **Business Priority** was created on the Case object. However, that field is not available when trying to add it to the data stream. What could be causing this issue?

   A. Custom fields on the Case objects are not supported for ingesting into the Data Cloud

   B. Utilize Salesforce's Dataloader application to perform a bulk upload from a desktop

C. The Data Cloud administrator does not need to do anything. After 24 hours when the data stream refreshes, it will automatically include any new fields that were added to CRM

D. The Salesforce Integration User is missing `Read` permissions on the newly created field

Answer: Option D.

Explanation: As we have already explained, before ingesting any field to Data Cloud, you need to have View All and Read permission on the object being ingested. Hence, D is the correct option. A and C statements are false. We cannot use Dataloader to perform bulk upload in the Data Cloud to solve our use case.

8. An organization wants to enable users with the ability to identify and select text attributes from a picklist of options. Which Data Cloud feature can help with this use case?

   A. Transformation Formulas

   B. Data Harmonization

   C. Value Suggestion

   D. Global Picklists

   Answer: Option C.

   Explanation: The Value Suggestion feature within Data Cloud enables you to recognize and pick text attributes from a provided list of choices. By utilizing value suggestions, you can establish uniform values across various data sources, leading to enhanced data quality.

9. Which three Data Model objects do Reconciliation Rules operate across?

   A. Individual

   B. Party Identification

   C. Contact Point Email

   D. Contact

   E. Lead

   Answer: Options A, B, and C.

   Explanation: Reconciliation rules operate across Individual, Party Identification, and Contact Point Email data model objects. Reconciliation rules guide Data Cloud in establishing the precedence of values for unified individual profiles in conflicting data within the data model.

For instance, in situations where two profiles possess distinct email addresses, reconciliation rules play a role in selecting the appropriate one for the unified profile. These rules can be applied to the Individual entity, symbolizing a person or entity, the Party Identification entity, denoting identifiers like social media handles or loyalty card numbers, and the Contact Point Email entity, representing an email address.

10. What should be the type of the Event Time Field while ingesting Engagement data?

    A. Mutable

    B. Inconsistent

    C. Immutable

    D. None of the above

    Answer: Option C.

    Explanation: The event time field chosen while ingesting engagement data cannot be changed. It is immutable. So before choosing the date, we have to be cautious. If the wrong time field is chosen, we must delete the data stream and configure it again.

11. Which data model type in Data Cloud defines interactions with a specific party,

    A. Sales Order

    B. Transaction

    C. Engagement

    D. Individual

    Answer: Option C.

    Explanation: For information related to interactions with a specific party, such as an email message or telephone call, we use the engagement data model.

12. Which field in the recommended source schema is not editable?

    A. Field Label

    B. Field API Name

    C. Header Label

    D. Data Type

    Answer: Option C.

    Explanation: Field label and Field API name are editable before ingestion as well as after ingestion of data from the source. Data type is not directly editable but you can create another field with the same value but a different data type by creating a formula field for the same. So we will also count that as editable. The Header Label is not editable at all. That makes option C the correct answer.

13. What three things happen when an admin clicks on identity resolution deletion?

    A. Deletes all custom data model objects

    B. Removes all unified customer data

    C. Resets all settings in identity resolution

    D. Eliminates dependencies on data model object

    Answer: Options B, C, and D.

    Explanation: Deleting identity resolution rulesets does not delete all custom data model objects. By eliminating that, B, C, and D are the correct options. Deleting a ruleset permanently removes all unified customer data, eliminates dependencies on data model objects, stops all processing of the ruleset, and deletes the history of previous runs. Option C seems to be doubtful, but since the three options are correct, we can mark that as true as well.

14. What are the two steps of data ingestion in Salesforce CDP?

    A. Map ingested data to existing ingested data objects.

    B. Map ingested data to data model with consistent semantics.

    C. Preserve data per source schema with ingestion to the data lake.

    D. Establish a connection with the source data via REST API.

    Answer: Options B and C.

    Explanation: You can eliminate options A and D as ingested data is not mapped to existing ingested data objects and you do not establish a connection via REST API. Therefore, B and C are correct.

15. What Salesforce CDP API enables simultaneous retrieval of customer profiles along with their calculated insights?

    A. Profile API

    B. Query API

    C. Calculated Insights API

    D. Metadata API

    Answer: Option C.

Explanation: There is no such thing as a profile API or query API. Metadata API is not used for retrieving customer profiles with calculated insights. We have calculated the insights API for that. Therefore, option C is the correct answer.

16. How should an admin view past processing for resolution rules in Identity Resolution?
    A. Run History
    B. Audit History list view
    C. View processing Audit Trail
    D. Click on the view Processing History tab on the identity resolution record page.

    Answer: Option D.

    Explanation: The processing History tab on the identity resolution record page lists all the past processing jobs for resolution rules. So Option D is the correct one.

17. How does an admin increase the consolidation rate for identity resolution?
    A. Add more matching rules to broaden the search for matches
    B. Change the ignore empty value option
    C. Change all reconciliation rules to the source sequence
    D. Reduce the number of matching rules

    Answer: Option A.

    Explanation: Adding more matching rules to broaden the search of matches increases the consolidation rate for identity resolution. So option A is the correct one.

Conclusion

Reading this book, completing the partner learning camp curriculum, doing all the hands-on experience and self-practice along with practicing mock exam questions will prepare you to ace the exam in the first go. Follow the process diligently and you will be successful.

With this chapter, we have come to the end of this book. Hope you had a great time reading and learning from this book. This was our attempt to demystify the world of customer data platforms and talk in detail about one of the leading CDP platforms in the market, Salesforce Data Cloud. Despite its continuous name changes, Data Cloud remains the most consistent choice for CDP implementation among the top companies in the world. We wish you all the best for a successful CDP/Data Cloud implementation and the consultant exam if you are planning to take the exam. Once a trailblazer, always a trailblazer!

Useful Links

1. Salesforce Data Cloud Documentation: **https://help.salesforce.com/s/articleView?id=sf.c360_a_product_considerations.htm&type=5**
2. Data Cloud trailhead trailmix: **https://trailhead.salesforce.com/users/strailhead/trailmixes/prepare-for-your-data-cloud-consultant-credential**
3. Data Cloud YouTube Playlist: **https://www.youtube.com/watch?v=sn-3qimlECic&list=PLOWi4YJyd0lS6pgKP0IxqlCeH7zZ0rJiJ&ab_channel=SingaporeSalesforceMarketersGroup**
4. Salesforce partner learning camp: **https://partnerlearningcamp.salesforce.com/**
5. Salesforce partner community: **https://partners.salesforce.com/**

Index

I

L

M

O

P

Q

R

S

T

W

Z